"Turner's pursuit of justice reminds you ~~of humor and compassion shows her human, and yes, vulnerable~~ have no choice but to bond to Turner as she takes you on the roller-coaster ride of police work. I'm proud of Turner and her willingness to share her stories in BEHIND HER MIAMI BADGE!"

GARY MARTIN HAYS
Attorney, Best-Selling Author,
TV and Radio Show Host
Board Member, Elizabeth Smart Foundation

"BEHIND HER MIAMI BADGE is an action-filled page-turner that will bring tears to your eyes, either from laughing so hard at the humor or crying from the tragedies. I am so honored to call her my friend, my colleague, and one of my heroes."

ANNA RODRIGUEZ
Author, Founder & Executive Director,
Florida Coalition Against Human Trafficking

"Get ready to be entertained and inspired. As a proud woman who worked in law enforcement, I know the challenges of pushing through in this male-dominated profession. Turner shows that a lot of determination and a little bit of estrogen can go a long way. Clark and Turner are successful in their first book in their Badges trilogy."

JANE DOUGHERTY-MCGOWAN
Police Officer, Retired,
NYPD

"Floy Turner's memoir is outstanding on several fronts: First it provides a snapshot of the era in U.S. history when women were first entering formerly all-male fields. More importantly, amidst today's controversy about America's police practices, Behind Her Miami Badge shows how one woman managed to do a difficult job with intelligence and humanity. Her war stories are often humorous and always illuminating, a darn good read."

PETER SWANSON
Newspaper and Magazine Editor

"Everyone knows that cops tell the best stories, and Floy Turner can keep up with the best of them. It was an honor to work with this pioneer who paved the way for women in law enforcement."

LISSA UDELL
Special Agent,
Florida Department of Law Enforcement

"Be ready to strap in and ride along with Floy Turner as she provides a realistic, emotional, and deeply personal view of what it means to be a law enforcement officer, and the considerations and biases she had to overcome as a female. I recommend this book to all considering a career as a police officer, and especially women considering this career path."

BILL KEARNEY
Author
Co-Owner, WBKEARNEY & Associates/EQYP

"A female trooper in the Florida Highway Patrol in 1983 was not a familiar sight. We were not always welcomed by our fellow coworkers and many times unwanted by the public we swore to serve and protect. BEHIND HER MIAMI BADGE is a factual accounting by Floy Turner, who was bound and determined to change those attitudes by showing that a woman could carry out the duties of a Florida Trooper. Her reflections in this book will make you laugh, make you cry, and will inspire you. It is a quick and brilliant read."

TRISH ENGLAND
State Trooper, Retired,
Florida Highway Patrol

"BEHIND HER MIAMI BADGE takes a realistic look at the emotional and psychological turmoil that women in law enforcement face. Floy describes the commonality of concerns that rotating shifts, high-risk assignments, mandatory overtime, and working in a male-dominated environment will have on her children and spouse or partner. She describes the discrimination by male colleagues and supervisors who jealously guard their traditionally male-dominated territory, and by wives of male colleagues who resent another female spending so much time with their husbands.

"Floy doesn't romanticize the job; instead she accurately depicts what women in law enforcement face, physically, psychologically, and emotionally. She also accurately depicts the rewards of being a woman in law enforcement.

"BEHIND HER MIAMI BADGE is a book that should be read by every woman who is considering a career in law enforcement and by every woman who has been in law enforcement."

JAYNE WEST
Detective, Retired,
Miami-Dade County Police Department

Behind
Her
Miami Badge

UNDERCOVER, THE COCAINE WARS, AND
LIFE IN THE FAST LANE

Floy Turner
and
Sherrie Clark

Storehouse Publishing, LLC
Saint Augustine, Florida

Storehouse Publishing, LLC
Saint Augustine, Florida 32092
www.StorehousePublishers.com
Author@StorehousePublishers.com

Book Layout ©2015 Storehouse Publishing, LLC

Ordering Information:
Quantity sales. Special discounts are available with the Publisher at the email address above and type in subject line "Special Sales Department."

Behind Her Miami Badge / Floy Turner and Sherrie Clark. —1st ed.

ISBN-10: 1943106029 (sc)
ISBN-13: 978-1-943106-02-8 (sc)
ISBN-10: 1943106037 (ebk)
ISBN-13: 978-1-943106-03-5 (ebk)

Library of Congress Control Number: 2015917500

Printed in the United States of America

Dedication

I want to dedicate this book to my husband Gary Carmichael, my love and my best friend, and to my daughters Kally and Mary Ellen. Life has blessed me with a loving family and friends who have supported my endeavors.

FLOY TURNER

I want to dedicate this book to my five children Devlin, Tristan, Liam, Micah, and Janna, the loves of my life.

SHERRIE CLARK

We would both like to dedicate this book in memory of the fallen Florida Highway Patrol Troopers, the fallen South Florida law enforcement officers, and the fallen New York City Police Officers. God bless their families, friends, and colleagues.

FLOY TURNER AND SHERRIE CLARK

Epigraph

The LORD is my shepherd; I shall not want.
He maketh me to lie down in green pastures:
he leadeth me beside the still waters.
He restoreth my soul:
he leadeth me in the paths of righteousness for his name's sake.
Yea, though I walk through the valley of the shadow of death,
I will fear no evil:
for thou art with me;
thy rod and thy staff they comfort me.
Thou preparest a table before me in the presence of mine enemies:
thou anointest my head with oil;
my cup runneth over.
Surely goodness and mercy shall follow me all the days of my life:
and I will dwell in the house of the LORD for ever.
--Psalm 23—

Disclaimer

The purpose of this book is to entertain while enlightening readers to what happened during 1980s Miami from the perspective of Floy Turner, a state law enforcement officer. It's based on actual events that occurred during her tenure as a Florida Highway Patrol Trooper. Turner has made every effort to recreate events, places, and conversations as accurately as possible from her memories of them as well as through research.

Turner's immediate family gave her permission to use their real names. Also, the actual names of those who have been written about in the news have been used. To protect the privacy and anonymity of everyone else involved in this book, she has changed their names, the names of places, and any identifying characteristics and details, and she has modified some of the circumstances, and any similarities to anyone you think you may know are coincidental.

This book does include very few words that some may find offensive. They are written as they had been spoken so that the stories retain their authenticity.

The authors and publisher shall have neither liability nor responsibility to any person or entity with respect to any loss or damage caused, or alleged to have been caused, directly or indirectly, or disruptions caused by errors or omissions, whether such errors or omissions result from negligence, accident, or any other cause, by the information contained in this book.

Contents

Acknowledgements

We'd like to thank everyone who played a part in the writing of this book, whether you were with us during this whole journey or jumped on and off at brief intervals. Each of you added just the right components that were needed to make this book what it is.

Although we both have different groups of people we want to thank, our appreciation crosses over to each other's supporters. We recognize that what you gave was for the benefit of the whole book.

We both want to give a special thanks to Floy's daughter Kally Turner for proofreading. You did a fantastic job. And thank you, Sandy Sledge, Vicki Mellon, and Jayne West, for your commitment in editing our book.

Floy:

I want to thank my husband Gary Carmichael, who has provided me with loving support through this endeavor. I love you. I also want to thank my other daughter Mary Ellen Haid for all of the support and encouragement she gave me in this endeavor.

I want to thank the PLOCK Book club: Freda Blackmar, Janey Fox, Shannon Harbour, Susann Hayes, Beth Jansen, Judy Lind, Karen MacClaren, Mary Morgan, Laura Rhodes, and Cherie Wilson for your encouragement and valuable feedback on our first three chapters.

To my friends at the Barco Newton YMCA in Fleming Island, Florida, I want to give thanks. Thank you to my workout buddies, the staff, and trainers for all of your support through this journey, especially the veterans, current military and their spouses who have sacrificed so much for our country.

Thank you, Diane Cope, Dr. Linda Fagan, and Ann Marie Griffin, my Homestead, Florida, friends for your support in the early days.

To Sara Ackermann, Diana Dennis, Ann Gill, Ethel Mcghee, and Treva Wheatley, the wonderful ladies at the First Presbyterian Boynton Beach, Florida, Evening Circle, thank you for inspiring me to tell my story.

A thank you is given to Rev. Mark Hults and Ed and Tish Tunstall at the First Presbyterian Church Green Cove Springs for counseling me about some of the unfiltered terminology.

Sherrie:

I want to give my heartfelt thanks to my husband Darryl Clark and all five of my children: Devlin Kidney, Tristan Kidney, Liam Kidney, Micah Clark, and Janna Clark. You all were always supportive and encouraging during the writing of this book, and your unending patience with me was noted and appreciated.

A big thank you to Debbie Dykes and Malaki for your neverending support and encouragement. During those times you happened to call me while I was writing and agonizing over every word, you patiently listened to me read aloud certain passages. Your honest and valuable feedback and suggestions helped sculpt some of the sections within this book.

Thank you, Rhonda Biondi and Kay Brophy, for your genuine interest in my endeavors that always comes with your cheerleader-like support—your words encourage me more than you know.

Dr. Michele Fleming, thank you for your wise counsel and sincere encouragement. You have been a great friend and wonderful sounding board.

Last but definitely not least, I want to thank my co-author Floy Turner who was and is such a pleasure to work with. I admire everything that you've accomplished. I have been honored to travel this path of writing this book with you, and I look forward to walking more journeys together as we work on the next two books in this fun and enlightening series.

CHAPTER 1

From a Dream to Reality

Nancy Drew. She had the life.

I loved reading her books while growing up in Eastern Kentucky. I remember being immersed in the mysteries she solved and seeing her bring criminals to justice. Her super-sleuth techniques inspired me as a girl in my early teens.

As an adult, I found myself married with two small children living in Miami, Florida. The only facet of my life that stayed the same was my love for mysteries.

Then Angie Dickinson became my next idol. She starred in the television series *Police Woman*, and her character Pepper Anderson led an exciting life. I wanted to be like Pepper, only the South Florida version of her.

I wasn't exactly a complete stranger to law enforcement. My husband was a policeman. Unlike many of the cops' wives, I felt jealous of his career and wanted to become a police officer myself.

He continually had to listen to me talk on and on about my desire to be a cop. In an effort to indulge my incessant longings, he arranged for me to do a ride along on a midnight shift with one of his friends. I was so excited!

The night of my ride-along, I arrived at the police station several minutes early. By the time the cops on the midnight shift strolled into the stationhouse, the excitement had become almost unbearable.

I spotted my husband's friend, my partner for the ride-along. He waved and began strolling toward me. A few of the other cops stopped him along the way to chat. As a result, his walk to me seemed to take an exceptionally long time.

I just wanted to scream and say, "Leave him alone!"

When he finally reached me, he smiled and stretched out his hand. He lifted his right eyebrow and asked, "You ready?"

Was I ready?! I thought I would jump out of my skin if we didn't get out of there. I couldn't wait to get into his patrol car.

We stepped outside into the fresh air of the warm night. I tried to temper my excitement, knowing my place was to follow his lead.

The overhead lights lit up the parking lot. Still, the night seemed darker than most because of the overcast sky.

I followed my partner to the patrol car. I walked around to the passenger side, planted myself in the front seat, and tried my best to look calm.

My partner got into the driver's seat after putting his equipment in the back. He looked over at me. He tilted his head and studied me, silently asking if I was *sure* I wanted to do this.

I smiled, hoping it encouraged him. He turned his head, looked through the windshield in front of him, put the car in gear, and off we went.

Well, be careful for what you wish. I wanted excitement, and excitement was what I got. We had only been on patrol a very short time when we got dispatched to a man walking with a gun.

We neared the address given and drove around the corner. We saw the armed man, and he obviously saw us. He raised his gun and pointed it directly at the front of our patrol car.

I momentarily lost my breath, not from fear but from the exhilaration of experiencing my first hit-the-deck adventure. I surprised myself by remaining composed.

Before the suspect had the chance to shoot at us, my partner maneuvered the patrol car out of the direct line of fire. He then jumped out with his gun already drawn and pointed it at the suspect. He squatted behind his car door, using it as a shield.

I thought, *What do I do if this gets out of control?*

I looked around to see what I could use in case my partner got shot. I realized that my only hope was the shotgun propped vertically between our seats.

My partner yelled, "Put your gun on the sidewalk. Turn around with your hands on your head, and get on your knees."

The suspect actually obeyed his commands and lowered his gun. My partner ran over to him, pointing his gun at the suspect the whole time. When he got close, he kicked the suspect's gun over to the side and out of his reach.

Standing behind him, my partner kept his gun pointed at the suspect with his left hand while placing handcuffs on his wrists with his right. He then pulled the guy up and onto his feet and walked him back to the patrol car.

On the drive back to the stationhouse, the incident played through my mind again and really sunk in, causing my heart to race. I realized how quickly a situation could escalate and how easily cops can be thrust into danger.

Unlike what we see happens on television after a cop makes an arrest, we spent the next four hours at the stationhouse writing reports and booking the prisoner. We were back on the streets in time to respond to a domestic-violence call where a very large woman had taken a high-heel shoe to her man's thin and boney face.

After a few good licks, he got mad and took a knife to her, cutting a few slices into her big belly. This was the first time I had witnessed domestic violence.

As dangerous as that night may have been, it only increased my desire to go into law enforcement. Maybe my husband coordinated this ride-along in hopes that I'd get my fill and squelch my yearning to fight crime. Whatever his reasons, I knew he didn't support my dream to pursue a career as a cop.

After that first night on patrol, I began to make friends in law enforcement. In the early part of 1981, an opportunity opened for me to become an auxiliary state trooper with the Florida Highway Patrol. This was a volunteer position that assisted the troopers with patrolling the streets and with traffic incidents. Before I could start, though, I had to attend a very basic law enforcement academy designed for auxiliary officers.

Over the next few months, I attended the auxiliary academy in the Fort Lauderdale area. Once I began classes, I knew there was no going back. I was hooked. This was the most exciting school I had ever attended.

During that time, I worked full-time as a dental assistant. All day long I looked at teeth, but all I could really think about was the academy. I couldn't wait to go back. So after a long day at work, I drove to North Miami to meet my carpooling buddy, a great guy named Joe Brown. I parked my car in the lot where he worked, climbed in his car, and we drove together to the Broward County Police Academy.

My day ended with my arriving home around midnight. The long days forced an adjustment in my normal routine with my two young children. Thank God for my mother. She picked up my daughters from school, took them home, and fed them. She then made sure they completed their homework before my husband got home from work. Fortunately, he started coming around to my way of thinking and became more supportive in my venture.

The constant thrill of the academy gave me an ongoing energy boost; however, I needed more than just energy. If I was going to pass the physical test, then I was going to have to get into top physical condition. I realized one of the best ways to increase my endurance was to start running. This would be another adjustment since I had never even exercised. Up until then, I had spent most of my time caring for children, doing household chores, reading, and watching television.

I thought, *Well, one more thing to add to my already busy schedule.*

Much to my surprise, I discovered that I really enjoyed running. I had found a passion that led to a lifelong commitment of staying in shape.

Next, I needed to supply my own uniforms, gun, gun belt, and handcuffs. My husband let me borrow a Smith & Wesson .38 caliber, model-19 revolver.

Shooting made me nervous. Holding a gun for the first time gave me the reality check of having something in my hand which had the potential to end a life.

I wasn't accustomed to firing guns, so I struggled with this aspect of the academy. Fortunately a couple of firearm instructors offered to give me additional training. They spent their own time at the range to help me obtain the score I needed to qualify.

Driving the academy's skidpan was crazy fun. The skidpan is a blacktop area that can be flooded with water to simulate a fast-moving vehicle hydroplaning. We were taught how to regain control of the car in those conditions.

The skidpan reminded me of Mr. Toad's Wild Ride at Walt Disney World. Back in the early '80s when I attended the auxiliary academy, we would pack the vehicle full of trainees before engaging in this exercise.

The trainees went from having fun with lots of laughter while speeding on the blacktop to a feeling of total panic and fear as the car spun around. As I look back on those days, I realize those kinds of exercises really prepared us for police work and the emotional roller-coaster ride on which we were about to embark.

One difference between the academies of the '80s and the academies of today was tactical training. Back then we spent a lot of time watching horrid film clips that taught officer survival. These films were really scary with lots of cops being shot and dying. They were definitely not for the faint of heart. Still, I couldn't wait to hit the Miami streets.

After finally graduating from the auxiliary academy, I was assigned to Miami Troop E. I appreciated the station's close proximity to downtown, the interstate, and the courthouse. Its Hispanic neighborhood boasted of lots of great Cuban restaurants. Miami High School was located across the street. The downside, though, was the hour commute from my home to the stationhouse.

At that time, the only other female auxiliary trooper functioned as the troop commander's secretary. Upon meeting her, I realized why she would probably never work in the field. She appeared too overweight to easily get in and out of a patrol car. Walking a few feet to file a paper seemed to cause her to breathe heavily.

She came across as if she were the one in charge, always barking out orders. She seemed to have issues with me simply because we shared the same gender. When she looked at me, she never smiled. Instead, she squinted her eyes and gave me suspicious glares.

I knew she considered me a threat, but I wasn't going let her stop me. I'm still bothered by the memory of her establishing the battle lines from the get-go and never becoming a mentor or champion for my success.

After working my first assignment with one of the troopers, she called and admonished me, snarling as she spoke. I could see her spitting out the words into phone receiver. "You *needed* the commander's permission for a ride-along assignment."

She didn't mind it when the guys did the same thing, and I knew that she was trying to use her position to bully me.

She wasn't the only one who tried to penalize me in law enforcement because of my sex. I was floored when I learned that a Trooper Wife's Association existed but not an association for the *husband* of a trooper or the *spouse* of a trooper. They limited this association membership, and thus this role, to women and wives only.

Back then law enforcement didn't really recognize female officers and the possibility that a spouse could actually be a husband as well. Miami did have a handful of female troopers, and some of them were married.

Amazingly, a lot of the wives didn't support my riding in the patrol cars with their husbands. Either they didn't want their man riding in a car alone with another woman, or they thought their husbands would have to look after me in a dangerous situation.

Some of the male troopers flat out didn't want women intruding upon their profession. Luckily for me, not all male troopers felt that way. A few were glad to partner up with a female.

Looking back, three of those troopers who supported me were black. Maybe they took pity on the fact I was a minority and not initially accepted.

I owe them a debt of gratitude. Whenever I wanted to ride along on a shift, they were quick to make arrangements for me to be their partner. I learned a lot from those men. They became good friends who encouraged my career path.

Taking It to the Next Level

In the late summer of 1981, an opportunity opened for me to apply for a full-time position as a paid trooper. Since I had already been volunteering with the Miami troop, I knew this was where I wanted to work.

Up until that time, the Florida Highway Patrol (FHP) had discriminated against hiring females, and consequently, it had not complied with the percentage guidelines for women on the job. Therefore, a federal mandate was issued forcing the FHP to mend its ways and bring on more female troopers. This turned out to be great timing on my part.

I want to make it very clear that I'm in no way bashing the troopers. I view that lack of initial acceptance as part of the historical framework for women in police work. I loved the highway patrol, and being a proud member of this agency was a turning point in my life. As a trooper, I worked with some of the most dedicated men and women in law enforcement.

On the other hand, my family now completely supported me and my desire to move forward in law enforcement. I looked quite awesome in the eyes of my daughters when they thought about their mom carrying a gun, wearing a cop uniform, and lugging around all of the other police equipment.

My husband recognized my commitment, and so he took the path of least resistance. He finally accepted the idea that this was my career choice.

The application process for any law enforcement job is tedious with background checks and lie detector tests. I had to travel to Orlando to take my oral board exam. The men who interviewed me seemed to be a group of well-seasoned good ole boys.

During the oral board exam, one of those good ole boys looked over the black rims of his glasses and tucked his narrow chin into his chest. "What would you do if someone ran from you in *Mi-am-ma?*"

I responded, "I'd chase them down and detain them."

The one who wore his blond hair in a crew cut asked, "What if you are hired and not sent back to *Mi-am-ma?*"

The southern drawl some of them used made the word *Miami* sound like another world separate from the rest of the state.

Well at that point, I got a little cocky. I knew they needed to comply with the federal mandate to hire more female troopers.

I replied, "If I don't get assigned to *Mi-am-ma*, I'll apply to Metro-Dade Police Department." I don't think any of them caught onto my newly acquired accent.

After my interview, I was told that I had sailed through the background check, but I knew I would. I did receive a few traffic tickets from previous years, but I never used illegal drugs, never broke the law, and I had been volunteering as an auxiliary trooper for a year.

I was quickly hired as a trooper trainee in December 1982. Although I was now on the payroll, I still needed to be sworn in to have any police authority, and that would happen when I graduated from the next FHP Academy class. Until then, the FDLE (Florida Department of Law Enforcement) police standards and liability factors prohibited me from carrying my gun and handcuffs on duty.

In the meantime, I had to return to Miami Troop E where Pete Gannon was assigned to be my partner. I was honored that he was the one who mentored me. He wanted to groom me so that I would be completely prepared to enter the academy. I too wanted to be prepared and applied every lesson he taught me.

I respected him and his accomplishments, especially the award he received in 1976 as Trooper of the Year. Pete was shot three times when he unknowingly walked into a coffee shop while it was being robbed. After three bullets to the face and neck blinded him, he lay on the floor with his right arm paralyzed.

Using his left hand, he pulled out his weapon from his left-hand cross-draw-holster and shot the robber. The robber ended up permanently paralyzed as a result.

Pete was bleeding to death because the bullet pierced his carotid artery. A nursing student walked into the coffee shop and used her training skills. She pinched the artery with her fingers, saving Pete's life.

When he arrived at Homestead Hospital, he had a few hundred dollars and a knife in his pants pocket. He retrieved both after being transferred from the gurney to the hospital bed in the emergency room.

He concealed the knife under his butt, but he gave the money to a nurse, telling her that he was in the middle of a divorce and didn't want his wife to get the money. He instructed the nurse to include all of the doctors and nurses in a big party if he died.

As he lay in the emergency room still blinded by one of the bullets, he thought he heard the bad guy being wheeled into an adjoining partition. Even though both he and the robber had a police guard assigned to each of them, his state of mind led him to believe the robber was still a threat and that he might try to attack him again. Pete tried to get his knife so that he could pull himself off the gurney in preparation for another round of fighting the robber. He may have been close to death, but he was determined to survive.

His attempt failed when one of the nurses saw him trying to pull something out from underneath his butt. She and Pete's guard found the knife, and the nurse gave it to another trooper.

His story is an example of survival, never giving up, and going after the bad guy. He recovered and eventually returned to duty, but his marriage didn't survive.

Pete's marital problems were more of the rule instead of the exception in law enforcement. Unfortunately, the inability for marriages to survive is a common problem for those in police work.

At times, I thought about the condition of my own marriage because I didn't want it to be one of the negative statistics. In the beginning of my career, though, I felt my husband and I were swimming against the tide. Despite the fact that I also worked, he insisted on treating me as a stay-at-home wife and mother. At this point, I could only hope and pray that he would come around and respect me in my profession as much as I respected him in his.

Welcome to the Florida Highway Patrol Academy

In March 1983, I received my next assignment—three months at the Florida Highway Patrol Academy in Tallahassee, Florida.

This academy was comparable to a military boot camp. Out of all the police academies in the state that trained either local or state police officers, the Florida Highway Patrol Academy was the most challenging.

I prepared myself for the mental and physical abuse that would inevitably be heaved upon all of us trainees. I was determined that no matter what, I would do my best and not give up.

I also made preparations for my children. Between my mother living nearby, my girlfriend and her husband offering to help, and my husband agreeing to do more of the child and household duties, I felt comfort in knowing that my daughters would be picked up from school, taken to ballet lessons, and homework would be completed while I was away.

I thought about how I had never been away from my children for more than a few hours. Leaving them for three months would be a life-altering experience no matter how many preparations I made. Still, I continued making plans knowing that doing so would make my absence more bearable for us all.

So on a Sunday morning in March, I kissed by family goodbye and boarded a small plane to Tallahassee, leaving behind my role as housewife. This undertaking would prove exceptionally difficult in more ways than I could have imagined.

As the plane left the gate and taxied on the runway, uneasiness overcame me. It dawned on me that the take off into the open sky was not only literal, but it was figurative too. I was taking off on a journey where I didn't have either a family member or friend in close proximity. As a result, I felt an aloneness knowing each passing minute took me further away from everything familiar.

Furthermore when I left Miami, I left behind a clear blue sky and temperatures in the low eighties, typical for South Florida at that time of year. When I disembarked from the plane in Tallahassee, a different scenario greeted me. A bitter wind hit my face, and I felt cold.

I stared out the cab window during the drive to the academy. The dreary colors seemed to accentuate my apprehension. The brown grass and gray skies made for lackluster scenery, one in which I would insert myself for the next three months.

I needed to put this feeling into perspective. I realized that my sadness came from missing my family, and I reminded myself why I was there. The thrill of entering the academy gave me a strong resolve to shake off this mood and immerse myself in this new role.

My first sight of the academy didn't help with my new resolution though. Instead, it caused my head to spin and not in a good way. I don't know what I expected, but in front of me stood two institutional-looking brick buildings. The only descriptive characteristics that came to mind for each of them were bleakness and gloom.

I found it hard to imagine that this dismal-looking place would be my home for the next thirteen weeks. My feelings ran from simple to complex. On one hand, I wanted this opportunity and welcomed this experience despite the grim sight before me. On the other hand, fear of what I was facing caused my stomach to churn.

I got out of the cab with my few belongings and approached the entrance to the first building. Once inside, the wall full of pictures and plaques of fallen troopers killed in the line of duty caught my eye. I studied them with a feeling of both sadness and pride.

I walked into the building and tried to shake off the cold chill. An odor that reminded me of pine-scented cleaner mixed with kitchen grease was overwhelming.

I made my way to the center of the building. The only audible sound was the tapping of my shoes on the gray cement floor. The noise echoed against the cement walls, and the volume seemed to amplify with each step I took.

A giant trooper who looked like he was over seven-feet tall greeted me. I was amazed a human being could be that big. Although he appeared friendly enough, one could find him intimidating just by his size alone. He gave me directions of what I needed to do at that time and where I needed to go to get it done.

I walked to the supply room and picked up sheets, a towel, my nametag, and my room number. After finding my assigned room, I unpacked the duffel bag I brought from home. I somehow managed to fit in it all of the items I was required to purchase for the academy, including my new uniforms.

They consisted of khaki shirts and pants, a web belt with a brass buckle, black patent oxford shoes, gray sweat suits, black t-shirts and shorts, black socks, and white v-necked t-shirts. The academy staff did allow us to make personalized choices for our underwear, athletic shoes, toiletries, and off-duty clothing.

When I met my roommate, she seemed likable, but we appeared to be polar opposites from each other both emotionally and physically. I was five foot ten, and she was five foot two. My blonde hair contrasted with her dark-brown hair. Whereas she lived in a small town, I hailed from cosmopolitan Miami where women wore makeup and got dressed up to go anywhere. I wasn't quite sure if my roommate even owned makeup since her face was void of any color the whole time we roomed together.

She started talking about not staying at the academy and going back home that first day. Tears pooled in her eyes as she talked about her husband and children and how much she missed them.

She did most of the talking while we set up our room. A couple of hours later, the recruits were directed to the review area in the main academy building.

The drill instructors introduced themselves and then ordered us to kneel on the concrete floor. This may seem to be an odd demand, but they used this tactic as our initial endurance test. By making us kneel for hours in that position, they were able to evaluate whether we were capable of putting mind over matter and push through our discomfort and tiredness.

After awhile my knees hurt badly, and then they started cramping before ultimately becoming numb. At least with the numbness, I could halfway comprehend the next few hours of dictates barked out by these instructors.

The lectures dispelled several myths, including the false security that we had finished setting up our rooms. The instructors provided a list of specific directives. They required a precise distance between the head of our bed and the wall. They told us the exact placement of our typewriters on our desks, and our desks could only contain one picture. Furthermore, our rooms must be free of any dirt or dust. The first inspection would take place in the morning. .

We finally were dismissed, and I lumbered back to my room. My exhaustion trumped my apprehension, allowing me to fall asleep immediately after laying my head on my pillow.

I woke up extra early the next morning to make sure everything was as it should be. When the counselor entered our room, I held my breath and silently prayed. He looked around with not even a hint of emotion on his face. He then used a ruler to ensure we didn't place items outside of the restricted measurement guidelines.

The instructors were tough on us. Word got out between the recruits that they expected us to fail at some blatant wrongdoing, mostly with our uniform. Either our shoes or belt buckle lacked enough shine, or a stray thread became visible, or our tucked-in shirts lined up improperly with our belt buckle and zipper line.

I wasn't immune from their reprimands. They constantly chastised me about my hair. They wanted it shorter and further off of my face and collar.

It became evident that a few class members would fail every inspection. If someone didn't meet academy standards, they punished the entire class. We'd be forced to run a couple of extra miles and do more push-ups and sit-ups.

This technique was used to instill an important lesson: we were all in this together. If we didn't stick together in training, we wouldn't rely on each other when the times got tough on the road.

We began losing class members from the start. The first one dropped out on the morning of day one. This resignation came right after kneeling on the floor for hours and listening to all of the rules and regulations. After that, it seemed like most of the recruits we lost disappeared overnight. We were warned not to ask questions about why or what led to their leaving. However, my roommate was still hanging in there, albeit miserably so.

Academy life required adjustment on a daily basis. One of the biggest had to be made by our digestive tracts. The academy didn't offer any culinary delights.

For instance, the mystery meat cooked in a heavy red sauce seemed to be the status quo, especially before or after extreme physical exercise. This dish had earned the name "Red Death."

Also, the staff always made it the meal of choice before dousing the class with tear gas. Mixing Red Death with tear gas produced a very nasty red vomit.

Another favorite food seemed to be fried mullet, which they always served on Fridays. I never understood why the command staff loved that greasy mess so much, but sure enough, fried mullet was enough to get even the command staff into the cafeteria. All of the recruits joked about how the grease from the mullet was used to fry all of the other food during the week. The French fries served several days later contained the evidence needed to support our claims. They carried the distinct fishy odor reminiscent of our Friday's mullet delight.

I tried to find the upside to those meals. Maybe they were simply part of the training program. Like the exercises performed to strengthen our arms, legs, and abdomens, the gut-wrenching fare they served must have been to strengthen our stomachs. Inevitably, most of us would need a strong stomach when forced to patronize all-night diners while working the midnight shifts.

The academy stretched us mentally and emotionally as well. I missed my children terribly and felt guilty that they were without their mother. During our thirteen-week training period, the academy allowed only one weekend off to spend with family. Perhaps the academy used this as an exercise to wean us from leaning on our family as our support system. This placed us in the position of needing to rely upon each other. After all, when we're out there on the streets and going fisticuffs with the bad guys, it will be our comrades in law enforcement who will help us, not our family.

I couldn't wait for that weekend when I would be able to spend time with my daughters. My husband and I had made the decision that he would bring them to Tallahassee to see me. I could then show them where I lived.

When the day of their visit arrived, I ran outside and paced in front of the first building, glancing at my watch every minute or two. They were scheduled to get there any moment. It just seemed as if those moments stretched on and on.

Finally, I saw our car driving toward me with my husband and two small blonde heads framing two smiling faces. As soon as the car stopped, the doors opened, and four sneaker-covered feet came running toward me.

I knelt down with my arms open, welcoming eight-year-old Mary Ellen and thirteen-year-old Kally. We hugged while both girls tried to talk above the other. I just held them tight, tears pooling in my eyes. Strands of their hair tickled my nose while their clean, fresh scent rushed through my nostrils. It was so good to have them with me.

The weekend flew by quickly. The girls toured the academy, and we spent most of our time on the agility course. They loved looking at the eight-foot wooden wall that all recruits had to climb up and over as one of the qualification exercises.

We also explored the city of Tallahassee and Florida State University (FSU). They loved the area so much that several years down the road, they both would decide to attend college there.

Over dinner Saturday night, the girls candidly described the dinners their dad made for them during my absence. Eyes rolled and noses crinkled as they made it quite clear that children *can* get really tired of eating hot dogs and fish sticks all the time.

We thoroughly enjoyed the weekend, and it turned out to be a good break for us all. When the time came for them to leave, which was much too soon, we all cried. I knew I would miss them, and I counted down the days for when we would be together again.

In the meantime, the academy pulled me to return to its merciless grind. As recruits, we worked from sunrise to sunset five days a week and on Saturdays until noon. We were given permission to stay out on Saturday nights until midnight. Afterward, the counselors conducted bed checks to make sure the recruits were in compliance with the rules.

I had come to the academy prepared for a lot of things. For instance, I had anticipated mind games to be the norm. I was ready to be yelled at and driven beyond my mental and physical capabilities. What I had omitted in my preparations and just really hadn't considered to be an issue was sleep deprivation and complete fatigue.

The one part that scared me the most was being gassed. We were informed that this event would take place at the range. After a lunch of Red Death, our instructors took us to the range where they ordered us to line up and march to the end.

While we marched, they threw tear gas in our direction over and over again. The high ground on each side created the perfect area to prohibit the gas fumes from escaping or even dissipating.

The abundance of gas overwhelmed me, and I panicked. I felt like I couldn't breathe and was being smothered to death. I prayed for the strength to endure this horrific experience.

When I could finally catch my breath, a significant amount of mucus kept coming out of my nose, and my eyes watered. But I didn't disgrace myself. In fact, I was proud that I didn't vomit, pass out, or stop.

I thought, *Well, at least I'm ready for any upcoming Miami riots.* I knew this would be the same type of tear gas used.

At least I survived, even though I could barely touch dinner that night because I still felt the effects of the gas. I hoped I never had to experience that again, but I also recognized the reality that I may. At least today's exercise removed any future shock factor.

About three-fourths of the way through the academy, a Hispanic-looking man walked into our classroom with his shoulders squared and head held high. His intense brown eyes quickly scanned the room. Yet I got the feeling that he took in every detail, from the smallest dust ball in the corner of the gray linoleum floor to the shape of each recruit's earlobe.

Our instructor introduced our visitor as DEA Special Agent Rios from Miami. "He's here to train you in narcotics," he explained.

Agent Rios walked to front center of the room and began speaking. His Cuban accent created an air of mystery and excitement as he shared his dramatic, real-life stories, captivating his audience of impressionable recruits.

He turned out to be an excellent instructor who offered a wealth of experience and information. Although he came across as smart, very self-assured with a somewhat-superior demeanor, he did seem a bit jaded. In fact, he didn't hold back on his cynicism, and his lessons reflected a man with a rigid mindset. None of these were uncommon characteristics for hardcore cops.

Special Agent Rios said, "You're crazy to wanna be troopers. You're not gonna make much money, and your lives are gonna be in danger. A couple of your classmates are gonna be killed before they can retire." (Unfortunately, the prediction about losing two classmates in the line of duty came true.)

Then Agent Rios said, "I don't know why anyone would want a job where they'd be picking off dead babies from windshields."

He also provided in-depth descriptions of all this gloom and doom. One of the recruits took Rios' message to heart and departed the academy in the middle of the night.

When word got to the academy's major-in-charge about Agent Rios' candid presentation, he called Miami's DEA office. He was straightforward when he told them that Special Agent Rios would never be allowed to set foot on the academy's property again. Years later, I reaped the repercussions from the major's call.

The Florida Department of Law Enforcement (FDLE) also came to the academy. They provided a training module about the horrific murder cases committed by Ted Bundy at Florida State University and Lake City, Florida. I was immediately interested in learning more about this agency. During that presentation, the thought entered my mind that maybe one day I could be an FDLE Special Agent.

I kept that aspiration in my head and heart in the years to come. I trusted that God would provide me with opportunities to not only prepare me for the challenge of protecting and serving, but to prepare me to become an agent for the FDLE.

At the time, getting through the academy and all of its requirements was my first and foremost task. As our three-month tenure began winding down, a lot of the pressure was alleviated, but I still had the firearm qualification looming over me.

I was issued a .38-caliber Colt Trooper five-inch-barrel wheel gun and a three-inch-wide gun belt with a cross-draw holster. My shooting had improved since becoming an auxiliary trooper, but I still felt some butterflies in my stomach at the thought of shooting a gun.

We went to the range every day during the final week of firearm training. On the last day, we stayed most of the night for a night shoot.

We boarded the bus in the wee hours of the morning to go back to the academy. While there, we had just enough time to change clothes and eat breakfast before having to return to the shooting range.

I felt dirty and exhausted. Furthermore, my entire being seemed to vibrate from the tension of not sleeping but staying awake way past what nature dictated. The overinfusion of caffeine from splurging on lots of coffee exacerbated my trembles.

In an effort to get my mind off of my shaking and my nerves, I chose to momentarily focus on the beautiful sky. Thankfully, it was a clear spring day, warm but not hot.

The distraction seemed to put everything into the proper perspective. I knew the challenge before me boiled down to mind over body.

Once again, this exercise prepared me for the street wars I might come across as a state trooper. I wanted this challenge, and if I had to crawl in the dirt and shoot without sleep, so be it. I needed to meet this head-on with determination, a good eye, calm breath, and a steady hand.

Then it was time for me to shoot. As I aimed my weapon, I reminded myself of everything at stake. I blinked my eyes a few times to clear the tiredness that tried to overtake me. Praying, I pulled the trigger repeatedly. My hand jerked up slightly with each shot. Before reloading, I studied the targets, feeling proud and excited to discover that the holes from my shots appeared well-placed. The instructors scored my tests, and relief flooded through me upon learning that I had officially qualified with a better-than-average score. I also gained confidence in my abilities.

The other component of the academy consisted of academics. They were never an issue for me with the exception of the algebraic formulas used for traffic-crash investigation. I've never been a math whiz, but I passed the traffic-investigation module with a decent grade. I ended up second in my class in academics.

A few days before the last week, we were given our uniforms. I noticed that they all came in men sizes. As a result, I had a substantial alteration bill once I returned home. Even after being altered, my shirts still had really wide arm holes and sleeves. Other than that, I managed to look professional. Plus I had the advantage of being slim and tall.

We then received our assignments during that last week. Half of the class, or twenty-six rookies, got assigned to Miami. I was delighted to be going back to my hometown, but the guys and one other female assigned to Miami from North Florida were not so pleased. They looked at it as a necessity but hoped to get out of Miami within a couple of years.

I think they all realized that time spent in South Florida would provide them with action-packed events. They would experience more serious police-related scenarios and challenges in Miami as compared to some of the less-populated areas of the state.

All who were assigned to South Florida made an additional five thousand dollars a year, which was a cost-of-living offset and increase. This part of the state was one of the most expensive places to live.

Our final day at the academy consisted of a long-standing tradition of washing and waxing all of the vehicles of the patrol fleet. This included patrol cars, marked and unmarked, and a couple of buses.

We washed and waxed from sunup to sunrise. The class mood was festive and fun. At that point, we had all endured thirteen weeks of intense training. Plus, we looked forward to reuniting with our families and beginning our new careers.

Then at last the time we had all been looking forward to finally arrived—the day of our graduation ceremony. I was ecstatic at seeing my entire family and a few of my friends from Miami. I mostly felt pride at having achieved my dream and my goal.

When the announcer called my name to come and get my hard-earned badge and credentials, it felt almost surreal. It seemed like I moved in slow motion as I walked across the stage. One thing was for sure, I couldn't quit smiling.

I looked out at the audience as my guests clapped. They too wore big grins on their faces. I thought, *Wow, I've really made them proud of me.* I realized that moment was worth the Red Death and tear gas and kneeling on the floor for hours.

My roommate managed to stick it out and graduate from the academy as well. However, the day after she returned home, she took all of her equipment to the stationhouse and resigned. What a waste of taxpayers' money. They must have lost about thirty thousand dollars on her salary and training. When I heard this, I realized that instead of talking her out of leaving the academy, I should have helped her pack. I shouldn't have been surprised, though. Back in the early 80s, the average length of employment for a female trooper was less than two years.

After the ceremony, my family and my girlfriend and her husband all drove to a local restaurant and celebrated. The glasses were clanging during the multiple toasts.

Once the celebrations ended, we drove back to the academy. This time around, I saw it through different eyes. No longer did I view it as a challenge but as the first step to my career in law enforcement.

CHAPTER 2

Welcome to Miami North

In May 1983, I returned home from the academy late at night. When we pulled into my driveway, I thought about how beautiful my house looked. I think I had gained a new appreciation for home and family.

Making my way to my front door, I took in a deep breath of the warm and balmy air. Yes, it was good to be home.

The weekend lay ahead, but for tonight, I wanted to relax and sleep in my comfortable bed again. I missed it as well as all of the other comforts of home while away at the academy.

I planned to use part of the next two days to mentally prepare myself for starting my career Monday morning as a Florida Highway Patrol Trooper. I couldn't help but feel excited about my first assignment—reporting back to the Miami station located in the heart of the Latin community.

In the meantime, I needed to do a lot of catching up with my family. We spent Saturday and Sunday swimming, shopping, and visiting friends. In between activities, we hung out with our two dogs in the backyard. The flurry of activities made the weekend fly by quickly.

Before I knew it, Monday had arrived. At around six thirty that morning, I peeked through my living room window and saw Trooper Pete Gannon pulling into my driveway in his patrol car. He had promised to pick me up and drive me to the station.

When I stepped outside my home, the sun was just beginning its ascent. Its tranquil beauty served to exacerbate my giddiness. Everything seemed so perfect.

I got into the passenger's side of Pete's patrol car. I didn't know if my jitters came from my excitement or from my lack of morning coffee. I knew that Pete always stopped at the same mom-and-pop shop for coffee and donuts, and I looked forward to the caffeine and sugar fix.

Yes, cops eat a lot of donuts. At least we did in the early eighties. Very few donut shops were robbed in Miami.

We walked into the coffee shop and found a booth in the rear of the small restaurant and sat down. Pete always selected a seat where he wouldn't have his back to the door.

I felt so proud to wear my uniform. I couldn't stop chattering about how I was ready to get started and how eager I was to drive the patrol car.

I paused long enough to realize that Pete hadn't said a word the whole time. More baffling than his silence was his tense facial expression. He hadn't smiled since we had sat down. He clenched his jaw while his eyes searched my face. I sensed he wanted to tell me something, but he either didn't know how or even whether he should.

While waiting for our coffee to arrive, I asked, "Pete, is anything wrong?" Now it was my turn to search his face.

His eyes bore into my own without his facial muscles relaxing even a little bit. "I don't think you'll be riding with me."

Of course it never crossed my mind that I wouldn't ride with Pete. I just assumed that I would continue under his mentorship since he had been my training officer prior to the academy.

Disappointment set in. First of all, Pete and I got along so well when he trained me, and this offered an element of comfort. Secondly, we lived in the same area of the city. This offered an element of convenience.

I knew that none of my classmates who moved to Miami lived near me. They had been instructed to move into the northern part of the city, and I had already been residing down deep in the southern part of Miami.

If Pete wasn't going to train me, I was curious about who would. I began naming other troopers who worked in the south end because, of course, it never crossed my mind that I would work anywhere else.

Pete just remained silent. He shook his head left to right with each name I mentioned, indicating no.

I became more confused, wondering what was happening. My mind raced while my stomach flipped and flopped.

I didn't feel so chatty anymore. My previous excitement just got doused with an overwhelming amount of letdown and uncertainty.

We finished our coffee before grabbing a donut. After climbing in the car, we headed north to the station.

Pete hit rush-hour traffic on the interstate before exiting and heading onto the crowded streets. As we neared the station, I looked out the window at all of the Cuban walk-up coffee windows and Cuban businesses that seemed to make up this part of town. The sidewalk activity, restaurants, and smells of downtown Miami had always energized me.

We pulled up to the station's chain-link gate that opened to the parking lot. It had a slightly battered appearance as though too many bumpers had kissed it upon entering or leaving.

Once inside the gate, we drove past a covered parking area to a larger one. Razor wire laid snuggly on top.

I looked around the bleak and disorderly lot. An assortment of vacant vehicles sat idle, giving the appearance of the stationhouse having more people in it than it actually contained.

I noticed a lot of wrecked patrol cars, a few late-model vehicles, which I assumed were seized from drug investigations, and a few other nondescript cars battered from crashes. They were probably evidence in fatality cases.

We entered the sand-colored building that looked like it had been built in the fifties. Our heels clicked on the terrazzo, a very popular mixture of concrete, sand, and stone that South Florida used to create flooring. Its dull and dingy appearance provided proof of many years of hard use, confirmed by the large cracks deeply embedded in the concoction. These rifts had formed so long ago that they had grown and now ran the length of the entire large squad room.

Undoubtedly, this old station had seen better days and looked older than it probably was. The lack of renovations and its outdated furnishings didn't help.

Metal chairs covered with weathered green vinyl complimented the long rows of narrow gray tables. I thought the dirt-stained walls could stand a new coat of paint. The musty smell of old wood gave the air a stale odor.

Troopers stood around talking while eating last-minute breakfasts of donuts and fried-egg sandwiches. I constantly kept a lookout for a rat or roach lurking nearby. I could just imagine it waiting for a nibble to fall in its direction. After all, this was Miami, and roaches and rats also enjoyed the flavors of South Florida.

The building's ambiance may have needed some help, but the undercurrent of excitement of new recruits arriving started to distract me from the sights and smells. My classmates provided camaraderie and a sense of comfort because of the bonding that took place during our time in Tallahassee.

We gathered together into one large group. A lot of conversation took place about new apartments and rental houses, what their wives thought of Miami, and schools for their children. Most of them expressed a desire to leave Miami as soon as possible and be reassigned to a troop near their hometown.

Not only was I the only female in the group, but I was the only female recruit assigned to Miami. The other female assigned to South Florida got sent to Key West.

All of the recruits were told to take a seat. I looked around for Pete. That uneasy feeling from hearing his news earlier remained with me. I thought, *Surely, Pete must be wrong.*

I tried to keep him in my peripheral vision, afraid that if I lost sight of him I'd somehow lose that connection. And if I lost that connection, I'd lose the opportunity to be assigned to him. I guess I was in denial about not having him as my field training officer.

A crusty, middle-aged sergeant took charge of this meeting. He stood behind an old scratched-up wooden podium and held a sheet of paper in his hand. After placing the paper on the podium's reading surface, he took a pair of brown-rimmed reading glasses out of his shirt pocket and put them on his face. He then peered over his glasses at the group of eager new faces sitting in front of him.

Looking back at his papers, he began reading the list of assignments for the rookies, including their squad and field training officer. Since this information was given in alphabetical order, I wouldn't hear my assignment until toward the end.

Four squads covered the north and south areas for two shifts. The day shift went from seven in the morning until three in the afternoon. The afternoon shift was from three in the afternoon until eleven at night. I wasn't sure as to which one I would be assigned to work. I hoped I would get the south end so that I could be close to home and the day shift since I had children.

I tried to prepare myself to hear that I wouldn't be riding with Pete. Still I was shocked at what the sergeant had to say when he finally called my name.

He informed me that I was assigned to a permanent midnight shift in the north section, and my training officer was Hank Jackson. I hadn't even considered that possibility.

The midnight shift was comprised of a combination of troopers from both the day and the afternoon shifts. Everyone's schedule rotated so that every trooper on patrol eventually worked all of the shifts. For instance, a trooper worked the day shift one month, and then the next month he or she worked the afternoon shift followed by another month of the day shifts and so on. This back-and-forth bouncing between shifts continued until about every sixth month when that trooper would be assigned to work the midnight shift. When he finished that month of midnights, he went back to the day and afternoon shifts for the next five months.

There was an exception to this unique scheduling practice. A few troopers worked all midnights due to their college-class schedules. My training officer happened to be one of those troopers enrolled in a college program. As a result, I would have to work the midnight shift consistently.

I tried to keep my composure, but I couldn't keep my mind from reeling as I tried to process this news. Logistically, I would be working about forty miles from home and driving across most of the county to get to work. All of the other recruits who lived close to the south area were sent to one of the two south squads.

Also with the midnight shift ending at seven o'clock in the morning, I would be forced to drive home in heavy rush-hour traffic. Driving in Miami during this chaotic time would add hours to my commute. All of this would take place while I tried to adjust to staying awake all night. However, I didn't know if one ever truly got adjusted to staying up all night and sleeping little during the day.

I wondered if the sergeant intentionally placed extra stress on me because I was a female. It sure looked that way to me, but I didn't dare express my feelings to this crusty ole guy or to any of my classmates.

Maybe he was trying to run me off so that he could get rid of me. If that was the case, he was in for a surprise. I wanted this job too much to let it go. In fact, I wanted to excel with a fierce determination.

Admittedly, my unexpected assignment shook me to the core. I had not anticipated this subtle type of discrimination, but I couldn't be one-hundred-percent sure if this assignment was intentional. I kept silently questioning his motive for this unforeseen turn of events.

As I mulled over my situation, I realized I needed to let go of my dismay and make the best of it. I drove myself home in the late afternoon in my own patrol car, and it felt good. Even though I was in training, it still provided me with a sense of independence.

I glanced at my watch as I pulled into my driveway. I didn't have much turnaround time since I had to meet Hank in the north end at ten thirty, a mere few hours away. Meanwhile, several things needed to be accomplished during that small window of time. I needed to cook dinner and help my girls with their homework. I also needed to familiarize myself with the items issued to me earlier.

Unfortunately, sleep didn't make the to-do list. Thank goodness my adrenaline was pumping from the excitement of setting up my car and acted as a much-needed stimulant for my upcoming midnight shift.

I opened my trunk and pulled out what looked like a large blue suitcase from the pile. It turned out to be a first-aid kit. Its top opened up and extended out like a small shelf. I busied myself examining all of the bandages, ointments, and bottled sterile water.

When I was a trainee and on the auxiliary force, I had been on the scene of a couple of fatalities. Seeing them up close made me glad I was with experienced troopers.

Then during my time in the academy, we had extensive first-aid courses. Still, I found the thought of actually needing to use all of these medical aids without any supervision a daunting prospect.

I finally finished going through all of the gadgets that came with my new job. Although overwhelmed, I felt confident that I at least possessed an understanding and knowledge of what I carried around with me.

After a nonstop afternoon and evening of doing, doing, doing, I finally finished donning my uniform, badge, and gun belt. I climbed into my patrol car to work my first patrol shift as a Florida Highway Patrol Trooper.

Before pulling out of my driveway, I managed to blurt out the code 10-8 over the radio. This told the dispatcher I was in service.

Using the radio was not as simple as people may think. The timing of when I talked to dispatch could be tricky. I tried to avoid talking over another trooper or "stepping on" another call. When I wanted to say something, I waited until all conversations and transmissions stopped. Then as I clicked the button to activate the mike, someone else started speaking. Some of the male troopers delighted in keying me out by activating their mikes and talking. They used this as an attempt to intimidate the new female rookie.

Most of the troopers, including myself, had small scanners in their patrol cars so that they knew what the local police were doing. We used ten signals while the county and local police all used a strange code referred to as Q signals. All of these transmissions ran together when they were broadcasted simultaneously. A new trooper could find listening to them challenging. To the untrained ear, it could sound completely confusing. Therefore, a trooper working in Miami needed to know both "languages."

I used my drive north to become even more familiar with the chatter and the codes in action. I paid close attention to make sure I didn't miss the dispatcher calling fourteen hundred, my personal call sign, in the midst of the constant transmissions.

I arrived first to our designated meeting spot—a semi-secure parking lot off of the turnpike tollbooth. As I waited for Hank, I thought about how things had not worked out as I expected. I could do nothing about the situation but accept it. Instead of looking at the glass half empty, I decided to look at the glass half full and adopt a positive attitude. Maybe the bright stars hovering in the clear sky was a good sign.

When Hank drove into the lot, he pulled his car next to mine. I gathered my gear and got out of my car.

I walked over to Hank's rolled-down window. He smiled and said, "Hi, Turner."

I returned his smile. "Hi, Hank. Do you mind if I drive?"

"No. I want you to sit and watch how I maneuver in and out of traffic."

A bit disappointed, I opened his back door and threw my stuff into his backseat. I then climbed into the front passenger seat. I looked over at Hank's six-foot-two frame that almost completely filled the driver's space from the floorboard to the roof.

His dark eyes watched me get situated onto my seat. "Ready?" he asked.

"Yep. Let's go."

I studied Hank out of the corner of my eye while he drove out of the parking lot. His dark mustache matched his dark hair, and his large barreled chest crammed into a trooper's uniform made him appear intimidating.

I found myself sitting on the edge of my seat. I had wanted action, and I was assured I would find action in Miami's north end. Nothing remarkable happened, though, which made me feel a little disenchanted. I reminded myself that I was only beginning my career and still had years ahead of me to experience all of the excitement one person should ever have. Still, I couldn't wait to be out on the street and on my own, since Florida troopers normally ride solo.

Throughout our shift, Hank taught me several lessons. They could be as minute as tucking a hand towel under your shirt collar to catching any spills when eating or drinking in the car. It could be as complex as assessing situations for possible dangers.

He also explained how our zone partner was our life link on the road. A zone partner is another trooper who works nearby. If things went bad, this is the person to count on for help since he or she worked in the same assigned area.

As a result, I learned that I must depend on my zone partner and squad members to keep me safe. I also needed to be vigilant in protecting those with whom I work. An important aspect acquired from working with others over time was the ability to tell if something was wrong by the inflection in his or her voice.

At the same time, it enabled the cop-against-the-world mentality that most rookies developed. Fortunately, this outlook settles down into a more normal and realistic attitude after a couple of years. I've always felt it might be a defense mechanism that results from frequent exposure to life-and-death situations.

I found myself liking Hank a lot. His demeanor impressed me the most. Besides his professionalism, I appreciated his low-key and patient mannerism.

We worked some of the most violent areas in Miami. Our zone ran the length of State Route 7 (SR 7) and covered a section of Interstate-95 (I-95) that crossed over Liberty City where the 1980 riots occurred. During this incident, eighteen people were killed, eight hundred people were arrested, and property damage soared to one hundred million dollars. We also worked the Overtown and Wynwood neighborhoods. They would become areas of future riots.

Within a few nights of working with Hank, I experienced my first crazy encounter with a suspect. While riding on SR 7 in the middle of Liberty City, we noticed a scruffy man on foot. He dodged in and out of traffic with no apparent concern for his personal safety.

His clothes were nondescript except for the grease and dirt that covered them. His shoulder-length brown hair was matted into clumps, and his brown eyes presented a wild, glazed look.

Hank stopped the patrol vehicle and looked over at me. "How will you handle this?"

I took in a deep breath. "Well, I would take a signal so the dispatcher knows where I am. Then I would get out of the car and speak to him."

And I did just that. I radioed to dispatch and then got out of the car. Hank followed behind me.

I approached the man and asked, "Why are you walking on the road and jumping in and out of traffic?"

His wild eyes glared back at me. "Fuck you, lady."

He then continued walking in the middle of the road and away from me. I was stunned for a moment. Then my training took over, and I realized I needed to take action.

"Hank, I need to get this person under control immediately to protect him and those driving on this road," I said, sounding braver than I felt.

Hank nodded in return. His eyes darted back and forth between me and the wild-eyed man.

I moved forward. "Get on the sidewalk," I ordered in the most authoritative voice I could muster at the time.

He turned and faced me before lunging at me.

I sprung back with my right side exposed toward him since I wore a cross-draw holster. If I had faced him and leaned my left side forward, my gun would have been exposed, making it too easy for him to pull it out of my holster.

I reached behind me and grabbed my handcuffs from its case attached to my gun belt. I approached him and then had to wrestle him so that I could put on the handcuffs. Fortunately, I didn't lose my balance, but I did grapple with both of his dirt-encrusted forearms.

Hank jumped into the struggle, and I noticed he wore latex gloves on his hands. I wished I had thought about that so that I could protect my hands too.

Together, we managed to handcuff this man and get him stuffed into the back of Hank's car. Then we drove very quickly to the Miami jail.

Thank goodness the jail was only about eight minutes away. The patrol car began to smell really bad. I was just about at the point of becoming very nauseous when we pulled into the jail's parking lot. I prayed I wouldn't throw up.

I led my nasty-smelling arrestee into the sally port, which is the jail's secured entryway. We stepped in between the two steel gates constructed out of a strong chain-link material that opens and closes by being rolled up and down.

Once inside this area, the gate we had just walked though closed behind us before the next gate opened up to the main jail. The design kept detainees from walking (or running) out.

Four Hispanic jailers stood by and waited on the other side of the second gate. I felt like I was trapped in purgatory. My arrestee kept trying to bump up to me, saying, "Fuck you, lady."

All of the jailers laughed and had fun at my expense. The gate rose up, and we entered the booking area. As I took the handcuffs off of my arrestee, he screamed "Fuck America."

He then spit at our patriotic Cuban jailers while lunging at them. The correction officers took great offense at his disgraceful quote and felt threatened by his menacing actions. They all jumped back at him, and the fists started flailing. Total chaos broke out, and many of the jailers joined in a free-for-all jailhouse brawl.

The fracas finally settled down. I grabbed my prisoner before he could do anymore damage. He needed to be put in a holding cell and confined until I could finish all of the paperwork required in the booking process. As a state officer, though, I didn't have access to the cells. They were under the control of the county.

I looked around for a corrections officer to assist me and lodge my prisoner in a cell. As if on cue, a corrections supervisor came over and grabbed my prisoner. He proceeded to fingerprint him before taking his picture. He then took him to the holding cell area.

I submitted his prints to the ID section located in the main headquarter building of the Miami-Dade Police Department. I then discovered that the man I had arrested was known in Miami as a "Marielito." This was the local term used for Cubans who participated in the mass emigration to Florida in April 1980.

At that time, Fidel Castro had allowed many of Cuba's prisoners and mental patients to board Miami-bound boats from Cuba's Mariel Harbor. This caused Miami to experience a higher-than-normal crime wave during the early eighties.

Not surprising was that my prisoner was identified as a career criminal. I ended up charging him with being a public nuisance, obstructing the highway, disorderly conduct, and resisting arrest.

As soon as I completed everything, I handed over my arrest affidavit and hurried out of that detention center and to our patrol car as fast as my legs would carry me.

We may have left the pandemonium of the detention center behind, but our prisoner's body stench remained in the car and played havoc on my sense of smell. I kept smelling hints of him as his odor continued to linger on my skin, hair, and uniform. I began to wonder if his scent had actually embedded itself permanently into my nostrils and olfactory nerves.

Over the next few days, the odor of his stale sweat refused to leave the confines of Hank's car. This turned out to be one of those lessons that you learn best from experience rather than word-of-mouth. No extent of imagination could have truly prepared me for that smell.

When you work midnights, your chance of arresting someone who stinks, vomits, urinates, or defecates in your car or on his or herself increases. I've seen other police officers keep large garbage bags in their cars for the unfortunate prisoners who soil their clothes. Rest assured that the odor becomes worse if the car is outside and "baking" in the hot Florida sun during the day. I strived to fight (and defeat) the battle of the odors by hanging little scented pine trees from the rearview mirror.

As a result of my experiences with my first arrest, I learned several valuable lessons. The physical confrontation made me see firsthand the potential dangers involved with using the department-issued cross-draw holster. So on the first day I had off from work, I drove to the police products store and purchased a secure right-side holster and ditched the other one. A few years later, the highway patrol followed suit and updated its troopers to all strong-side holsters.

Additionally, my first booking experience at the jail motivated me to become a quick study in the area of hygiene. Although my germ-freak disposition and life on the mean streets butted heads, I eventually learned to adapt. I began keeping a spare uniform in my patrol vehicle plus towels and toiletries. Also once I arrived home from working a shift, I took off my uniform and shoes in the laundry room located in the garage.

All of my patrol cars had cloth seats and no rear cage. I learned how to combat the damage caused by whatever excrements were expelled or rubbed into the rear seats. I made mental notes of the locations of every store in my district that stayed open all night. After each smelly incident, I'd go there to purchase disinfectants. You could then find me cleaning my car in the store parking lots because at this point, the scented pine trees had no effect.

From Super Heroes to Super Glue

Hank and I took our meal break around four thirty in the morning.

Many times, we ate at a twenty-four-hour chain restaurant close to an on-ramp for I-95 near Liberty City. It became the go-to eating establishment for law enforcement in this particular area. On just about any given night, the backroom could be filled with troopers and police officers. The dim lighting gave the room a hint of mystery to the other patrons. It also allowed us to "hide" from the public so that we could recharge, if only for thirty minutes. The excitement in the room always seemed to energize us as we ate together and shared "war stories" from our evening experiences.

All of the waitresses paid a lot of attention to the needs of their law enforcement customers. One reason was that some women just find a man in uniform attractive or sexy. However, I've never known of any man to think that about a woman in a police uniform.

Another reason was that they wanted to make us feel welcome. Having cops around gave the waitresses a sense of safety, especially since the restaurant was located in an area known for criminal activity. The rental car lots in the vicinity attracted lost tourists, which in turn attracted thieves. Like a lioness waiting for her unsuspecting prey, these thugs watched for those cars with Z license plates that identified the vehicle as a rental. Once spotted, the vehicle's inhabitant became a target, and thus, a victim. If the criminals couldn't snatch a rental car, they resorted to committing other crimes. Several years later, this area would earn its name as "The Triangle" after a series of murders took place within its boundaries.

During the early 1980s, we couldn't take our radios with us into the restaurant because only senior troopers were given handheld portable radios. For the rest of us, our stationary car radios created some inconveniences. For instance, when conducting traffic stops we had to extend the car radio cord out of the driver's side window and loop it over the car's spotlight. We needed to insure that we could reach the mike in an emergency or just to be able to communicate easier.

Another challenge was leaving our car for our meal break. If we wanted to hear the transmissions while eating, we could only take our portable scanners with us. If the transmission required a response from us, we had to run back to our car to answer on the radio.

One night an emergency call came across Hank's scanner, dispatching us to an accident with injuries. We bolted out of our seats, threw money on the table, and ran outside. Upon exiting the confines of the restaurant's cool air conditioning, the night's mugginess and heat slammed against us like a sledge hammer, momentarily taking my breath away.

Our car was located at the far end of the row of patrol cars parked in front of the restaurant. After reaching our vehicle, I pulled the keys out of my pocket since Hank now allowed me to drive. I tried to insert it into the door's lock, but it wouldn't go into its keyhole.

I thought I was doing something wrong. After all, why couldn't I get my key into the lock?

I threw the keys to Hank. He couldn't get the key to slide into the lock on his door either.

I looked around and saw our backup troopers, who had also run to their vehicles. They too struggled with trying to insert their keys.

We took our flashlights and started examining the door locks. I could see a hardened drip that had wormed its way down from the lock in my door.

About the same time, Hank thought he knew what had happened. While we were on a meal break, some prankster had filled our locks with super glue.

One of the troopers got into his trunk to retrieve a slim jim. He took this thin piece of metal and inserted it between the driver's door window and the weather stripping to jimmy the lock.

While he worked on my door, I heard a clinking noise inside its frame. The window's glass dropped down into no-man's land. Although it didn't break, it did manage to slip off of its track and fall to the bottom of the door.

Hank and I finally were able to head to the accident. We drove at a high speed, so Hank and I couldn't talk over the loud roar of the wind blowing through the opening where my door's window had once been. It didn't matter anyway; we were too tense to talk. I seethed with frustration and anger as I worried about the accident victims who had been on hold waiting for us.

Thank God the Miami Fire Rescue had already arrived on the scene by the time we got there. Still, I couldn't help but wonder about the possible consequences that could have erupted from that prank.

What if Fire Rescue had been on another call? What if the injured had to wait longer and consequently died? What if the unsecured scene turned into a hazard on the roadways, causing additional collisions and possible deaths? What some idiot thought was funny could have resulted in life-or-death situations.

Later on, Hank's deduction was confirmed. We learned that someone had doused the door locks of both the trooper and county police cars parked at the restaurant with super glue. Some of the locks needed to be replaced at the taxpayers' expense, and we lost valuable time responding to an emergency. This didn't include the few hours we spent on paperwork explaining how our vehicles got damaged. These reports got submitted up the chain of command.

Needless to say, we altered all future meal plans. We began eating at another restaurant on the north end of Liberty City. It offered counter seating with a large picture window. This allowed us to keep a vigilant watch on our patrol cars at all times. Additionally, the bright lighting over the counters provided ideal conditions for report writing. The eatery soon became a favorite with all the cops on the midnight shift.

We never had anyone mess with our patrol cars again. This incident turned out to be a valuable lesson learned, and thank God, the only damage incurred was fixable.

Together We Stand

After spending two months on patrol with Hank, I had finished my field training and was deemed ready to leave his nurturing nest, fulfilling yet another phase of my career.

Not only did Hank reinforce the techniques taught in the academy, but I learned a lot just by watching him. Some things that stand out in my mind today is how much I admired Hank's ability to keep a level head in each predicament we found ourselves. I witnessed how he put into practice the lessons he meticulously explained to me. I saw and experienced his most important lesson firsthand: keeping safe and protecting those with whom we came into contact, all the while making sure we went home at the end of our shift.

Another important lesson I learned was to look out for all of our brothers and sisters in blue. Law enforcement officers need to stick together regardless of any personal issue we may have with each other. We don't even have to know him or her. The bottom line is, if we don't have each other's back, then who will?

I know that during those precarious times in my career, I felt relief when another city, county, state, or federal officer stopped to assist me. Some of these officers were on-duty, and some were not. Whether it's on the streets of Miami or in some small town in the middle of nowhere, we stand together to fight for justice.

This knowledge provided me with comfort as I stepped into this new chapter. Importantly, I did so possessing the confidence I needed to do my job and to do it successfully. I was able to understand more clearly that what had initially appeared to be a curse turned out to be a blessing. My soft demeanor had been toughened but not calloused; my naivety transformed to a wisdom that can only be garnered from surviving the crime-ridden streets of a large metropolitan city.

Looking back, I often wonder if that ole crusty sergeant had placed me with Hank for that specific reason. Maybe he thought I was too soft, too naïve for this job. He was right. Maybe he took it upon himself to indirectly groom me. Maybe his intention was to ensure that I obtained a new perspective on—and in—the toughest neighborhoods in Miami.

If so, he succeeded in his mission. Because of everything Hank poured into me, I acquired a necessary understanding of my job and my environment. I learned how to not only function but to survive in a massive area in the inner city where violence totally impacted the residents. I learned how to react to danger and adapt. I learned how to see through the eyes of the average citizen who must endure gangs and lawlessness and poverty's influence on both.

Maybe in my naivety, I had been too eager, too quick to judge that sergeant, thinking that my comfort should have been the priority when it came to assignments. Perhaps that ole crusty sergeant was wiser than I had given him credit to be.

Hank and his midnight shifts turned out to be one of the best on-the-job trainings a rookie could experience and endure. If not for my assignment with him, I know that I would not have been as prepared and equipped for the events that lay ahead of me in the years to come.

CHAPTER 3

Trooper on Her Own

I got assigned back to the south squad on Pete's shift. Although at first I only knew Pete, I soon got to know the other two guys, Jacob Trotter and Dean Trout, and the other female, Jackie Hays. She concluded our five-member squad.

At first the others were friendly enough to me, yet they were understandably reserved. In this kind of atmosphere where we literally put our lives into the hands of others, trust was a huge issue. The way you received trust was to first receive respect, and you received respect by proving you could handle yourself.

Pete helped a lot in the acceptance area by smoothing the way for me. He gave me the thumbs up that demonstrated he had already vetted me and that I had passed the test. His approval went a long way with them. Still, I had to prove myself. Once I did, they could let down their guard and relax around me.

The five of us ended up developing a bond that's hard to describe. Suffice it to say that we shared a closeness that at times went deeper than family. In fact, we became family.

We worked together in the deep south end of Miami-Dade County. Whether we were meeting for coffee or backing each other up on traffic stops, arrests, or car crashes, we were there for each other through thick and thin.

We each brought our own personalities, strengths, and weaknesses to the squad. The one trait that we all shared, though, was a dedication to the job.

Both Jacob and Dean were single, ambitious, attractive, and took great pride in their appearance. Here was probably where the similarities ended.

Jacob had never been married, which at first glance was hard to believe. He seemed to be the overall great package for a woman looking for love.

He could never be caught with a hair out of place. He always wore a smile, and he was smart, an excellent communicator, and well-read. His favorite book genres tended to be the classics and history. I thought his love for reading probably contributed to his wonderful writing skills. He wrote impeccable arrest reports using correct vernacular, grammar, and punctuation.

He wanted more from this job and from life. He talked frequently about going to school to earn his master's degree.

Jacob and I shared similar tastes in food, especially Italian pasta. Dean, on the other hand, watched everything he ate. For instance, he preferred chicken over beef as his form of protein.

Dean had been married, but it obviously didn't work out because he and his wife divorced. He was actually more of a guy's guy, into mechanics, working on cars, and he previously served as a U.S. Marine.

He earned the unofficial award as the tallest member of our squad. He balanced his six-foot-four-inch height with a muscular build that he maintained with weight lifting. He exhibited great features which included a perpetual smile, beautiful light-blue eyes that twinkled, and light blond hair.

Dean's clean-cut appearance served his handsome face well. His expressive eyes gave away his thoughts or feelings whether he wanted them to or not. Every time I looked into them, I felt as if I were looking into his very soul. When happy, his eyes lit up and twinkled, and when sad, they darkened and became more fixed on people or things.

He was also the squad's chick magnet and continuously dated different women. His good looks caused the cop groupies to flock his way because he fulfilled the ideal of a dream man wearing a uniform. His activities always entertained the rest of the squad members.

He loved to joke around and told the corniest jokes, like how he spilt his coffee down the front of his uniform shirt. It didn't matter if anyone else found his jokes funny because he sure did. He loved to laugh, even if he had to laugh alone, which happened many times.

However, he could immediately switch into a somber demeanor. He took his job very seriously.

He and I shared a lot of commonalities. We both lived in Homestead, a farming community south of Miami. In addition, our children were about the same ages.

Pete was the third male member of our squad. He had his own quirks, such as being in the middle of a divorce from his fourth wife. We always joked that he didn't know how to date, only how to marry.

Jackie Hays was the other female. She and I made a great team and enjoyed working together. Although female troopers were few and far between, it just happened that Jackie was assigned to the south. She had been a trooper for about a year, and until my arrival, she had been the rookie of the squad.

Although she was about ten years younger than me, we bore an uncanny resemblance to each other. We were about the same weight, except that I was a few inches taller than her five-foot-seven-inch frame.

When we drove down the highway, our blue eyes, fair complexion, and blonde hair that was cut just about our shoulders made us difficult to tell apart. Differentiating became even more challenging when we wore our Stetson trooper hats.

Later on we laughed about our physical similarities. We shared an ongoing joke that if we felt someone was going to complain to headquarters about one of us, we would give the other's name.

As a cop, getting complaints was part of the job. After all, we worked in an industry where the majority of our "customers" were never pleased with our work.

In reality, neither Jackie nor I never really gave the other one's name during those few times we received a minor accusation. Often the complaints came from drivers who had been issued a ticket. They just wanted to vent.

When the calls came in, they got transferred to the sergeant or lieutenant on duty. He then asked the caller questions, such as whether the cop displayed rudeness.

Afterward the sergeant or lieutenant would call one of us to ask about the specifics of the incident. After we answered his questions, the complaints never went any further. Usually at that point, the caller just dropped the complaint.

There were some complainants, though, who insisted on pursuing their grievance. If so, then they were instructed to go to the station to file a formal complaint.

Looking back on my career as a trooper, I can remember how I caught hell from drivers when I gave them a speeding ticket. However, years later in my career as a special agent with the Florida Department of Law Enforcement (FDLE), I helped put away a lot of bad guys. They ended up going to prison for decades, and they never complained. Yet most of us know friends or family who have been hurt, or even killed, in motor vehicle accidents.

People just seem to get irate over traffic tickets. The driver actually believes it was the cop who ruined his day, not his actions. Of course, getting a traffic ticket on a holiday like Thanksgiving and Christmas exacerbated their anger. I must admit that I tried to avoid writing tickets on those kinds of holidays, unless the driver went way beyond the limits for public safety. "Have a nice day" is the worst thing a traffic cop can say to someone after writing him or her a ticket.

Most of the time I tried to put myself in the driver's shoes. If the car looked old and on its last wheel, and the driver appeared not to have much money, I only gave a warning. If the driver appeared to be unable to afford the child safety seat, I sent them to the local hospital or clinic to obtain a free one.

My job as a trooper involved stopping cars all day. Evolving into the extra roles of psychologist and social worker became natural.

I've always wanted to seek justice for the weak, those who just seem to need that additional assistance. I stayed especially sensitive to families in need, those parents down on their luck without the necessary skills to acquire a better life for their children. However, I responded quite differently to parents who abused or neglected their children.

One winter morning while on patrol during rush-hour, I came across a certain situation involving a parent and his kids. I had observed an old, dirty, and battered four-door sedan stopped at a red light, and the taillights were out. I activated my overhead lights and gave a quick yelp with the siren, signaling to the car to pull over to the side of the road.

When I walked up to his car, I noticed four children in the front and back seats. They all appeared to be young enough to attend elementary school. They wore dirty, worn-out clothes, and their hair needed to be washed and combed. They bounced all over the car as if they just consumed a donut-and-Kool-Aid breakfast.

The driver's wrinkled clothes looked similar to those of the children. His thin and weathered face contained a set of dark, sunken-in eyes.

He turned toward me but didn't look me in the eyes. "I'm taking my kids to school," he muttered without any emotion. He then turned to stare back out of his front window. After that, he didn't say anything else.

I walked back to my patrol car parked behind him. After running his driver license, I discovered he had a bench warrant for his arrest. His failure to appear in court for a fraudulent check had finally caught up to him, literally. I guess he thought that if he didn't talk to and interact with me, I'd just go away.

I felt bad for these children and knew that they needed to get to their school immediately. I made arrangements for another trooper to transport them.

"Sir, would you please step out of your vehicle," I said in a soft yet authoritative tone.

His chest rose slightly before his body momentarily froze. He then lowered his chest and head simultaneously in acceptance of his defeat. After opening his door, he slowly got out of his car.

I walked close to him. "There's a warrant for your arrest, and I'm going to have to take you in. I don't want to arrest you in front of your kids, so I'll wait until after they leave before handcuffing you."

His chest rose again, but this time his eyes softened in appreciation. He nodded his understanding and agreement.

I watched until the patrol car that transported the children to school drove out of our line of vision. I then said, "Okay, turn around so that I can place the handcuffs on you."

He did exactly as I told him. Still, he didn't mutter a word.

With Homestead's small-town environment, I found out the name of some of these children's teachers. A couple of days later, I ran into one of them. I told her about my concerns regarding the youngsters arriving to school late that morning.

She jokingly said, "These are horrible and disruptive children. I wouldn't worry so much about getting them to school."

Since then, I've often thought about those children and how they turned out.

I came across so many needy families with children. I felt compelled to do more. So I approached the twenty or so members within my church circle with an idea that had been brewing in me for awhile.

While the president discussed upcoming events during one of our meetings, I thought, *This is the perfect time to ask them.*

I raised my hand. When the president acknowledged me, I said, "I was wondering if you would assist me in a project." I then explained the situation. "I want to make nonperishable food boxes for these disadvantaged families."

I looked around the room. Every face wore a big smile, and eyes were stretched wide open in excitement as heads nodded emphatically.

I heard several responses. "What a great idea." "Yes, let's do it." "I really like that idea," and so forth.

Inside, I felt a big sigh of relief. I knew I had a willing crew to help bring my desire to a reality.

We gathered together small white cardboard boxes that food caterers used. We placed small packets of raisins, packets of cheese crackers, protein bars, and cookies into each one of them.

I kept some of these boxes in my trunk and gave them to each and every needy family I pulled over for traffic infractions. Not only did I spare them a ticket, but I gave them some food to boot. Maybe this would help some of their hungry kids.

When supplies got low, the ladies made more boxes. This project turned out to be an ongoing success.

Over the course of a few years, the ladies made over a hundred of these boxes, and I had the honor of distributing each and every one of them.

Too Close to Home

Marijuana was the primary drug imported in South Florida from 1960 to 1970. Then from 1970 through the 1980s, a more lucrative and intense drug came on the market—cocaine—and it replaced marijuana. Most of the cocaine was smuggled from Colombia to Miami via boats and light aircraft.

The cocaine trade was a different beast than the marijuana trade. It created the infamous Miami cocaine wars, which were known for extreme gun violence as a result of a 1979 shootout involving drug dealers. This shootout became known as the Dadeland Massacre, and it introduced the infamous phrase "cocaine cowboys."

Throughout the '80s, a lot of the U.S. experienced an economic slump, but Miami was booming. Its economy benefited from the drug money coming into its bountiful city and vicinities. When I shopped in my favorite department store Burdines at the Dadeland Mall, I couldn't help but look at all of the beautiful displays. I didn't possess much disposable income, but I had fun trying to choose an item on which to splurge if I had the money. However, I saw well-dressed women standing next me who bought expensive items in mass quantity. I suspected they were Colombians.

It wasn't uncommon for Colombians to fly to Miami just to shop. Drug money was spent and invested all over South Florida. Money was being made, and money was being spent while murder escalated, and the casualties could be found in the most unlikely places.

On a clear morning in 1984, I drove my youngest daughter to her elementary school where she was a school safety patrol member. Upon arrival, she got out and walked into the building.

I needed to look over my daily schedule. I couldn't remember if I had court that morning.

I decided to drive down a dead-end road that ran parallel to the school's fenced physical education field. I planned to drive to the paved end and turn around. I could then monitor the school's morning traffic while I looked through my calendar.

When I neared the end of the road, I saw what looked like a crumpled body. It lay across the grass near a gate that led to the field.

I pulled to a stop and got out of my car. I walked over to get a better look and saw a young woman wearing a rose-colored sleeveless top and blue jeans.

Her back faced my direction. I could see a cascade of long brown hair from the back of her head.

When I leaned over, I was shocked to see that her entire face was gone. I hadn't received extensive death investigation training at this time in my career. However, I was fairly certain she had been executed with a shotgun.

I thought about my daughter, and my maternal protection automatically kicked in. I radioed dispatch and said I needed immediate backup to secure this crime scene. I requested they notify Miami-Dade homicide to respond.

I then jumped in my car and drove around to the front of the school. After running into the office, I told the school secretary Nancy to make sure the staff kept all children away from the field. I explained that I had just discovered a dead body near the physical education field.

By this time, I was running on pure adrenalin with the idea of my child or another child seeing the body. I felt like this was just too close to home. I only lived a mile away.

I later learned that this woman was a victim of a drug execution that happened in my own "backyard."

The Tell-Tale Signs of the Broken Taillight

One hot and muggy night while on patrol, I noticed an older model green Thunderbird without taillights driving south on U.S. 1. When I lit up my blue overhead lights, the driver sped away.

I radioed to dispatch that I was in pursuit of a suspicious vehicle. After giving the car's description, license plate, and direction of travel, I heard several other troopers chime in over the radio notifying dispatch of their intent to back me up and join in the pursuit.

My heart raced as I followed the car heading east from Homestead into Leisure City. We then made a few fast turns into a neighborhood.

The car came to a stop. The driver jumped out and broke into a full run. I parked my car next to his and then jumped out to chase him. I gave his description over the radio: male Hispanic, long hair pulled into a ponytail, white t-shirt, and black jeans.

Times like this one reminded me of how grateful I felt now that we had been issued portable radios. It certainly simplified some important functions of my job. The state came through with the funding to buy them. The ability to carry them with us during a foot chase came in handy, and not a moment too soon.

I kept the driver in my eyesight as I ran after him. The next thing I knew, I saw my zone partners Pete, Dean, and Jacob out of the corner of my eye. They too were running, and I was so thankful that they had showed up to help me apprehend this guy. They instinctively knew my mission, and they ran just as hard as me to complete it.

The driver tried hard to evade us for a reason. I didn't believe it had anything to do with a dysfunctional taillight.

Before I knew it, my zone partners caught up to me, and the four of us formed what appeared to be a small army. There was no one else I wanted with me at that time than my team. I knew them and had grown to trust them with my life.

We all ran through a middleclass neighborhood. We passed one concrete-block house after the other with all of them looking similar in design. The only difference seemed to be the pastel color each one displayed on its exterior frame.

My eyes never left my suspect's back. I watched his dark ponytail quickly swish to and fro each time one of his feet hastily hit the ground.

I felt relieved to see him run up to the front door of a pink house, open it, and then disappear through its doorway. I knew our foot pursuit had come to an end.

We barreled through that same front door of the small house. We immediately found ourselves smack dab in the middle of a small room that I assumed acted as a living room. I spotted my suspect about four or five feet away with his back still to me. By now, I would recognize that ponytail anywhere.

He turned toward me when I was about a foot away from him. His dark eyes locked onto mine and slightly narrowed. I'll never forget the hatred that emitted from them. He looked deviant, mean, and very angry.

That moment shared between us seemed to have lasted several minutes, but in reality it only lasted a split second. I didn't take his abhorrence personally; I got the sense that he loathed all cops.

Before he took another step toward hiding, running into another room like the kitchen, or making himself comfortable, the four of us pounced on him. I straddled his back and wiped the sweat from my forehead to prevent it from running into my eyes. Then I reached into the triangular-shaped black-leather case strapped onto the back of my belt. I pulled out my handcuffs from the case and quickly placed them on our runaway driver.

Within my peripheral vision sat a couple of men on a sofa watching a basketball game. They looked quite comfortable in their shorts, wife-beater tank undershirts, and flip flops.

Neither one said a word to us; they just continued watching television and drinking their beers as if we weren't even there. Maybe the police barging into their living room during the night was a common occurrence. But then again, maybe they figured that if they ignored us, we would go away.

If they wanted the latter, then they got no argument from us. We ignored them and went away, walking out with our prisoner.

I was relieved that Jacob and Dean offered to escort him back to our cars. I needed to catch my breath and refill my lungs with air. I didn't know if my heart raced because of running so hard or as a result of the pumping adrenaline that a cop experiences during any pursuit.

As we got closer to our parked cars, I saw Jackie walk to the trunk of the suspect's car and open it. "Come quick! You're not going to believe this," she hollered over her shoulder.

The shaking of Jackie's head intrigued me. All of a sudden, my adrenaline surged back through my body like a drug, invigorating me with newfound energy. It almost catapulted my body to the trunk. I sensed that she had discovered a missing piece to this puzzle.

I looked inside the trunk and saw a young, dark Hispanic woman with her hands and feet bound by brown rope. She cried as her small and thin body shook uncontrollably.

Her face contained scrapes and bruises that retained the shape and size of a man's fist. Her clothes and hair were damp from the heat within the trunk.

Jackie untied her feet, and I untied her hands while Pete called for Fire Rescue. We then helped her out of the trunk.

I asked, "How did you end up in this trunk with your hands and feet tied?"

Her eyes stayed glued to the ground. In between sobs, she spoke in a shaky voice. "This is...Antonio's car. He...he used to be...to be my boyfriend. I was going to leave him, but he found out, so...so...so he threatened me. He said that if I ever broke up with him, he'd...he'd...he'd get even. I broke...broke up with him anyway.

"When I...I got home tonight from work, I got out of my car, and...and Antonio grabbed me. He...he hit me so hard I could barely move. He then...he then tied my hands in front of me and...and made me get into the trunk. I knew he would hi...hit me again if I di...didn't do what he told me to do. After I got into his trunk, he...he...he tied my hands and feet together."

She reached up with quivering fingers to lightly touch a bruise on her cheek. Her eyes closed as she cringed from the pain.

"He told...told me, 'I'm...I'm going to take you to the Everglades and f...f...feed you to the gators.' He would. I was...was so scared. I just knew I was going to...to...to die tonight."

Antonio's plans contained one big flaw. He left her in the trunk facing its opening. While he drove south on U.S. 1 toward the "Glades," she used her fingers to pull on the wires and disconnect the taillights.

Jackie said, "As soon as I arrived, I started securing the area. That's when I heard a soft banging sound in the rear of the car. I had just opened the trunk when you showed up."

About four hours later, I had the opportunity to conduct an in-depth interview of this woman. She was still frightened, not yet over that horrific and traumatic event.

I learned that she had suffered relationship abuse from Antonio. He had gained power and control over her through manipulation tactics, isolation, physical force, and violence.

At some point in their relationship, she had begun to stand up for herself and let him know that he wasn't going to abuse her anymore. Then she left him. He made good on his threats and kidnapped her.

In the United States, nearly one in four women report experiencing violence by a current or former intimate partner. What could have helped to protect this woman? A useful tool is a threat assessment. When domestic-violence advocates and the police collaborate together to perform this evaluation, the risk of lethality can be identified. Still, an abuser may become lethal without notice.

A safety plan, which is a personalized plan to reduce the risk that a victim will be hurt or killed by the abuser, is advised. It also includes an advanced plan to assist the victim to avoid dangerous situations.

I've often wondered what would have happened to this woman had I not noticed the broken taillights. Would she have been murdered in the Everglades? Did God intervene, and did He use me as His tool to rescue her?

Trooper or Secretary?

I had been on my own and riding solo for a few months. While I appreciated Hank's nurturing hand, I must admit that I loved my independence.

One morning when leaving my home to go on patrol, I notified dispatch that I was back in service. Dispatch responded immediately to inform me of a 10-5. This is the radio code that instructs an officer to go to the stationhouse. Because dispatch was so quick to give me that code, I thought, *Has she been waiting for me since early morning to give me that code?*

I had no idea what they wanted with me, but I wasn't concerned. On the other hand, I wasn't happy to leave my zone.

I immediately drove to the stationhouse and parked. As soon as I walked inside, one of the supervisors spotted me and quickly walked to me. "Turner, go upstairs to the captain's office."

"Yes, sir," I said, more confused now than ever.

When I entered the captain's office, he looked up from his desk. He spoke in a condescending tone as he waved toward a smaller desk. "My secretary called in sick today, so I need you to fill in for her." He then looked back down at the papers on his desk, signaling that I was dismissed to begin my new role.

My mouth dropped, and I think it almost hit the floor. My stomach churned as I felt my internal heat rise. I couldn't believe this was happening.

First of all, I've never been a typist and had minimal office skills. Plus, the state had spent a lot of money to train me to be a trooper, not work in an office.

I complied, of course. He was my superior officer. I couldn't help but wonder how many of my male classmates were called into the station for this type of assignment.

I suffered through the day, hoping it would be the first and last time I was ever asked to fill in for his secretary. I sat at my little desk and answered the phone and handwrote messages on a pink message pad. There was no way I was going to type. Instead, if I wasn't answering the phone, I spent my time shifting and shuffling papers around the desk.

My compulsiveness came out in full force, and I took my frustration out on cleaning, dusting, and wiping down the desk and phones repeatedly. I felt totally out of my element and except for the cleaning, I didn't want to be productive in this job whatsoever.

The next day, I forgot all about that office duty. I was assigned back to where I belonged: with my squad.

However, a few weeks later, this same incident happened again. I got called back to the stationhouse as soon as I reported my on-duty status to dispatch at the start of my shift. This time, I knew what was happening, and I knew I needed to put a stop to it once and for all.

I walked into Lt. Wells' office. I guess I should have been timid and intimidated by his rank, but I was so mad, I wanted to spit nails. My anger gave me the confidence to approach him and speak out on my behalf.

He looked up from his papers with a deadpan expression. I met his eyes with my own and held his gaze. I squared my shoulders back. My voice was strong when I spoke. "Lt. Wells, I'm a trooper, not a secretary. I've spent three months training at the trooper's academy to be a trooper. I've put forth a tremendous amount of effort to become a law enforcement officer. I didn't do all that I've done to be called off the road to type and file."

His blank face contorted into an angry glare. He frowned, and his eyes narrowed. He said, "When I became a trooper, I was just damned happy to have a job and never questioned my superiors."

I could tell that he didn't like my challenging him, but I refused to cower. "I'm a grown woman. I've had many jobs, but the one I've been trained for is the job of a trooper."

I forced my eyes to stay locked on his. I felt I might have made an enemy, but so be it. I knew I had to take a stand. I had no doubt that I was in the right, and he was in the wrong. He needed to understand that this bordered on harassment.

Many years later, his daughter became a trooper, following in her father's footsteps. I suspect by that time, his attitude toward women in law enforcement had changed. I wonder if he remembered the way he had treated me and how he would have felt if his daughter had been treated the same way.

Times were changing, and more women were entering the workforce, breaking the gender boundaries. For the longest time, my own mother couldn't understand my career choice. She always expressed confusion over why her daughter was a police officer and her son a nurse.

On one occasion, my mother talked with my zone partner Dean. She asked him to look out for me on the road.

Dean replied, "Floy can take care of herself, and she looks out for all of us".

I really appreciated Dean's vote of confidence in my abilities. He was such a standup guy.

The Jackie-and-Jacob Incident

The evening shift was always my favorite.

I went on duty at three in the afternoon and made it back home by eleven. Many nights, though, I got home late because I got tied up with an accident investigation or with processing an arrest.

The most challenging part of working the evening shift, though, was not spending time with my family. A law enforcement profession places a lot of stress on the officer's families.

When my children attended elementary school, they loved my being a cop. Once they got in high school, they hated it. Having a mom as a cop outright embarrassed them. Maybe some of their friends made some derogatory remarks about cops. I don't know. My daughter Mary Ellen's disdain went as far as even hating the Ray-Ban sunglasses I wore on patrol. She called them cop sunglasses.

My marriage lacked solidity. My husband stayed busy advancing his law enforcement career, finishing college, and earning his master's degree. I worked a lot of overtime to pay for my children's activities like dance and music lessons.

The hours my husband and I worked didn't leave any time to develop a stronger relationship between us. I felt like we were two ships passing in the night with him going his way and me going mine.

Since we both were driven by our careers, neither of us gave our marriage a lot of effort. Admittedly, the job came first. We learned firsthand how this lifestyle can take a toll on a marriage, and ours was not immune.

For instance, it seemed that I ate most of my meals with Jackie. She did eat dinner with my family on a lot of evenings, though. She was single and enjoyed being with my children.

We also shopped for clothes together and helped each other with our yard work. During the shift, if I needed to go by to check on my children, she covered for me. I covered for her if she had an errand to run or needed to stop by her house.

Covering meant that if Jackie was called to an accident, I informed the dispatcher that I would take the call. She did the same for me.

Jackie dated Jacob, but they kept their relationship quiet. Only our squad knew about them.

Jacob had been previously engaged to a city cop, but she broke his heart and left him for a homicide detective. I figured Jacob dated Jackie on the rebound.

One day Jacob called in sick. Jackie tried to reach him on the telephone to check on him. He didn't answer the call.

She asked me to cover for her and then drove a few miles out of our zone to check on Jacob. Since she had spent a few nights with him and had helped care for his Golden Retriever, she had a key to his apartment.

When she arrived, she opened the front door and entered. She walked toward the bedroom calling out his name.

She could see straight down the hall into his bedroom. He was in bed with another woman, and they were in the middle of having sex.

Jackie later told me that Jacob saw her and jumped off the bed fully nude. She recognized his partner as the waitress from The Good Luck Diner. The woman sat up, pulling the sheets over her bare chest.

Jackie turned around and stormed out of Jacob's apartment and returned to the zone. She radioed me to meet her.

I heard something different in her voice, and I didn't like it. Concerned, I agreed to meet her at the location she gave.

When I saw Jackie's parked patrol car, I pointed my car in the opposite direction. I pulled up next to her so that my driver's door was within a foot or so from her driver's door. Her sunglasses hid her eyes, so I couldn't read their expression. I could, however, see her set jaw, downturned lips, and what looked like wet smudges on her cheeks.

She told me what had happened. She was obviously very hurt and lamented about Jacob being a pig.

For the next few months, we endured a lot of drama between Jackie and Jacob. The tension between them intensified, creating a serious gap in the camaraderie of our close-knit group. The strain of not taking sides disrupted the once-enjoyed dynamics of the squad.

For instance, Jacob and Jackie refused to eat meals together, which made it tough on the rest of us. We were placed in the position of having to choose.

Regardless, I never ate my favorite dish again at what we began to call the "Bad Luck" Diner.

There for awhile, Jackie withdrew more than Jacob. She didn't want to be around him and avoided him at every opportunity. Of course, she couldn't avoid him all of the time because she did have to work with him.

Usually, Jackie and I ate together while the guys ate somewhere else. Although I missed them, I felt she needed me. She told me that she had fallen in love with Jacob. As a result, she was suffering through some major emotional pain.

At times, I caught her glancing at Jacob. At other times, I caught him eyeing her.

Believe it or not, but something positive did come from what soon became known throughout the troop as the "Jackie-and-Jacob incident." It provided reinforcement that getting sexually involved with coworkers is not a good idea.

Within a few months, however, we were just a team with a bit of history. Jackie and Jacob pushed aside their differences when it came to the jobs we faced within our dangerous work environment.

Still, this event continued to have a negative impact on our once-happy close-knit squad. Outside of work, Jackie kept her distance from Jacob as much as possible. She seemed to carry a broken heart for quite some time afterward. But I never asked.

On the other hand, Jacob appeared to have moved on from the "Jackie-and-Jacob incident." He also appeared to have recovered from his broken engagement with the city cop. But I never asked.

The other question I never asked was, who did Jacob get to replace Jackie as his dog walker.

Those Slithering Snakesters

I have never liked snakes. If truth be told, I'm terrified of them.

It's not that I'm afraid of being bitten by one. I'm simply repulsed by them in general. I don't even like to look at pictures of snakes or watch them on TV or in movies. Getting within a hundred miles of one is too close for me. In fact, I vividly remember how I used to shudder every time I drove past the Miami Serpentarium.

Honestly, my aversion could probably be defined as Ophidiophobia, which means an abnormal fear of snakes. Some people can commiserate with my weakness. However when you're a trooper, I'm positive that divulging it around a specific demographic, such as other troopers, is not in your best interest.

During one winter-night's shift, I was patrolling U.S. 1. I felt so relieved to be in my warm patrol car and out of the cold. Even though it was three in the morning, the stars lit up the dark sky. The contrast between its grayish color and the ebony landscape allowed me to see the tops of the trees swaying from the wind.

I noticed a small car driving very slowly along a desolate stretch of the roadway. As I got closer, I saw that the vehicle in question was a MG convertible sports car. It kept crossing the middle line, leading me to believe that the driver had been drinking.

I put on my overhead lights and drove behind him. I then gave a flicker of my siren.

He pulled over to the side of the road immediately. I parked behind him but at a slight angle for safety purposes.

I got out of my car, ready to address an inebriated driver. I approached the two-seater, which had its top down.

When I shone my flashlight into its tight interior, my eyes widened in horror. I thought, *Surely, this isn't what it looks like.*

In that same second, logic assured me that it was what I thought—a huge snake completely covering the cramped section behind the front seat.

My heart jumped into my throat as my body involuntarily recoiled backward a couple of feet. In my mind, though, that wasn't far enough. I then took a couple of more steps back, totally repulsed and almost shaking.

After a few moments and through a sheer force of will, I calmed myself down. I kept my distance from the man's car and yelled, "You can continue on with your destination, and be careful." I then said a silent prayer for him to get home safe and sound.

I always figured he must take that vile snake out with him whenever he drank, possibly to avoid a DUI arrest. One thing I knew with certainty that night was that his tactics worked on this trooper.

My second encounter with my hated species occurred on the road to the Florida Keys, otherwise known as *the stretch*. Its long highway didn't have any turns, turnarounds, or exits.

One day while on patrol, I drove my car on a part of the *stretch* that had a canal running parallel to it. Someone had parked his car on the shoulder.

The only person without a vehicle was a man walking alongside the road carrying a burlap bag. I pulled in front of him and stopped.

After getting out of my car, I approached him. "What are you doing?"

He didn't look up but continued searching the ground for something. "Collecting rattle snakes," he responded in a nonchalant tone as if he was informing me that he was looking for rocks.

I certainly believed him because dead pigmy rattlers were scattered all over that part of the road. I immediately got in my car and drove away as fast as I could and as far as I could. At that moment in time, I had no problem with this guy collecting all of the snakes in Florida.

I never shared this fear with my colleagues because if I did, I'd probably find a snake in my car. Sometimes cops can be great pranksters, especially when it came to their comrades. In law enforcement, it's easy to pull some stress-relieving pranks during downtimes. Cops will take advantage of whatever is at their disposal to get a few laughs.

For instance, I had been part of a joint task force that included law enforcement officers from different agencies. It had been formed to cut down on a crime spree occurring in a small neighborhood south of Cutler Ridge known as Goulds. Not only had some small stores been robbed, but several johns had been robbed, and one john had even been murdered.

One night, I worked with some county officers. We conducted surveillance near a local hangout called the "store porch," which was basically a store with a long porch where some guys hung out and drank.

My eyes slowly and continuously canvassed everything within my line of vision. The darkness was almost overwhelming and always seemed more intense in Goulds. Perhaps the huge ficus trees looming over the sidewalks and roadways contributed to its eerie atmosphere, especially in the middle of the night.

We all seemed to suffer from a bad case of boredom. One of the duties you won't see listed in a cop's job description is long and boring nights of just watching, waiting, and well, nothing. Some cops, however, can only take so much of not doing anything until they have to create their own action. So when one of the county officers came across a large black snake crossing the road, he couldn't leave well enough alone. He remembered that another officer had found a suitcase in an alley.

So the two of them put their heads together to come up with what they must have thought was a brilliant idea—put the found snake in the found suitcase. Then they placed the suitcase on the side of the road next to the store porch. Next they gathered all of the nearby surveillance units with binoculars and waited for a car to stop and take it.

Finally a low-slung Cadillac fully loaded with passengers drove by the suitcase, slowed down, and stopped. A rear door opened only wide enough to snatch the suitcase and pull it into the unsuspecting car.

Within moments, bodies poured out of the car, including the driver. This provided these cops with lots of laughter. This also gave them a story to share with those who had the misfortune of not being on the scene to witness this entertaining episode for themselves. As for me, I couldn't leave the area fast enough. Just knowing that a snake was in my general vicinity was too close for me.

I became a victim to another fun exercise the county officers practiced. Whenever they arrested a transvestite, they located a female rookie and requested she conduct the pat-down search. Naïve to this prank, I started the search on one of their female arrestees. Working my way down the prisoner's body, I slid my hand between her legs since prisoners have been known to hide illegal and potentially deadly items in that area. My hand froze when I felt something that made me realize she was really a he.

I fell for that request once and only once. Not only was I embarrassed, but I felt terrible for the prisoner. He was certainly a true victim of this cruel joke. Of course, this type of behavior wouldn't be tolerated in today's society.

Still, cops are known to have fun at the expense of others, and that wasn't the last time they had fun at my expense. One night when I left the jail, I noticed someone had placed a large dildo on the hood of my patrol car. Although I had my suspicions, none of my squad ever confessed to this act. I just took it and threw it in the parking lot's trashcan.

As a trooper, though, this sex toy was more common than one may think. While searching under car seats, I came across more of these devices than I care to mention.

Strange what some folks will hide in their cars.

Farewell to an Officer and a Gentleman

One midsummer day while on patrol, dispatch assigned me to a job of a disorderly person in the farmlands of South Miami. I drove to the area and saw a dirty, scruffy-looking man with long greasy hair walking close to a busy two-lane roadway.

I watched the traffic swerve to avoid hitting him. I was afraid that if I didn't intervene, he would either get hit or cause a vehicle crash.

I pulled over to the side of the road in front of him. As I approached him, he reeked of alcohol. Drool escaped his dry lips and dribbled down his unshaved chin.

After introducing myself, I requested he walk a straight line while touching his finger to his nose. He looked at me with a scowl before going on his merry way.

Obviously, he had absolutely no intention of complying with my instructions. I could tell that he was going to put up a fight with whatever I did.

I radioed my location and notified dispatch that I needed assistance. I heard Pete say he was on his way. Inside, I let out a sigh of relief. I wasn't surprised though. He had always been there for me.

I went to pull my guy out of harm's way. When I put my hands on him, he tried to jerk away from me. I refused to relinquish my hold and almost dragged him into the grass close to a chain-link fence that ran parallel to the road. He physically fought me the whole time by elbowing and kicking me.

I needed to gain control of him, so I pushed him into the fence. The heat and humidity created a slippery situation. Sweat flowed freely on both of us. It made it difficult to maintain a firm grasp on his dirt-covered arms. He continued to struggle while I continued to try to pin him against the fence in order to cuff him.

When Pete arrived about eight minutes later, I had the prisoner handcuffed. My uniform was torn and dirty. Sweat ran down my forehead and mixed with a tint of blood from a scrape I had received when the suspect knocked me into the fence.

Pete grabbed my prisoner, placed him in my car, and then looked over at me. He said, "You look like a mess. Come with me."

I followed Pete to his car where he retrieved his first aid kit from his trunk. He turned around and saw me standing next to him.

His eyebrows creased as his dark eyes explored my face before stopping and examining the scrape. He gently wiped it with antiseptic. He then picked up both of my hands and observed my knuckles. This altercation had scraped them raw.

These slight injuries worried him, so he suggested I go to the clinic and file a Report of Injury. He offered to book the prisoner for me after I finished the arrest paperwork, and I accepted. I found it touching to see Pete's display of care and concern for my well-being.

Over the years, Pete and I had become very close friends. I learned to look to him for advice on the many strange situations we encountered. He was very well-known, and most law enforcement officers in the south end of Miami respected him.

A few days after this incident, Pete called. "Hey, Floy, can you come over to my apartment now?"

I thought it an odd request, but I didn't hesitate to tell him I was on my way. He obviously wanted to talk to me about something.

About a half an hour later, I arrived at his front door and knocked. He opened it immediately as if he had been waiting for me on the other side.

I almost recoiled backward in shock when I first glanced at his unusual demeanor. I had just seen him a few days earlier, but I felt as if I was looking at a stranger. Before me stood a worn- and defeated-looking man wearing military-pink uniform pants and a white t-shirt, both of which looked slept in, and black combat boots.

He greeted me with a half smile. "Thanks for coming, Floy. Come on in."

I studied his pale, almost translucent face. Prominent dark circles bordered the bottom of his beautiful brown eyes.

I followed him down the short hallway. As I walked behind him, I noticed for the first time just how thin he looked. The heavy wrinkles on the back of his neck contained a fading reddish hue.

He led me into his small, typical bachelor's kitchen. The bare-boned décor and furnishings had seen better days.

I sat down in one of the scarred brown chairs at the metal card table that Pete had turned into his kitchen table. Large coffee mugs with highway patrol logos littered the faded-green felt tabletop.

Pete took a few steps to the wall containing a small white refrigerator and a small white stove. A coffee maker seemed to overwhelm the limited space that the beige laminate countertop provided.

He pulled out the full glass carafe from the coffee machine, revealing drip stains created by many past coffee pots. Pete then poured two cups and brought them to the table. After he sat down, we both began sipping the hot brew.

His big brown eyes looked deeply into my own eyes. He spoke in a husky voice. "I've been diagnosed with terminal cancer, Floy."

I froze and became speechless. His proclamation rocked my world.

Looking back over the past couple of weeks, I recalled noticing that Pete had been coughing frequently and was always congested. Cancer never crossed my mind.

He kept his eyes steady as he continued gazing into my eyes. "I plan on telling the rest of the squad after I tell the troop commander."

I looked down and stared at my coffee cup. I tried to keep my composure and fought hard to hold back the tears. I studied the cup's highway patrol logo as if seeing it for the first time, yet nothing of its design registered.

Pete had played a huge role in my life and in my career. In addition to having a mutual trust and love for each other, I considered him to be my guardian, my protector, and my mentor.

Without looking at him, I whispered, "What's next?"

I surprised myself for being able to articulate those two words. I knew that if I talked too much, I would lose it. Plus, I didn't know what to say. I kept my head tilted down and my eyes on my coffee cup.

Pete said, "I'm supposed to start a series of chemotherapy treatments within a week. After I get done with them, I gotta have some radiation treatments."

I could feel his eyes boring onto the top of my head. I forced myself to look up and into his eyes. He looked a bit blurry, and I realized I hadn't been too successful with my attempts to not shed any tears.

In addition to perceiving Pete as my hero, I had a lot of feelings for him. I admit I probably suppressed a crush for him and was physically attracted to him.

I wanted to take Pete in my arms to comfort him with more than a brief hug. I was afraid that if I did, it would cause me to go someplace that I shouldn't go.

The combination of my feelings for Pete created a concoction of complex emotions. None of them contributed anything positive to the welfare of my marriage that was already in jeopardy.

I believe my strong faith in God kept me from having an affair, but my faith didn't keep my heart from sinking. I wondered why I had been placed in this set of circumstances. Pete must have read my mind.

"Floy, I called you here to let you know about my sickness, but I also want to show you where I keep all of my personal papers and my will. Here's a list of my family members who I want to be notified of my death."

I just stared back at him, my eyes opened wide. I could only give him the nonverbal response of a nod, signaling that I would take care of everything.

His eyes never left mine. He wrinkled his forehead as his eyebrows pushed together. His nonverbal question asked if I was okay.

I hugged Pete. I forced a smile on my face. "Don't worry. I'll be here for you and whatever you need." My voice cracked, betraying my smile.

Leaving his apartment that day, my legs felt as if heavy weights had been strapped onto them. I got into my car and sat, staring through the front window of my car. I unleashed the held-back tears, and they poured from my eyes, down my cheeks, and dripped from my chin.

I then looked up at the outside of Pete's apartment, trying to make sense of his news and our conversation. My hands tightly gripped the steering wheel. Bowing my head, I silently prayed for him to be healed and for me to be strong.

Within a short time after that day, Pete was admitted to a major cancer institute to begin his treatment plan. I visited him every few days while he was in the hospital.

Unfortunately, nothing worked, and he had to be placed in hospice. All of us on the squad divided our time looking after Pete as he continued to rapidly decline.

Toward the final week of Pete's life, our troop commander made sure all of the squad received time off the road so that we wouldn't leave Pete alone. We were his family.

The last night of Pete's life, Jacob, Dean, and I stayed with him as he went in and out of a coma. At times I couldn't look at him, his once rugged body diminished to skin and bones. As he lay still, he appeared so small in his hospital bed.

I glanced around the private room in an effort to momentarily distract me. It also gave me an opportunity to hold back the tears and be strong. The dreary brown walls, brown tile floor, and forest-green drapes pushed to the side did nothing to encourage me.

Pete had always been so strong, and now was no different. He fought for every breath. When lucid, he tried to smile, but I could tell the pain was too intense to endure.

I sat down next to him on his bed and held his hand. I wanted to be strong for Pete but soon gave up my attempts to hold back my tears again. I allowed them to fall unashamedly.

Jacob and Dean stood next to me. I heard sniffles and knew that they too were crying. No one spoke; we simply couldn't.

Dean frequently bent over us to place a cool towel on Pete's forehead and lips. My heart broke with each struggled breath, yet it rejoiced that he had taken a breath and that for the time being, he was still with us.

Memories of our times together deluged my mind. I longed for them to return and for us to make more memories. Flashbacks of joking and sharing with each other placed a brief smile on my grief-stricken face.

Pete opened his eyes slightly and stared into mine. He managed a weak smile. I felt like he was trying to tell me that it's okay.

I smiled in return and nodded. I wanted to tell him that it's not okay, that I wanted him alive and well. I wanted to tell him that I needed him. I wanted to tell him...

Before I could finish my thoughts, I watched Pete slip back into a coma. I reflected back on all of those times I had considered telling him about my true feelings. Now those opportunities were gone.

Our paths had crossed at a time when I had already committed to another. I knew that if not for my marriage and strong moral convictions, we probably would have developed a deeper relationship. I also knew that if a physical relationship had ever developed between us, it would have been built on our mutual love and respect for each other.

Of course I felt guilty about having these feelings for Pete, and now I felt a great loss. Regardless, I could have never gone against my beliefs and yielded to this temptation while married to another man.

Pete's chest now heaved up and down dramatically with each breath. I realized that my loving friend was at the end of his life. Watching him suffer was the hardest thing I had ever faced.

And then it happened. Pete took one more breath and then no more.

The room grew stagnant. Jacob, Dean, and I still didn't speak. I believe that at that time, a collective breath had simultaneously been sucked out of everyone in the room.

Pete was gone. I continued clasping his hand. I refused to let it go.

Finally, Jacob placed his hand on mine and gently removed them from my friend's hand. When I stood, my legs wobbled and almost collapsed under the extra weight of my aching heart.

I didn't dare take my eyes off of Pete's lifeless body. Maybe subconsciously I thought that if I stared long enough, he'd open his eyes. Then we could all give a sigh a relief that none of this really happened. But the realization that it did happen and that Pete was gone caused a fresh flood of tears to pool in my eyes.

The three of us just turned and lumbered out of that room, leaving my heart behind. We hugged out in the hallway, trying to gather strength from each other. I longed for my friend and prayed silently for God to help me endure this excruciating pain.

When Pete's body left the hospital that night, the entire squad followed the transport van to the funeral home. The caravan pulled into the parking lot of a southern mansion complete with large white pillars and a front porch illuminated by bright lights. We watched as they took Pete's body into the rear of the building.

We agreed that each member of our squad would take turns sitting by Pete's lifeless body at the funeral home every day and throughout every night. We wanted to continue with this ritual until Pete's funeral service.

When my turn came, I walked into the funeral parlor and to the entrance of the room that held Pete. I took a deep breath before stepping through the doorway and onto the dark floral carpet. Rows of chairs sat in the middle of the room, and a few couches lined its dark-paneled walls. The air was almost stifling, and I wished they would open the windows.

I plodded slowly to the oak coffin. When I touched it, I didn't feel Pete's physical presence. I got the sense that he was at peace with God and in a better place.

I refrained from shedding any tears. Maybe I could contribute my ability to compartmentalize and detach during that time to my cop training. I felt I owed Pete the respect of being dignified and maintaining a brave front.

When it came time for his service, our squad and three more troopers served as Pete's pallbearers. While holding up the heavy casket, my legs shook from both its weight and again from the weight of my broken heart. We finally made it to the hearse where we placed his casket for his final journey.

We drove to the cemetery and carried Pete's coffin to his grave. Rain poured down from the skies as if heaven was crying too.

Returning to normal duties seemed strange without Pete. Our squad never overcame the void caused by his death.

I refused to cry outwardly for the first few weeks after that day in the hospital room. Inwardly, though, my heart cried and mourned as my soul shattered into a thousand pieces over and over again.

For the next several months, seasons, and years, I felt empty and alone. My heart continually grieved for my comrade, my mentor, my hero, and more importantly, my dear friend whom I loved. In fact to this day, I still carry feelings of love for Pete.

I valued his mentorship. He laid the fundamental groundwork for me in becoming a respected law enforcement officer. His sincere thoughtfulness, sensitivity, and caring guidance encouraged me and showed me how to excel by believing in myself and thus in my skills. This not only made an ongoing impact in my career but in my survival in a job that has a higher mortality rate than most professions.

He gave me something that no one or nothing, not even death, can take away from me. Pete *believed* in me and always made me feel special. He made me feel wanted as a fellow officer and as a person.

Pete will always own a piece of my heart. He was and will always be my brother in the thin blue line.

CHAPTER 4

Field Training Officer

I missed Pete so much.

My heart refused to heal. The memories constantly rubbed themselves into my deep and gaping wound, preventing it from closure.

I tried to work through my sadness. During those times when I remembered a special moment we had shared, I'd experience another crying spell.

Life went on without Pete, though. A few months after burying him, my supervisors selected me to take on an additional assignment. Despite the fact that I had only been a trooper for about three years, they asked me to become a field training officer (FTO).

I felt honored to be chosen. Of course I did look forward to the slight pay increase. Nevertheless, I mostly looked forward to the opportunity to share my experiences and guide and mentor new troopers. I wanted to help them progress in their career. The only downside was all of the paperwork required to record and document the trainee's progress.

Prior to starting my new assignment, I was required to report to Tallahassee for two weeks of FTO training. So in December 1983, I packed my patrol car to take on my new endeavor.

I kissed my family goodbye and drove away. On one hand, I would miss them, but on the other hand, I couldn't help but feel excited.

I made it to the highway and drove all the way to the academy in Tallahassee. The further north I drove, the more the temperature dropped. I welcomed the change in climate from Miami's fairly consistent higher temperatures.

After arriving at the academy, I noticed a different attitude toward me this time around. No longer a cadet, the trainees looked up to me. They showed me the same kind of respect that I had shown veteran troopers when I was a cadet.

Once I completed that two-week period, I returned back to Miami as a trained FTO. A new female trooper named Jenny Simpson got assigned to me.

When Jenny reported to our squad for the first time, I was immediately impressed with her. Although she looked to be in her mid-twenties, she exuded authority and confidence that commanded respect. Her shoulders were squared back while her chest pushed forward, displaying a straight posture. She briskly walked toward us, her dark brown eyes focused on me before briefly scanning the rest of my squad.

I introduced Dean, Jacob, Jackie, and myself to her. They all smiled and said hi, but their eyes remained guarded, and their smile appeared forced. She would not be truly accepted by them until she proved herself.

Their lack of warmth didn't seem to affect her at all. She gave each of them a genuine smile. Her white teeth created a stark contrast against her smooth, dark-brown complexion.

When she opened her mouth, she spoke with a warm and cute southern drawl. Before we had a chance to ask where she got her accent, she offered up, "I'm from South Cay-rolina."

But Jenny had more going on than her appearance and her twang. She had just earned her master's degree in criminal justice. I had a feeling that Jenny would excel during her training period.

One of my first tasks as her FTO would be to take her to view an autopsy at the office of the medical examiner, or the M.E. Back in those days, a trooper was mandated to witness all autopsies performed on the victims of the traffic fatalities they investigated.

The M.E.'s office was located behind the county's Jackson Memorial Hospital. It had a refrigerated trailer that acted as a surplus storage unit for all of the bodies. Law Enforcement also stored vials of blood drawn from DUI suspects in its locked refrigerator.

Most of the DUIs took place during the midnight shift. I found myself frequently having to walk through the super-cold section late at night to log in the vials. This was probably not one of my favorite tasks. The dim lighting accompanied by naked corpses lying on gurneys presented an eerie and grotesque atmosphere, especially when alone.

I scheduled Jenny to view an autopsy during one of her first training days. That morning we arrived early for our eleven-thirty appointment.

As we walked into the building that housed the morgue, I glanced at Jenny to see how she was handling this. I was glad but not surprised to see that her facial muscles looked relaxed.

I signed us in before heading to the autopsy room. Jenny looked around and then walked about a foot behind me.

The frigid temperature covering us from head to toe provided more stimulation than a cup of coffee. However, the cold did nothing to hide the distinctive odors of formaldehyde, bleach, and decaying flesh. Together, they produced an overwhelming and nauseating sensation to the recipient's olfactory nerves.

I led the way into a large aesthetic-looking room with several strategically positioned tables containing sharp stainless-steel instruments. More of the same kind of tools hung from brackets attached to beige walls.

A couple of tall ladders placed off to the side remained unutilized for the time being. At the appropriate times, they would be climbed by autopsy techs so that they could take pictures of assigned bodies.

Hoses lay near floor drains to facilitate washing away and disposing of blood and other biohazard liquids. A circular saw used for cutting through skulls and other thick bones stood out amidst the other furnishings and equipment.

Long stainless-steel gurneys were lined up side by side. Each one held a still, cold, and naked body waiting for its turn to be examined and scrutinized in the most minute of details.

Hovering over one of the tables stood a heavyset man with thin graying hair and wearing a set of very thick glasses. He seemed clumsy in his gait when he stepped away to grab something from another table. While making a Y incision on one of his guest's chest, he gave his technician his lunch order.

He then turned to Jenny and asked, "Do you want to place an order? Right after I finish the autopsy, we can eat lunch together and discuss the findings."

Jenny was less than enthusiastic at the opportunity to break bread in this bleak environment. "No, thank you," she graciously responded. "It's not my lunchtime yet."

During the autopsy, Jenny handled herself just as I anticipated. She showed interest, asked questions, and didn't display any outward signs of uneasiness.

I thought back to my first experience witnessing an autopsy. Before I went, some of the troopers had advised me to place Vicks Vapor Rub under my nostrils.

I never tried to disguise the smells with vapor rubs or creams. I just thought that if I wore a face mask, I wouldn't be able to get a whiff of some of the odors. I learned quickly that the smells released from an autopsy were never pleasant, and they change drastically according to the postmortem condition of the body. I started wearing a face mask later on in my career once law enforcement agencies began stressing the biohazards that could be emitted and breathed in during the process.

About eight years after training Jenny, I attended an advanced homicide class at the new state-of-the-art medical examiner's office. It had been built across the street from the previous location.

The training offered a barbeque dinner in the building's atrium. While savoring the tangy pork sandwich, I couldn't help but think of Jenny. She had since been promoted to sergeant and moved to the Florida Keys, but I wished she was with me to enjoy this meal. She and I had some good times together.

Jenny and I also experienced some weird situations during her training period. Probably the strangest one was when we stopped the driver of a late-model Jaguar. While on patrol on U.S. 1 in Cutler Ridge, we witnessed the sports car weaving in the lanes across from the mall.

Jenny and I glanced at each other. She raised her eyebrow, and I took in a deep breath. I thought, *Here we go again. Another possible drunk driver and so early in the day.*

I reached over and flipped the switch to turn on my emergency lights. The Jaguar pulled over immediately. I parked behind it and glanced over at Jenny another time.

I opened my door, and the sun's intense heat immediately rose from the blacktop and stopped me momentarily from getting out of my car. The atmosphere felt almost suffocating, and the glare of the sun tried to penetrate through my sunglasses.

I slowly and cautiously walked to the left side of the Jaguar. Jenny also got out and walked to the trunk on the passenger side of the car. From that position, she could observe my interaction with the driver without becoming a target.

A pair of alligator-skin boots exited the driver's door followed by their owner, which turned out to be a slender Hispanic man. He wore a peach-colored Latino-style silk shirt that was well-coordinated with his peach-colored pants. His left wrist flashed from the gold Rolex watch encasing it.

He kept his left side pointed in my direction as he stepped away from his door. When he looked at me, the corners of his lips curved upward, yet his eyes didn't match his attempt at a smile.

As soon as he turned toward me squarely, his right side fell within my line of vision. I immediately spotted a bulge under his shirt.

I yelled, "Gun!"

I lunged toward him, grabbed him, and spun him around. He offered no resistance as I pushed him away from the door and onto the front quarter panel on the driver's side. I pulled up his shirt and removed a 9-mm semi-automatic GLOCK pistol out of his belt.

About that same time, a woman who I assumed to be his wife jumped out of the passenger's side of the car. With lips pressed together, eyes narrowed, and fists clenched, she rushed at me. Since her eyes were focused on me, I knew I was the object of her wrath. Evidently, she was going to defend her man.

Jenny yelled, "Stop where you are! Ma'am, place your hands on your head!"

This command had zero impact on this charging woman who looked like a fancy, frilly dressed bulldog on steroids. Jenny ran after her in an effort to stop her.

The woman turned on Jenny, and they began to physically fight. Both eventually landed on the ground and rolled around in the dirt.

When the man saw the brawl between his wife and Jenny, he became combative with me. I managed to call for backup since I had to deal with an extra gun while trying to handcuff him.

Out of the corner of my eye, I saw a very large cat jump out of the passenger side of the car. It must have been well over the size of any domestic cat I had ever seen.

I couldn't do anything about it now. I needed to spend all of my energy on my wiry guy.

Finally, I managed to pin him against the car with his arms behind him while tucking his firearm into the back of my belt. About the time I felt the final click of the second cuff on my prisoner's hand, Jenny subdued the bulldog of a woman. She then "cuffed and stuffed" her into my car. Fortunately, my trainee was a good street fighter.

Before I had a chance to put my arrestee in my car, his strength coupled with his wiriness enabled him to squirm out of my grasp. We began dancing around the car as I tried to apprehend him.

Jenny rushed over to help from the opposite direction. Between the two of us, we had him cornered. As soon as I grabbed him, he started squirming again in another attempt to escape.

The next thing I knew, all three of us were on the ground. With Jenny's help, we managed to pin him against the side of the road.

I heard the tires of cars driving close-by on the graveled shoulder and stop. I glanced up and saw that our backup troopers had arrived: Jacob, Dean, and two others.

Jacob rushed over to us and asked, "Are you two okay?"

Jenny and I must have looked like a mess. Our uniforms had gotten dirt all over them during our struggles.

I said, "Yes," while Jenny nodded her head and took in a deep breath.

Dean and Jacob grabbed my noncompliant prisoner, hogtied him, and placed him in the cage in the back of Dean's car. We dubbed the backseat "the cage" because it was separated from the front seat by a sheet of Plexiglas.

I then noticed a small child, who looked to be about three years old, exit the car. Before I had a chance to react, he ran over to the street side of my car.

He was way too close to the busy highway. I ran and grabbed him, pulling him out of harm's way. Jenny took him and walked him back to our patrol car. Of course, the little guy was terrified and had huge tears pouring from his big brown eyes.

Because of all the craziness occurring on the side of a busy highway, we drew the attention of drivers passing by us. Rubber necking ensued. All of a sudden I heard the squeal of brakes and a loud crash followed by one car slamming into another.

Jenny checked on the people involved in the wreck, and I began to look for the cat. I radioed to the dispatcher to have a fish-and-game officer respond to my location as soon as possible. I wasn't about to wrestle an animal that probably had sharp claws and big teeth.

I spotted the cat in a field adjacent to the road. It didn't look like an ordinary house cat. It appeared much larger than a bobcat, yellow in color, and beautiful.

When the fish-and-game officer arrived, he snagged the cat with a lasso on a stick. The cat turned out to be a young Florida panther.

The authorities placed the cat in a cage and drove off with it. I'm not sure where they took it initially.

When I had the chance to stop and study my prisoner's driver license, I noticed he lived off of Krome Avenue west of Miami. Many cocaine cowboys resided in this area on large acreages, and many were known to have exotic animals. There was talk of one drug dealer who even had a couple of giraffes on his estate.

I radioed dispatch, and I told her that we had two prisoners and a "tiger in the tank." After completing the arrest paperwork, I transferred the "bulldog" wife from my car to another trooper's car. He drove her to the county substation about a mile away from the scene.

Soon after, Jenny radioed to dispatch for a member of the state child-welfare agency to meet her at the station. She removed the little boy's carseat from the Jaguar, placed it in one of the other trooper's car, and then they drove away with this cute little guy. I always felt sorry for children who witnessed their parents' arrest.

I then requested a narcotics-sniffing K-9 to search the prisoners' car. When the dog and his handler arrived, they slowly walked around the vehicle. The dog sniffed and sniffed but didn't discover any illegal substances.

All of this commotion from the driver and his wife resulted in numerous charges, which ended up being pled down to lesser offenses. The state credited both arrestees with time served and fined them. The largest fine turned out to be not having a permit to obtain a panther.

The cat was finally placed into a rescue preserve for a period of time. Maybe by now, he's out roaming the Florida Everglades at night.

Road Rage

Right after the "Kitty-Cat Car Stop," a term fondly given to the Panther incident, Jenny and I decided to patrol Krome Avenue. We had this deep-seated desire to take a look at where our recent arrestees lived. Maybe we would come across them again. We were sure they were associated with the cocaine trade.

We headed north on the two-lane highway in the midst of an agricultural area. Both the dark cloud-covered skies hovering overhead and the imminent rain created an eerie setting in front of us. It felt like we were driving into a scene of the *Wizard of Oz* just before the tornado carried off Dorothy and Toto.

The dispatcher radioed us. She gave the report of a gun-wielding man in a white Chevrolet SUV chasing a silver Toyota close to our location.

Jenny glanced over at me from the driver's seat. I picked up the mike and informed dispatch that we would respond.

Jenny turned on the overhead police lights and siren. She then proceeded to drive us to the area. Neither of us spoke as the tension built. We looked to both sides of the road and straight ahead, trying to spot the described vehicles.

All of a sudden, I broke the silence and yelled above the siren. "There they are on the right!"

Both vehicles sped parallel to us on a dirt road. Dust billowed as they raced alongside us.

Jenny immediately turned onto a dirt road to our right. My body involuntarily fell slightly to the left during the turn. She pushed down the accelerator pedal even more in an effort to catch up and join the speeding caravan. The engine roared, showing its power. I subconsciously checked my seatbelt to make sure it was tightly secured.

I felt a little uneasy when I saw a canal further off to the right. I envisioned Jenny losing control and the patrol car taking an involuntary dive into the water and us with it.

The Toyota slowed down. The driver ducked in his seat and pulled over to the side of the road before coming to a complete stop.

We continued to chase the SUV with lights and sirens. I saw that the road was about to end up ahead. If we kept this pace, we'd find ourselves stuck in the middle of a cornfield.

Jenny was a heck of a driver. I glanced over at her. Her chin jutted forward and her eyes stared straight ahead. I knew this SUV didn't have a chance against a determined Jenny.

Sure enough we caught up to it about a hundred yards past the parked Toyota and fortunately just before the end of the road. The SUV began to slow down and then stopped.

I made a mental list of possibilities that could transpire with its armed driver. Still holding the mike, I called in our location and requested a backup because of the reported gun.

After we came to a stop, Jenny and I jumped out of our car with our guns drawn. We used our car doors as a shield. My heart raced with adrenaline mixed with a healthy fear of the unknown.

Jenny extended the PA system's cord out of her opened door. I placed my gun sights on the driver.

She spoke into the microphone. "Stick your hands out of your door window. Reach over and open the door from the outside. Then step out of the vehicle with your hands on top of your head."

Thank God the driver followed her commands. He exited the SUV facing us, his barrel chest accentuating his burly build. His dark sunglasses hid his eyes, so it was difficult to read his thoughts and intentions. He wore a blue baseball cap over a massive amount of wild brown hair. His mane reached down his jaw line, around and over his chin, and extended above his upper lip. His jeans and plaid shirt completed the picture of what a stereotypical lumberjack might look like. Thank God he complied with us.

I kept my gun sights on him while Jenny ran over and handcuffed him. She then walked him back to our patrol car and placed him into our backseat. He didn't give us anymore trouble.

We drove back to the victim and found him still parked in his Toyota on the side of the road. He just sat in his seat and looked frozen. His eyes were wide and stared out his front windshield, and his face was pale. Jenny did a u-turn so that we could park behind him.

We approached his car from both sides. Jenny lightly tapped on the window of his door. He jumped as if the noise caused him to come out of a trance. He then jerked his head to the left and saw Jenny.

Her smile must have encouraged him. He opened his door and exited his vehicle.

He looked like the total opposite of Grizzly Adams sitting in the back of my car. He wore dress pants, a white shirt, a tie, and shiny shoes. No hint of facial hair resided on his clean-shaven face.

His hands shook as he pulled off his sunglasses. His clenched jaw revealed his tense state. "Thank you. My heart sank when I saw that two women were coming to my rescue. I thought I was done. I watched what you did, and I was amazed. Now I know that you two can handle any situation."

I appreciated his words, but I think Jenny appreciated them even more. We don't always hear gratitude.

We told the victim to move his car closer to the perp's SUV. We followed him in our car.

Once there, Jenny and I got busy securing the scene. We searched the perp's vehicle and found the loaded handgun.

Jenny said, "I'll start on the paperwork." She pulled out an evidence form for the gun and a towing form for the SUV.

At that time, Jacob arrived as our backup. He wanted to know if we were okay and if we needed help.

I said, "No, thanks. I think we've got everything under control right now."

I then walked back over to the victim. "I need to take your statement. I need to know what exactly happened here." I held my clipboard and pen in my hand ready to write.

He looked over at my car. His wide and staring eyes stayed glued to my backseat and its occupant. "I don't know this guy. I was just at a convenience store down the road. I was in line waiting to pay the cashier for my soda when he got in front of me. I told him to get in the back of the line and wait his turn."

The victim tore his eyes off of my backseat and turned to look at me. "He wanted to argue with me. I told him I was in line first, and I stood my ground. Then when I pulled out of the store's parking lot, he pulled out behind me and started following me and chasing me in his SUV. The guy drove alongside me and pointed a gun at me. I sped up to get away, but I thought he was going to kill me. I think if he had caught up with me before you two arrived, he would have."

Just as we finished writing our reports, I glanced around and saw Jacob walk over to the canal. He called out to us to come and look at what he found in the water.

I wasn't quite sure I wanted to see, yet curiosity overcame me. I glanced over at my car to make sure Grizzly was still in the same place where I had left him. I looked over at the victim. I think he was still too traumatized to move.

I said, "We'll be back in a moment."

His eyes opened even wider as his eyebrows raised in an unspoken plea, begging me not to go far.

I tilted my head in the direction of the canal's bank. "I'll just be right over there," I assured him.

He hesitated before nodding slightly. I don't know if he was letting me know he understood or if he was giving me permission.

Jenny and I walked over to Jacob. He pointed to a white spot in the canal. "I think it's the roof of a car."

I had to agree. It had the same shape as the roof of a car., and I couldn't think of anything else with that shape and size that would be in those waters.

The tow-truck driver arrived to tow the suspect's SUV. He then walked to the canal where we all stood.

Jacob said, "Yeah, I think that white object is a car."

The tow-truck driver looked to where Jacob pointed and stretched his neck to get a better look. "Hey, I've got my diving gear in my truck. I can dive into the canal and check it out."

Jacob thanked him. After the tow-truck driver hooked up the SUV, he walked back over to us with his diving gear. He put it on and went into the water.

Jenny and I stayed and watched. We wanted to make sure nothing happened to the tow-truck driver, and we also to see what he found.

He emerged above the water and swam to the shore. He took off his face mask and lumbered up the bank.

"Yep, it's definitely a car," he reported with a smile on his face. It appeared that he was enjoying this adventure.

Satisfied, we thanked the driver. I turned to Jacob and said, "We're leaving to take our prisoner to the nearest county police substation to book him. We still got a few hours of paperwork ahead of us, so we'll leave this new development with you."

Jacob just nodded but kept his eyes fixed on the canal. He then started slowly walking south along its shore.

After arriving at the substation, we ended up charging the suspect with aggravated assault. When we ran his record, we discovered that he had a list of other violent felony convictions.

I've always been envious of the police on television shows after they arrest someone. They're never overloaded with paperwork and go from one exciting event to the next.

However, this isn't a realistic depiction of police work. In addition to experiencing hours of boredom, we have to endure tons of report writing.

The next day, Jacob told me that he had stayed at the canal for quite awhile after we left with our prisoner. As a result, he pulled five vehicles out of the water.

He had found a new fishing hole, but instead of catching wiggly and scaly creatures, he reeled in stolen vehicles. During the next few days, he recovered almost thirty stolen vehicles from areas along the canal. Some were stripped down and used for parts. Others were probably stolen for joy rides or transportation then later dumped.

Jacob had discovered his niche. For the next year or so, he spent many hours looking into the vast canal areas located west of Miami.

You Never Forget Your First (Trainee)

On a slow Saturday afternoon, Jenny and I headed north on U.S. 1 outside of Cutler Ridge. We observed a female driver cutting in and out of traffic at a high rate of speed.

Jenny said, "Look at her. I gotta pull her over before something happens."

She reached over and turned on the lights and sirens. She then increased her speed to catch up to the swerving car.

The driver appeared to have no interest in pulling over and complying. Moreover, she drove even faster, and so did we as we continued pursuing her.

My adrenaline started pumping again as my body prepared itself for some kind of action. Again, my fingers automatically caressed my seatbelt buckle to ensure it was secure.

A few miles later, the swerving driver finally pulled over, jumped out of her car, and ran. Jenny pulled off to the side of the road and stopped as well. We both jumped out of our car and chased after this woman.

I was thankful that I was a runner and in shape for such an event. As we followed close on her heels, I focused on the pink and green curlers that covered her head like a colorful helmet. They looked as if they were glued to her scalp. In fact, they were the only thing on her body that didn't move or jiggle with each hammering step she took.

For a heavy woman, she could run fairly fast. Jenny and I were faster, though, and caught up to her after a couple of minutes. We then pounced on her. After a quick struggle, Jenny was able to handcuff her.

We both took an arm and pulled her up to her feet. Between her tight pants and low-cut floral blouse, I made a mental note not to move her too much in the wrong direction for fear that something would joggle its way out of her attire.

All the way back to my car, she spewed obscenities at us, thrashing her head from left to right to left again in an obvious attempt to make sure she gave us both an earful of her ranting. Each time she faced me, her mouth opened wide with each lewd word she directed at me, revealing her shiny gold front tooth.

Finally, we made it back to my car, and Jenny put her into the backseat. I thought about what she had done and shook my head. I didn't know if she drove that way out of incompetence or pure callous negligence.

I turned around from the front passenger seat and said, "What you just did, do you realize you're putting innocent people in danger?" The potential consequences of these incidents made me angry.

Our arrestee didn't share my line of reasoning, though. She continued to complain. If she said once, "The only reason you stopped me was because I'm black," she said it fifty times.

I ignored her accusations and asked for her identification. After running it through the system, I discovered that she had a suspended driver's license. No wonder she ran. She didn't want to be caught.

Jenny filled out the paperwork, charging her with the driver's license offense and resisting arrest. The woman continued pulling the race card, alleging our actions had everything to do with the color of her skin.

Although initially humorous, her mantra got old. She obviously refused to accept responsibility.

Jenny shook her head and rolled her eyes. She looked at the woman in the backseat and spoke in a very calm voice. "Ma'am, I'm the one who arrested you, and I'm also black."

Afterward, we both had forgotten about this woman's statement. Then months later, we were summoned to the courthouse for a jury trial relating to our arrest of her.

During my testimony, her attorney asked, "Is it not true the only reason you stopped my client was because she was black?"

I looked over at the woman sitting and watching me. She wore a smug smile that showed her shiny gold tooth.

I wanted to laugh as those memories flooded my mind. I suppressed my snicker, but I don't think I was too successful at suppressing my smile.

I looked at the jury. "No, sir, her race had nothing to do with the reason why we stopped her."

Without removing my eyes from the jury, I proceeded to tell them the circumstances for the traffic stop. Her attorney then dismissed me as a witness. Jenny was then called to testify.

I watched the facial expressions of the jury members when Jenny walked into the courtroom in her trooper uniform. Their eyes widened in surprise, and some of their jaws dropped. I knew they no longer believed the defendant.

When the verdict came back, we had a conviction. I had been right about the jury.

Over the next several years, Jenny and I laughed about that trial. People come up with some strange excuses for their bad driving behavior.

In total, Jenny and I rode together for a couple of months. Just like I had predicted, she was an excellent rookie. She had a keen ability to adapt and learn the concepts necessary for survival as a trooper.

She and I made an uncanny pair, but we got along really well and enjoyed working together. We remain good friends to this day.

After I trained Jenny, I was assigned to another female trooper named Sara Wheatley. She was about my height with light brown hair.

I liked Sara. The perpetual twinkling of her blue eyes did nothing to deter her serious and ambitious temperament. However, we didn't encounter any of the wild situations that Jenny and I shared.

After Sara, I was assigned to another rookie, former army soldier Daniel Lopez. He was tall (about six foot two), dark, and handsome. His previous military experience trained him to follow directions and put him in tactically fit condition. Also, his easy-going disposition made working with him a pleasure.

The one situation with Daniel that stood out in my memory was the car stop of a very drunk female driver who refused to exit her vehicle. The woman annoyed me with her nasty and foul use of four-letter words, so I let Daniel take over the stop.

He had been standing behind me and walked closer to the woman. His professionalism and level headiness prevented him from overreacting. He was always very polite to women.

I figured this driver would give him a tough time, maybe even resist arrest. She did give him a jolt, but not in the way I had expected.

When he finally talked her out of the car, she stepped out and pulled up her t-shirt, revealing her naked breasts. I rolled my eyes at her dramatics and shook my head.

I had had my fill of her drunken state. Now it was my time to take over this car stop.

I moved Daniel out of my way and grabbed her. I received a lot of satisfaction clicking my handcuffs onto her bony wrists.

Being exposed to so many drivers and passengers under the influence of alcohol or drugs made me realize how these substances can bring out the worst in people. This woman was just one example.

Daniel made a great trainee, but he ended up joining another police department. I last saw him when I had gone back to finish college years later. He happened to be enrolled at the same college on the G.I. Bill. As it turned out, the teacher and the student received their diplomas on the same graduation day.

Sometimes You'd Like to Forget Your Last (Trainee)

My final FTO assignment wasn't so easy. I found my patience challenged with a hotshot male named Denny Romano from Miami.

Denny stood five foot five. His fine brown hair framed a baby face that contained a pair of deep-set brown eyes. Weightlifting created his stocky build and left him with a bit of a macho attitude. He probably cared as much for the idea of my being his training officer as I cared for the idea of him being my rookie.

Time with Denny wasn't always so difficult. He gave me some great laughs with some of his antics.

One of the funniest incidents pertained to a bar fight we responded to at the local strip club. We had been driving on U.S. 1 when county officers sped by us with lights and sirens. We followed them to the front of this club known as Tease Me, Please Me.

When responding to places like strip joints, protocol required more diligence. A male trooper must be accompanied into the club by a female officer for any needed interviews. Her presence would detract from any allegations of improper misconduct against the male officer.

Denny and I hurried behind the county cops to provide backup and security. I stepped inside the club and got smacked with the repulsive odor of stale sweat, stale beer, and a mustiness that all combined with the smell of cheap perfume.

I could see that the fight had ended. The county officers were taking a few men out in handcuffs.

Before we had a chance to leave, we heard a lot of screaming and yelling in the rear of the club. Denny ran through a wide-opened door in the direction of the hollering sounds and found that he had stumbled into another world. To his shock and delight, he found himself standing in the strippers' dressing room and in the midst of a bunch of barely clad women.

However, barely clad may be an overstatement. Just like the room's exposed and naked light bulbs, many of the women were also exposed and naked. The only item worn were high-heeled shoes. Small pasties and G-string panties hung from every fixture attached to the purple walls.

Some of the women milled around on the tacky floor. Others were bent over stained vanities while looking into mirrors and adjusting their pancake makeup.

The ruckus came from two women who stood face-to-face, verbally fighting with each other. At least they were the more conservative of the bunch and wore G-strings.

Denny squeezed in between them to break up the impending fight. In doing so, he found himself standing in front of an exceptionally tall woman. Her spiked heels raised her up to a height that placed his line of vision directly in front of her naked breasts. His widened eyes became fixated, spellbound, on the nipples before him.

I said, "Earth to Denny. The fight's over. We're leaving now."

I needed to get him out of his stupor because my words and suggestions weren't working. Denny seemed to have a hard time peeling his eyes from their focal point.

I had to laugh. I grabbed his arm and pulled him out of the danger zone. Once he was no longer in front of the naked breasts, their power over him broke.

He gave a half smile, I assumed because he was still slightly drunk from the memory. We managed to leave the club, although I don't think that image left Denny for quite some time.

Afterward, I received a lot of enjoyment sharing that story with my squad. This incident was just too funny to keep to myself.

On another night, Denny and I were looking for a fugitive who had escaped from a prison in the area. Our search led us to an abandoned building west of Miami.

Not only was the area isolated, but the dilapidated building didn't have any electricity. The lack of stars in the black sky and the still fog acting as a shroud gave the structure an even more creepy appearance. As a result, we both had our guns drawn. Our non-shooting weaker hands held flashlights crossing our line of sight.

Denny walked in front of me and to my left. When we rounded a wall, we saw a light and a gun in front of us.

I knew we were looking at our reflection in a mirror. On the other hand, Denny hadn't come to the same conclusion at the same time. His entire body visibly shook as he raised his shooting hand and pointed it at the mirror.

Thank God he didn't fire. Later on, he admitted that he almost did.

I wrote these kinds of incidents off as normal rookie knee-jerk reactions. Some actions, though, could not be excused so easily.

Toward the end of each rookie's field-training period, the FTO sits in the passenger's seat. He or she wears regular street clothes that conceal the FTO's gun, radio, and handcuffs.

The reason for the civilian attire is to provide the rookie with the simulation of having total control. The FTO judges the rookie's conduct and actions prior to releasing him or her to normal duties.

While on patrol during this phase of Denny's training, he stopped a car with nonworking taillights. He approached the driver, and I walked to the passenger's side. He told the driver to exit the vehicle.

The driver obeyed. He looked at Denny, his eyebrows pulled down in confusion. "Why did you stop me?"

Denny gave a curt answer. "Your taillights are out." He snapped out his ticket book.

The driver smiled and said, "I appreciate knowing this. Okay, I'll get it fixed."

Denny started writing. Without looking up, he said, "I'm issuing you a ticket for no taillights."

The driver's head jerked back as his eyes widened in surprise. He shrugged his shoulders and shook his head. "But I didn't realize my taillights were out. I'll be glad to get them fixed."

Denny didn't say anything and continued writing. When he finished, he told the driver to sign the ticket.

By this time, the driver didn't seem so humble. He looked down as he kicked at the gravel and then up into Denny's tight-lipped face. The driver's own tight facial expression let me know that he was very angry indeed.

I wasn't comfortable with Denny's entire demeanor, and I wasn't comfortable with the way this was going.

I felt it would have been appropriate for Denny to issue the driver a warning or a correction card for an equipment violation. He also could have explained to the driver that if he got his taillights repaired, he could take the proof to any law enforcement officer. The officer could then verify and acknowledge the repair, and the ticket would be dismissed. Unfortunately, Denny never offered this option.

The driver was now really annoyed about receiving this ticket and refused to sign it. In Florida, the driver's signature on a ticket is not a confession of guilt but a promise to appear in court if summoned for lack of payment.

At that point, I felt I needed to step in and try to keep this incident from escalating any further. I walked over to the driver's side. I calmly tried to explain the purpose of his signature and why it's needed.

I don't think it would have mattered what I said by that time. The driver was livid. His face was red, and his stance was stiff as he leaned forward and yelled, "Just try and arrest me!"

My attempt to rectify this situation was too late. Denny looked at me when the angry driver once again refused to sign the ticket.

I looked at Denny and shrugged. "Do what you must."

I walked a few steps away and called for a backup. I anticipated a fight from this guy, and I anticipated correctly.

Denny and I danced around the driver's car to capture him. We boxed him in and were in the midst of getting him under control when Jacob arrived. When we finally managed to get the driver handcuffed, I put him in the backseat of Denny's car.

Jacob walked over to me and asked, "What happened to cause this fight?"

I was exasperated and frustrated and not in the mood to talk. I felt terrible that I didn't stop this train wreck beforehand.

"Don't go there," I said and walked away.

The next morning I walked into my favorite captain's office. "I'm done with Denny," I told him in a firm tone.

I felt justified in recommending he not be allowed to finish his probation period. My report reflected the details leading to my decision.

The captain decided to give Denny another chance. He placed him with an FTO who ultimately recommended he be released from probation and become a trooper.

Denny later lost his job with the Florida Highway Patrol for a collection of offenses. I had heard that he had not followed proper court procedures, had failed to maintain proper chain of evidence, had overused his sick days, and he had ventured out of his patrol zone. He was hired by a small police department where he shot himself in the leg. He claimed he had been shot by a driver during a traffic stop. He fabricated that entire incident because he wanted sympathy from his girlfriend who was leaving him.

I always felt terrible about the driver who went to jail for not signing the ticket. I sure do wish I could have a do-over with that traffic stop.

Not only was I done with Denny, but my experiences with him made me decide that I was also done with FTO training.

That was when I knew it was definitely time to move on.

CHAPTER 5

The DUI Task Force

The timing and the opportunity couldn't have been more perfect. When I decided to leave my FTO position, I found out that the Florida Highway Patrol was forming a new task force for apprehending those driving under the influence of drugs and alcohol.

Thus began the DUI Task Force in late 1985. According to the description, it would operate from seven o'clock Wednesday evening through three o'clock Monday morning.

When troop headquarters dispersed a notice that applications were being accepted, I couldn't help but get excited. I immediately applied for the position.

The request had to go through the chain of command for approval. My less-than-enthusiastic captain was in charge of the selection process. He appeared to have a long memory from when he tried to make me his substitute secretary. During my interview, he seemed disengaged and uninterested. I knew that my past of standing up to him had come back to haunt me. He rejected my application and instead chose a male trooper for the assignment.

However, things had a way of working out. The trooper who made the final cut decided he didn't want to join the task force after all. This opened the door for me.

I was thrilled to belong to this prestigious group. Since I was the only female on the squad in the Miami area, I felt some pressure about doing my absolute best and rising to the challenge.

Dean was also selected. Although I knew all of the other troopers, I didn't know them as well as I knew him. Of course, I hadn't worked as closely with them as I had with Dean.

The task force had its perks, but it also had its challenges. For instance, I was no longer dispatched to traffic crashes, but since many late-night or early-morning crashes involved drunk drivers, I volunteered to investigate them if I was in the area.

Also as part of this unit I was expected to make two to three arrests during the shift. The increase in arrest activity created more dangerous situations for me. These challenges seemed slight, though, when compared to having to attend court in the mornings after working all night.

The relationships I established with my team more than made up for the challenges. Those of us working the south end of the county became a close-knit group. We knew we were going to need to back each other up on these cases, so we all agreed to work in close proximity. Still, we did come across circumstances where we weren't able to get to each other quickly.

I encountered one of those situations early on during a very rainy and dark night. I observed an older gray Toyota weaving all over the road. I stopped him on the southbound side of U.S. 1.

The driver exited his vehicle and stood a moment, albeit a bit wobbly. He looked quite comfortable in his shorts, t-shirt, and sneakers. He took an exaggerated step and then staggered toward me, glaring with glazed, bloodshot eyes. He smelled like alcohol and spoke with a slur.

I told him to place his finger on the tip of his nose. He didn't follow my directions. I knew I had enough probable cause to effect an arrest.

While handcuffing him, he became very combative. I grabbed his wrist, and we began to struggle. Then both of us landed in a huge mud puddle.

I wasn't afraid. Instead, I couldn't quit laughing at this hysterical occurrence. I felt like I was mud wrestling.

I managed to get on top of him. I then straddled him in an effort to get his other wrist into my handcuffs.

All of a sudden out of nowhere, I heard someone yell, "Hold on! I'll help you. I'm a state attorney."

I turned my head in the direction of the announcer. The first thing I saw was shiny brown loafers with tassels. As my eyes travelled up, I saw a dark suit. My next marker was a loosened red and navy-blue striped tie over a white oxford-cloth shirt with its top button undone. I then saw a great smile that led to a pair of big brown eyes and light brown bangs covering his eyebrows.

Even through the mud, I could smell his lime-scented cologne. I smiled again as I thought it added a tropical flair to the situation.

His eyes twinkled, and his smile shifted to lopsidedness, reflecting a bit of mischievousness. He seemed more than up to the challenge of a mud-wrestling contest. Then the next thing I knew, my knight in shining armor jumped into the mud and joined in this ridiculous free-for-all.

He grabbed the driver and put him in a headlock. The three of us rolled around in the mud. The nasty substance felt both slimy and gritty against my face, neck, and hands, and my uniform stuck to my body. I began to lose my sense of humor and started hating every minute of this venture.

On the other hand, my hero seemed to enjoy the challenge. Finally his perseverance paid off, and he successfully subdued the jerk.

I took advantage of the help and slapped the cuffs on my driver. After putting him in the back of my car, I turned and thanked the attorney. We then exchanged names and information.

I discovered that his name was Mike Benton, and I wouldn't see him again for many years to come. When I became a special agent with the Florida Department of Law Enforcement (FDLE), I found out Mike had become a legal advisor for the FDLE at the Tallahassee headquarters. I made a point at that time to stop in his office in Tallahassee and renew our acquaintance.

I also enjoyed relaying this story to my colleagues over the years. After all, I must have been the only FDLE agent who rolled around with Mike in the mud.

Children of the Labor Camps

Miami had its share of migrant labor camps. Its inhabitants worked long, hard hours under the hot Florida sun picking vegetables. Families had to perform this back-breaking labor to make a living in order to survive.

These families didn't stay long at any given camp, though. Parents followed the agricultural crop seasons from state to state. As a result, the children in these camps moved several times a year. Between all of the moves and being too busy contributing to the family income as teenagers, a lot of them never finished high school.

I wanted to do something for these children, so I spearheaded some initiatives to help them. Since I was a member of my church and the Women's Club in Homestead, I recruited their assistance to provide funding for extracurricular activities for the children, such as music and dance lessons, and for the clothing they needed for recitals and community presentations.

To further my efforts, I collaborated with a married couple named Manny and Maria Gomez. They were originally from labor camps but had the opportunity to attend college, graduate, and obtain master degrees.

Manny and Maria were the community leaders for the local migrant population. Both of them were dedicated to providing educational opportunities to the labor camp children.

I had visited this couple in their home several times. We also attended social functions together because we shared mutual friends.

One night I arrested a Mexican male driver for being intoxicated in the area of the labor camp. The arrest took place without incident, and the driver pled guilty in court.

After the court appearance, I didn't think anymore about the arrest until about six weeks later. I got called into the station and was told that a migrant human-rights association had filed a complaint against me. They alleged that I harassed migrant farm workers by unjustly targeting them through driving violations.

You could have knocked me over with a wet noodle. I felt mad, violated, and victimized by this injustice aimed at my personal ethics. This group had no idea what kind of a person I was and how I had tried to help them.

The internal review officer interviewed me under oath. I provided him with a list of my activities that assisted the labor camp families. I also provided him with the names of my friends Manny and Maria Gomez.

I asked Manny and Maria to write letters for me to the highway patrol and to the farm worker's coalition that had filed the complaint. This issue stayed unresolved for months. Dealing with it took time away from my duties of protecting the public.

Eventually the compliant was deemed unfounded. The association never apologized to me.

I still continued to assist and champion for the needy children. A few years later when I was assigned to the Felony Drug Interdiction Unit, I investigated a child fatality at the same intersection where I had arrested the intoxicated Mexican driver.

Officer-Involved Shooting

During my DUI Task Force days, some of the county police seemed to have gotten tired of all of the drunks we brought to their substation for processing and booking. Our additional prisoners caused them to have to use their county transport van to make extra trips to the main jail. Depending on the location of the substation, the jail could be an hour away.

Furthermore, our prisoners caused their booking room to stink with the stale smell of alcohol and body sweat. This didn't include the strong odor of urine-soaked pants worn by those prisoners who either couldn't hold it or were too drunk to care.

One night around eleven, Dean and I were leaving the substation located in an affluent area of Miami. We stepped outside into the February cold and stopped to speak with Officer Steve Johnson, one of the county officers we both knew and liked. Steve stood about five foot eleven. He was thin and had dark hair with a mustache.

Each time I saw Steve, he displayed a very pleasant demeanor. That night, though, I saw something different. Within his brown eyes lurked an intense sadness and a dark depression.

His face seemed taut, and he only gave a half smile. We began a casual chat with him, but as the conversation progressed, it got very weird. He talked about his problems with his live-in girlfriend. He was also considering moving to Alaska to become a police officer where he would make fifty thousand dollars a year.

I thought, *You must be nuts. Who would leave the South Florida climate to go freeze? Why would you want to go so far away and start your career over?*

His comments seemed abnormal. It wasn't just what he said, but how he said it. The inflection in his voice didn't vary a bit. It remained monotonous. Without a doubt, Steve was not himself. Looking back, I can see how the darkness in his eyes reflected his conversation with us.

Dean and I wished him our best, and then we went back to patrol the roadways. About two o'clock in the morning, we stopped to have a roadside conversation with a few county officers.

They told us that about an hour ago, they had answered a call to a local restaurant where Steve and his girlfriend were involved in a bitter argument. They separated the couple and took Steve home. They asked the girlfriend to spend the night with one of her friends until Steve cooled down.

According to the officers, Steve had been drinking. Just as the officers finished telling us this story, an emergency tone and broadcast came across their radios. The dispatcher announced a shooting had taken place, and then she gave the address.

I looked at the county officers, and each of them shared the same stunned expression: wide eyes and opened mouth.

One of them exclaimed, "Oh, my God! That's Johnson's address."

The other said, "This is not good."

We all jumped in our patrol units and sped to Steve's house.

Upon our arrival, we heard screaming and crying coming from inside the small concrete-block home. The high-pitched tone told me that it belonged to a female, more than likely the girlfriend.

I rushed through the front door and toward the screams at the back of the house. There in the hallway that led to the bedrooms stood a small and petite young woman with her back to the wall. Her hands, face, and body were covered with blood.

She appeared to be using her right arm to brace herself against the wall and her left hand to cover her abdomen. She bent forward slightly as if she was going to throw up. The inside of her eyebrows were raised as her tear-filled eyes stared at the floor in front of her.

The object of her fixation was Steve. He lay on the worn yellow carpet, the left side of his face resting in a pool of blood with his gun next to him.

Looking at Steve, I had no doubt that he didn't survive the gunshot wound. From what I could tell, the bullet entered the right side of his head.

This scene felt surreal. We just had a strange conversation with Steve, but I still couldn't grasp that he was gone.

I walked over to Steve's girlfriend to see if she needed anything. I didn't question her because I didn't want to interfere with the homicide investigation.

She kept telling me she needed to go to the bathroom. I took her to the county police station where she used its facilities. I stayed with her to make sure she didn't wash her hands. The homicide detectives would want to test them for gunpowder residue.

When she finished, I took her upstairs to the detective bureau and waited. Once the homicide detectives arrived, I turned her over to them.

After I left the station, Dean and I went for a cup of coffee. We needed the release of talking about such a horrible incident. I knew I wouldn't be able to sleep once I got home.

Since that night, I've often thought about Steve, especially since his death was ruled a suicide. Could I have said or done anything different during my conversation with him that might have prevented his death?

I also wondered why his girlfriend chose to ignore the advice that the officers had given her at the restaurant. Why did she return to their house? What happened?

Only Steve and his girlfriend know the real truth. Only those two know whether she pushed Steve's buttons to the point that he felt he had no other option but to put a gun to his head and pull the trigger.

An In-Custody Incident

While patrolling an area known for street prostitution, I became familiar with the first names of most of the "regular girls."

Tammy was one of those "regular girls," very thin, older than her years, medium height with dirty, stringy blond hair. Track marks on her arms divulged that she was a heroin addict, and her face always bore open sores.

Tammy probably would have been attractive if she had fared better in life. Working the streets as a prostitute is hard without a good chance of survival. I suspected Tammy had AIDS.

She told me that her sister was also a prostitute. I believed that Tammy and her sister were victims of child sexual abuse, physical abuse, and psychological abuse.

I never arrested her. If I saw her get into a car, I stopped the car and told her to get out. I did arrest some of the men who stopped to pick her up for paid sex if they were drunk or I saw drugs in their cars.

I frequently wondered about her customers. Were their spouses clueless as to their husband's secret sex addiction?

It seemed so vile to me that a man would expose his wife to the possible diseases he could carry home from this type of sexual interlude. I always hated the movie with Julia Roberts and Richard Gere where prostitution was glamorized. Certainly, Tammy's life was void of any glamour.

During one hot and miserable night, Dean and I decided to patrol the highway area where Tammy normally worked the streets. The vicinity contained large ficus trees that bordered a blacktop strip. These types of trees possessed long roots, and a web of them hung from all of the branches. Just enough wind blew, moving these hanging roots and leaves. They looked like skeletal arms swaying to music created by the whistling wind. The full moon provided good visibility and illuminated these eerie effects. I felt as if I had entered into a horror movie.

Dean patrolled not too far away from me, and he encountered his own horror. He radioed to dispatch that he had stopped for an incident involving a female disrupting traffic. He then gave his location before attempting to get the woman to safety.

Accordingly, the woman who pranced in an out of traffic wore a red wig, low-cut red top, cutoff shorts that exposed the lower half of her buttocks, and high-heeled shoes. I had no doubt that she was another "regular girl."

By the time I arrived to back up Dean, it looked as if he had everything under control. He had the woman on her knees on the side of the road and was in the midst of handcuffing her.

Nevertheless, things can change in a moment's time, so I ran over to him just in case. While he double-locked the cuffs with his handcuff key, she turned her face into his arm to try to bite him.

Just as her mouth was about to make contact with Dean's skin, I took the quickest action I could. I hit her with my foot.

Dean jerked his head back, and his eyebrows furrowed. He had no idea what she had tried to do. My kick wasn't strong enough to hurt her, but it did stop what could have resulted in Dean being exposed to AIDS or some other contagious disease through a nasty human bite.

This didn't stop this woman. She rolled over and started kicking strongly, using her stiletto heels as weapons. Her radical and combative behavior must have been brought on by the full moon or by a lot of ingested cocaine or both.

Dean and I moved around her in a frenzy until we could finally grab her legs and remove her fashionable weapons. We half carried and half dragged her to the caged area of Dean's car and placed her inside.

She immediately began to kick at his back windows. We had to remove her from the car and hog-tie her for the trip to the station. Fortunately, the station was just a couple of miles away.

Whenever a combative prisoner is hogtied, the danger of them having breathing problems exist. I rode with Dean so that I could keep an eye on her. She fared well with no further incidences.

Another night while at the station, I glanced into the booking area and saw Jackie sitting at the report-writing desk. She had a scruffy-looking handcuffed male prisoner shackled to the bench behind her.

A few minutes later, a county officer walked into the room. He stopped when he saw Jackie's prisoner. He noted that his head was bent down, his chin was tucked onto his chest, his eyes were closed, and his chest wasn't moving up and down.

The officer walked over to her prisoner and leaned in to get a better look. He then yelled, "Turn around. Your prisoner stopped breathing."

Jackie did as he said, and her eyes widened when she saw the condition of her arrestee. She and the county officer took off the handcuffs and shackles, placed him on the floor, and began CPR. Fire Rescue was called by another officer.

I had been in the cell area during this time. I came out to find a chaotic scene.

A mere few minutes later, Fire Rescue arrived. Jackie seemed to be in shock as she watched them continue to perform CPR on her prisoner. She shook and trembled, and her face took on an ashen hue.

Fire Rescue took the prisoner to the hospital a few minutes later. Once there, he was pronounced dead on arrival.

I knew she felt terrible about this man dying right behind her. An investigation ensued where Jackie was interviewed in-depth about her actions during and after the arrest. That in itself can be a traumatic ordeal, even if you've done nothing wrong.

Jackie was cleared after the autopsy. Results showed that her prisoner had died due to a heroin overdose.

Have Gun, Will Travel

One busy night, I had arrested several different people throughout my shift. Before processing prisoners at a police station, protocol required us to secure our firearms in a designated location. In this particular station, officers put their guns in a drawer in the sergeant's area.

I didn't complete the booking process for my last prisoner until the early morning hours. By then, I just wanted to go home. My head pounded from a headache, and I was so exhausted that I walked out of the station and forgot my gun.

About the time I got home and started to remove my gun belt, my doorbell rung. When I answered the door, I saw Jim, a county officer standing in front of me with my gun in his hand.

He asked, "Did you forget something at the station?"

My embarrassment and uneasiness over my negligence drastically increased the pain in my head. I learned from that mistake and never forgot my gun again.

At the time, that was my only gun. The incident made me realize the depth of my vulnerability if I didn't have my gun for some reason. What if the man who just came to my house wasn't a cop but a burglar, or worse, someone meant to do me and my family harm? I wouldn't have had my gun to protect us.

At the earliest opportunity, I went shopping. I purchased a second weapon, a Smith & Wesson model .38 with a two-inch barrel. I also bought an ankle holster for it.

From that point forward, I always wore that gun on my left ankle as my backup patrol weapon. I knew a trooper who had been shot and killed on a traffic stop when he fought with a suspect who was able to remove the trooper's issued weapon from his holster.

I had decided that if my duty gun in my holster was ever taken from me, I had one more chance to fight for survival.

Courthouse Sentiments

With making so many arrests, I frequently got summoned to court hearings and trials after working all night or on my days off.

One morning, a plea bargain had been offered to a defendant. He decided he wanted a jury trial. As a result, jury selection was scheduled to begin after the lunch hour.

I felt exhausted after working all night. Once my shift ended, I went home and got the children off to school. After that, I took a shower and headed off to court to check in to let them know I was present for trial. I planned to then use the court's lunch hour to sleep in my car. My napping plans got interrupted, though, but in a good way.

I had gone inside the courtroom to see if the trial was still going to continue. After it emptied, I walked over to the judge's staff assistant to ask her.

She assured me the case was moving forward and then said, "By the way, the judge wants to see you in his office."

I was curious as to what Judge Harry Barber wanted, so I walked to his chamber area. Upon entering, I saw his secretary gathering her purse. I supposed she was about to go to lunch herself.

I said, "Judge Barber wants to see me."

"I'll let him know you're here," she said with a smile and disappeared through a door behind her. She came back a minute later. "He'll see you now."

I walked through the same doorway that the secretary did and into an oversized office. The masculine décor consisted of dark wood and navy-blue wallpaper.

A large, elderly man sat at a large wooden desk covered by a sheet of glass. A stack of papers in front of him held his attention. The downward tilt of his head displayed a bald spot in the midst of his grey hair.

He looked up at me and smiled. I could almost swear I saw a twinkle in his blue eyes. Their color was so vivid that they demanded your complete attention, ultimately distracting you from his portly size.

Judge Barber had earned an excellent reputation as a fair judge and was nothing less than an icon. In addition to being very well-liked, he possessed a commanding demeanor.

The smile faded as the inner edges of his eyebrows creased downward. "You look tired, Trooper Turner." He stood and began putting on his suit jacket. "The reason I called you in here was to offer you my office while I go out to lunch. You can sleep on my couch." He pointed to the brown leather sofa located to the left side of his desk.

I looked at the couch with its deep cracks from many years of wear. At the time, I considered it the most beautiful couch in the world.

I thanked the judge. As soon as he left his chambers, I sat down and almost sunk into its soft cushions. At the time, I considered it the most comfortable couch in the world. One thing was for sure, it felt much better than my cramped patrol car.

From that time on, if I had an afternoon trial, I had a place to sleep. I had never heard of another officer sleeping in the judge's chambers. I determined that my napping arrangements shouldn't be discussed with any of my colleagues.

I always wondered why Judge Barber was so gracious to me. I was in his courtroom constantly for a couple of years, but so were a lot of the other DUI Task Force members.

Clearly, he liked me, and I found favor with him for whatever reason. One time, a defense attorney became very antagonistic to me while I was on the witness stand. Judge Barber became very curt and annoyed with him.

On another case, the judge told the defense lawyer, "Trooper Turner is very professional and wins most of her DUI trials."

These attorneys were young as were most of the attorneys in the court's misdemeanor traffic division. It became a great training ground for them as well as for rookie police officers. Many of the lawyers went on to become defense attorneys.

Actually, I enjoyed partaking in the Miami courthouse setting. Although the surrounding areas were very worn and dirty, they energized each and every one of my senses.

Even the smells became nostalgic. I associated the courthouse with the aromas emitted from the tobacco products and the fragrance of hot dogs being grilled on vending carts that lined the building's sidewalks.

During working hours, you could always find people from all walks of life standing on the main steps chatting. They could be police officers, lawyers, defendants, street people, and those who were just released from the jail located around the block.

Many mornings, a dead chicken waited on the courthouse steps to greet those who arrived first. These sacrificed chickens meant a serious case was on the docket for that day. Drug traffickers used this voodoo practice to ward off evil spirits.

Goats were sometimes the sacrifices for those cases heard at the federal courthouse. I guess the Miami drug dealers were more frightened of the federal system and thus required a larger sacrifice.

The inside of the building always seemed to be in decay. The terrazzo floor contained cracks and embedded dirt that looked as if it had been swooshed around by dirty mops. The stained walls retained years of brown and grey streaks and smudges that could be seen even with the interior's poor lighting.

High-backed oak benches lined the walls and were marred with initials of those who had sat on them for too long. The elevators always seemed to be in maximum-capacity mode. A courthouse visitor could wait forever to find an elevator with enough space to accommodate him or her and everyone else who was waiting.

I always took the escalator up as far as it would go. Then I transferred to the elevator. At that point, they were fairly empty as compared to the main and lower floors.

Once I walked those hallow corridors of the courthouse, I quickly discovered that my already-stimulated senses intensified to an intoxicated level. I could feel the powerful emotions of those traversing in and out of the courtrooms' heavy wooden doors. The excitement and drama acted as my drug.

High-profile cases had been tried in this old building. For instance, serial killer Ted Bundy was tried here in June 1979, as a result of a change of venue from Tallahassee where he committed the brutal murders of the Chi Omega sorority sisters at Florida State University.

As I thought about that case, I was reminded of the brutality and evil that these walls had beheld as the state pursued justice. However, I began to sadly see and learn firsthand that justice on this earth can slip through the cracks of its worn terrazzo floors. Sometimes, the hands of justice are tied, and the wicked freely walk public streets as their victims grieve their lack of closure.

Despite this disquieting fact, though, I have faith, faith that one day every man and woman will be held accountable for his or her sins, whether it be in this life or the next.

CHAPTER 6

Back to Patrol Life

In 1986, I decided to leave the DUI Task Force and return back to patrol. I had been with them for two years, and I needed to get back to a normal life, well, back to as normal a life as one can have in law enforcement.

By now, I had gained a lot of experience making arrests and testifying in court. Although wonderful for my career, it had come at a price. The long hours of working all night and into the morning became too grueling on me physically. The odd hours also created stress on my family.

My greatest challenge in law enforcement was providing a healthy and productive home environment anyway, and my DUI Task Force hours exacerbated this challenge. I felt that my girls were forced to fend for themselves on many evenings, which wasn't conducive to their wellbeing.

Fortunately, they had a lot of positive despite the situation. First of all, they knew without a doubt that they were loved.

Secondly, I raised them to love God and the Bible, and we had always been involved in church and its activities. As a result, a solid biblical foundation and a love for God had been instilled in them since they were young. I knew it had played a big role in developing their strong character and unwavering integrity, both of which still remain with them today.

However, I knew they needed a well-rounded life. This would require my providing an atmosphere that enabled them to cultivate their talents through a focus on education. So going back on patrol gave me a schedule that allowed me to be with my daughters more and at a time when they needed me the most.

I hadn't been back on patrol for long when all of my squad got briefed about a string of bank robberies committed by two extremely violent men. They were reported to be driving a black Monte Carlo that they had carjacked from a victim who they had shot in the Everglades. The victim survived and reported the crime to the police.

About a month later on the Friday morning of April 11, 1986, Dean and I grabbed a cup of coffee at Tony's Donuts located in Homestead. We talked about the bank robberies and how more banks seemed to be robbed on Fridays than any other day of the week. We agreed that we would be especially vigilant that day in looking for that Monte Carlo.

After we finished our coffee, we went back on patrol. I pulled onto the U.S. Highway 1 south of Cutler Ridge. The sun was already hard at work, and I had to pull my visor down to reflect its vicious glare.

At around twenty minutes after nine, an intercity emergency signal patched into my highway patrol radio. My body stiffened as I listened to the communication center of the Miami-Dade Police Department (MDPD) sound the alarm. It reported a police-involved shootout south of Kendall Drive off U.S. 1 in Pinecrest, formerly known as Suniland.

I heard the MDPD officers as they responded. Their anxious voices blasted through my radio reporting that it involved several shooters and that they were unable to enter the shooting area.

My heart raced as I envisioned the worst. I knew their high-pitched shrieks were the combination of adrenaline, terror, and frustration because I too was feeling those same emotions. Heat then rushed through my body as the responding officers yelled how they couldn't identify the good guys from the bad guys.

The shooters were using cars as shields, but none were marked police cars. One, however, was a black Monte Carlo. Some speculation commenced over the radio as to whether the FBI was involved because of the Monte Carlo. We all knew that the FBI worked bank robberies and drove unmarked cars.

As it turned out, eight FBI agents were exchanging gunfire with those two violent bank robbers. We later discovered that the criminals' identities were Michael Platt and William Matix.

The agents' firepower was no match against the robbers' weapons and ammunition. Five of the agents didn't wear vests. Most of them used five- and six-shot revolvers to fight back, which required too much time and effort to reload. In exceptionally stressful situations, the delays can lead to deadly results.

Back in the 1980s, the FBI and law enforcement in general were not issued high-powered guns but revolvers. In addition, police agencies provided very little tactical training to their officers. This combination made the agents ill-prepared for a shootout, not due to any fault of their own.

In contrast, Platt's and Matix's military training and high-capacity semi-automatic weapons gave them an unfair and lethal advantage over the FBI agents. Platt shot and killed two of the agents—fifty-three-year-old Benjamin Grogan and thirty-year-old Jerry Dove. Five other agents were shot, three of whom were seriously wounded.

The robbers then had the audacity to climb into their murdered victims' vehicle to get away. However, Special Agent Edmondo Mireles, Jr. refused to allow that to happen. Despite the fact that he had been shot in the forearm of his shooting hand, he aggressively moved toward the robbers, shooting and killing both Matix and Platt. His courageous action finally ended the gunfire altogether.

I listened as the arriving officers and troopers entered the area and began to triage. They continued to transmit their reports, making me almost feel as if I was with them at the crime scene. Chills ran up and down my spine and a profound sadness overcame me because of the two heroes lost during that firefight.

This shooting later became termed the Bloodiest Day in FBI History. The follow-up action reports that always accompany these events forced the FBI and most of the nation's law enforcement agencies to alter their tactical firearms training. This shootout as well as other well-documented police shootouts caused firearms trainers, gun makers, and ammunition providers to develop new and more aggressive training standards. All the while, firearm companies and ammunition manufacturers joined with American police agencies to develop high-capacity firearms and better-performing bullets. Their purpose was to combat the high-powered military weapons that criminals had adopted for their illegal activities.

Sometime after the Bloodiest Day, MDPD Homicide Detective David Rivers conducted a forensic examination of all evidence, including witness statements and interviews. He then began a multi-year-long training review about the FBI shootout, traveling throughout the country, meeting with firearms instructors and police academy instructors.

Many recognized Detective Rivers' review process as being the best officer safety training available at the time. The mid-to-late-eighties is recognized as a pivotal time for American law enforcement with the emerging development of new ammunition, weapon designs, and more aggressive tactical training.

Later on, I would work with some of the FBI survivors who had been wounded during this shootout. I respected these brave men and considered myself to be very fortunate to not only get to know them but to learn from them as well.

Their courage and commitment inspired me. They proved that they never gave up the fight, even when they faced adversity and possible death.

The Attack on the German Tourists

The King Motel in the Goulds area was a decrepit, single-story concrete-block building with peeling white paint and fading green trim. The parking lot consisted of potholes and crumbling asphalt.

A lot of traffic traipsed in and out of the motel doors, probably due to the interest in the "working girls" who pranced their wares across the street on the highway's shoulder. Rumor had it the rooms could be rented for an hourly rate. Also about three hundred feet north was a locality known for street narcotics, robberies, and a host of other fights and criminal activities.

In the early part of 1987, a German couple had decided to come to Miami for vacation as the result of an advertisement they had seen. The pictures made a room at the King Motel look like a room at the Ritz but for far less money. The unsuspecting tourists arrived in Miami with high expectations.

They must have driven their rental car to the motel in the dark of night so that they couldn't see the true condition of their vacation spot. I could only imagine their reaction when they walked into Miami's version of the Bates Motel.

The couple didn't get much time to consider the ramifications from staying at this particular establishment. Unfortunately for them, a local criminal had been loitering in a dark area under a large ficus tree waiting for his next victim. When he saw the vulnerable tourists, he saw a great opportunity. He didn't waste any time.

Within just a few minutes of them arriving in their room, the thug calmly walked over to its frail, plywood door locked with a pushbutton doorknob. He then proceeded to kick it in. After entering the room, he brutally beat the male, beat and raped the female, and then took all of their money, jewelry, and valuables.

This attack on the German tourists made headlines in *The Miami Herald* and on all of the local television stations. If there is one aspect of sensitivity in Miami that will draw the community together, it's when visitors are violated.

The Miami-Dade Robbery Unit interviewed the couple. The husband gave a statement, but it was his wife Freda who really nailed the suspect with her identification of him. She had the image of her rapist imprinted in her mind. When shown a photo lineup of suspects, Freda immediately focused on the picture of Sonny Wright.

Sonny turned out to be a career criminal and had recently been released from state prison. His pictures were distributed throughout law enforcement agencies in Miami.

I hoped to come across Sonny when Jacob and I worked in the vicinity three days later. While patrolling the nearby area of Perrine, I spotted the profile of a tall, skinny, dark-complexioned male who was dumpster diving. He even sported the goatee that Freda had described as well as the curly black hair and black eyes.

I stopped to investigate. As soon as this man turned toward me, I recognized him to be Sonny. I called Jacob, who was about a block away.

Before he arrived, I casually walked over to him. "Hey," I said. "you doing okay? You looking for food?"

He stood up in the dumpster and looked at me, his eyes steady and revealing no expression. He didn't answer. I could tell from his relaxed posture and facial muscles that he didn't seem to realize I knew he was the rapist.

He pulled himself out of the dumpster empty-handed and stood before me, his jeans and t-shirt rumpled. I wasn't sure if the wrinkles were from the dumpster or from wearing those same clothes for a few days.

I continued talking as I reached behind me and grabbed my handcuffs. Before he knew what I was doing, I caught his left wrist with one of the bracelets, quickly turned him around, and grabbed his right wrist and clicked on the other bracelet.

Just as I was putting him in my car, Jacob arrived. I said, "Hey, can you watch my prisoner while I do the paperwork?"

I then notified my chain of command about this arrest. I also suggested the highway patrol public information officer (PIO) disseminate an immediate press release. This would ensure that my agency and I would receive the credit for apprehending this dangerous felon.

After I completed all of these tasks, Jacob and I transported Sonny to Metro Robbery at MDPD headquarters. Upon arrival, I was floored by the media response. Jacob and I did the "perp walk" with Sonny for the media. The "perp walk" is that infamous walk in front of the cameras with the handcuffed prisoner. The media loves footage of the bad guys being walked into jail by law enforcement. We were filmed and shown on the nightly news on all of the television stations, thanks to a well-connected PIO. Now all of Miami knew that the troopers had taken a vicious criminal off the streets.

The true hero in this case, though, was Freda. Her swollen face with eyes almost forced shut from her malicious attack and her sore body didn't break her spirit in the least bit. She demanded justice for herself and her husband and protection for women who could be Sonny's future victims.

Well-wishers from all over Miami presented Freda and her husband with offerings of clothes, meals, luxury hotel rooms, and money. The members of our beautiful city came forward in a display of goodwill toward this couple.

The diverse citizens of Miami made me proud. The way they pulled together and offered assistance to these victims reaffirmed why I loved this city.

System Failure

In 1987, President Ronald Reagan came to Miami for a visit, and I was excited to be selected to work the detail. My job was to clear the interstate where the motorcade passed.

On the day of the president's visit, I got reassigned to be inside one of the toll booths where the motorcade came through. I watched as the MDPD and Florida Highway Patrol (FHP) motorcycles approached, leading the black SUVs that held the secret service tactical units and their high-powered weapons. They then sped by the booth.

All went well. After the motorcade got out of my sight, I returned back to my zone.

Weeks went by, and I unexpectedly received a subpoena to attend court for a Motion to Show Cause for failing to appear as a witness in a case. I didn't know why I received this subpoena and checked with the highway patrol. They didn't have a record of me receiving a subpoena for the day in question, which just happened to be the day of President Reagan's visit.

I responded to court. When Judge Maria Ortega saw me enter her courtroom, her body stiffened, and her eyes squinted as she glared at me. I got a bad feeling about her.

She said, "Trooper Turner, I am planning to hold you in contempt of court for not appearing for the trial of this defendant you arrested."

Attorneys, the court reporter, and her assistant all stopped what they were doing. Everyone's eyes were trained on me waiting for my response.

I said, "I never received that particular subpoena, your Honor."

She then set a hearing date to address her charges against me.

I envisioned me spending the night in the cockroach-infested jail behind the courthouse, so I immediately went to see my friend Paul Hunt. He happened to be one of the high-ranking prosecutors for Miami State Attorney Janet Reno. Later on, Reno would become the U. S. Attorney General.

I sat in his office in front of his desk. "Paul, I'm afraid I'm in trouble with Judge Ortega." I then told him about her threat.

"I can go to the hearing with you if you'd like," he said.

I didn't hesitate to take him up on his offer.

When the time came for me to show back up again in court on this case, Paul came with me as my attorney. Judge Ortega took offense to him representing me against her charges of contempt.

She immediately stated, "Why is Janet Reno sending her big guns into my courtroom?"

Paul ignored the question and instead said, "On the day in question, Trooper Turner worked an important detail. In addition, she had not received notice to come to court for that date. At this time, your Honor, I'd like for the court reporter to read back the transcript when Trooper Turner was last in court on this case."

The court reporter complied. The transcripts revealed that the judge had stated she wanted me back in court on the day in question. The court reporter continued reading the transcript, but no record existed that I had replied back confirming to the judge that I would be returning. I suspected that I had already left the courtroom when the judge made her statement.

This judge was new and probably thought that she could hand down a verbal order in court without needing to follow through with a subpoena, which is not normal. Paul insisted that I was never made aware of my need to be in court on that day. Without issuing me the subpoena, the judge couldn't prove otherwise.

Finally Judge Ortega relented and reluctantly dropped the contempt charges, so I didn't have to spend the night in jail. She was a one-term judge with a poor record. I was elated during the next election when she lost to her opponent.

Just Another Night on the Job

On a clear, cool Halloween night, I drove my patrol car on SW 200 Street across from the Cutler Ridge Mall when something caught my eye.

A man stood at a gas-station pump swinging a crowbar. His target was another man lying on the ground with his hands in front of his face. I notified dispatch and immediately drove into the station. I then jumped out of my car and pulled my gun and not a moment too soon. The crowbar-armed guy was about to strike the head of the man on the ground.

I yelled, "Police! Drop your weapon!"

This guy stopped in mid-swing. He then just looked at me, smiled, and reraised the crowbar to finish what I had interrupted. My gun sights were aimed on his chest, and my finger was on the gun trigger, ready to pull should he not heed my order.

Fortunately, he must have realized I meant business because he chose not to follow through with the swing. He threw the weapon to the concrete. I kept my gun aimed at this maniac until Dean arrived and handcuffed him.

Fire rescue treated the victim on the scene while I took his statement. At first he didn't want to speak to us, but after encouraging him to cooperate, he finally and reluctantly told me what had happened that led to this altercation. In summation, the fight had ensued over a stripper at a nearby club.

I drove the prisoner to the Miami jail, and Dean followed me. When I walked past those old, nasty, crowed cells, one of the inmates exposed his erect penis. He began to masturbate as he yelled to me in Spanish from his jail cell.

I expressed my annoyance to Dean and the prison guards. They all just laughed at my indignation.

Dean asked, "What are you going to do, Floy, arrest the pervert?"

I even had to laugh at Dean's comment since he was right. It would take more time and effort to add additional charges to this prisoner. It had been a long and evil shift already, and I just wanted to call it a night.

Since my shift was ending, I made the smart decision to go home. I drove slowly in the direction of my house, hoping and praying the whole way that I wouldn't be dispatched to another call.

When Life and Death Weigh in the Balance

On an evening in October 1987, my love for mankind was challenged, and the reality of the life-and-death career that my comrades and I had chosen slapped me in the face.

My husband and I had attended a Chamber of Commerce dinner in Coral Gables. This was an elaborate affair. I had taken great care to purchase a beautiful, low-cut turquoise dress from my girlfriend, Ann Maria. She owned my favorite dress shop in Homestead.

During the middle of dinner, my husband's police station notified him that one of his officers named Dan was seriously injured. He was being taken to Jackson Memorial Hospital. All we were told was that an investigation at a nearby movie theater was taking place as a result.

Because the assistant chief of police was also at this dinner, my husband asked him and me to go to Dan's house since I knew Dan's wife well. He wanted us to tell his family about his condition and then take them to the hospital.

We all three then hurried out of the dinner and sped out of the parking lot in unmarked police cars with activated lights and sirens. My husband drove to his police station, and the assistant chief and I drove to Dan's house.

When we arrived, we quickly walked to Dan's door, hoping to get to his wife before she heard anything on the news. When she opened the door, she saw our serious and stress-filled faces void of the usual smiles. She collapsed to the ground, and her world went with her.

The first words out of the assistant chief's mouth were "He's alive, but he's badly hurt."

We all then rushed through the dark night to the hospital. I know we were all praying that he wouldn't succumb to his wounds.

We were then told the details. Dan had been working an off-duty job at the theater when a disturbance occurred. Three juveniles stabbed him multiple times, but they were now in custody at the police station. We were told that Dan didn't want to fire his weapon because he was in a crowded group of kids.

He suffered greatly from these wounds. Dan had been knifed in both his front and his backside, and both of his lungs had collapsed.

Five weeks later after being released from the hospital, Dan died from a heart attack at the young age of forty-one. In addition to being a Vietnam veteran, he had been a law enforcement officer for eighteen years.

The medical examiner ruled that his death was due to the heart attack, not the vicious injuries he received protecting his community. This ruling had negative repercussions for Dan's family. The families of fallen officers received state and federal dollars for their sacrifice, and his demise was not perceived to be a line-of-duty death.

My husband persevered as a champion for Dan's family through efforts to have the medical opinion of one person overruled. His persistent determination led to Dan's family receiving some of the funding.

When the world was privileged to have Dan a part of it, he was known to love his family and to enjoy his boat. Both in life and in death, whether on the battlefield of Vietnam or on the battlefield of the Miami streets, Dan proved himself to be an American hero all the way to the very end.

One Person's Trash Is Another Person's Treasure

Nothing like talking with another cop over a meal or a cup of coffee. In fact, two officers can accomplish a whole lot while sharing this ritual. Frequently, the time is used to connect, sometimes to vent, sometimes to sit silently together and ponder the previous event or experience, sometimes to talk shop, and sometimes to do all of the above.

I had been with the Florida Highway Patrol Trooper for six years now. The longer I stayed on the job, the more I appreciated these times with another officer. Very rarely did I refuse the chance to indulge, so when Jackie and I discussed meeting for lunch, I couldn't refuse.

Pulling up to the diner, I saw Jackie's patrol car, so I parked mine next to it. The cool November air of the overcast day caused me to hurry into the diner's interior. Once the sun's glare was no longer a threat, I removed my sunglasses and saw Jackie sitting at a booth and facing the door. We waved at each other, and I made my way to her table.

We hadn't had much of a chance to talk lately, so we were eager to hear about each other's recent happenings. She caught me up on the new love of her life, a trooper who had recently transferred to Miami, and I caught her up on life with my girls. We talked about the upcoming holidays and how 1987 seemed to have flown by.

We laughed like regular girlfriends except our accessories consisted of a gun and a pair of handcuffs. Suddenly, Jackie's smile disappeared. She looked down at the table, tearing the paper that had once covered her straw into tiny pieces. Her eyebrows were furrowed together as she raised her head to look at me.

"Floy, Tallahassee called me, well, more specifically, the patrol major called. He wants me to be part of a new task force they've put together. Evidently, there's been a lot of complaints from families and tourists. Supposedly, when they stop at the Gainesville rest area on I-75, several of the men get approached by prostitutes."

Her eyes searched my eyes for a response. At this point, I didn't know enough to respond one way or another.

She continued. "This major told me that they're concerned for families with children traveling to Disney World, and they don't want them exposed to that stuff. Obviously, this could hurt tourism, and they want to do something so that it doesn't continue. So they want single female troopers to work undercover as prostitutes."

Admittedly, I became green with envy. Jackie, on the other hand, was less than enthusiastic about the opportunity. Her eyes fixed on mine, her eyebrows now lifted in the middle as if she were pleading her case to me.

"Floy, I don't want this assignment. First of all, I don't want to work out of town and be away from my boyfriend. Secondly, I don't want to pretend to be a prostitute. I think it's repulsive."

She wasn't interested? Boy, oh, boy, what I'd give for this chance! I had been looking for something like this since FDLE Special Agent in Charge Drew Milton approached me a couple of years ago. He suggested that the FDLE might be a good fit for me if I could obtain some investigative experience. An undercover assignment like this would fulfill that requirement and thus give me a better chance to be hired by the FDLE. However, I couldn't understand why the major only wanted single female troopers, and quite frankly, I was a bit miffed by it.

I could only assume the reason why. He couldn't imagine a husband approving of his wife working undercover as a prostitute. On the other hand, the Tallahassee command never mentioned the need for any of the males to be single.

Jackie ended up going to Tallahassee a couple of weeks later for her undercover training and subsequently participated in her first assignment. When she returned, she said, "I don't want to do this anymore. It's disgusting having all of these men eyeing me with lust and soliciting me to have sex with them. Plus, my boyfriend doesn't want me to work out of town."

Her disdain was my opportunity to get my name before the major. If Jackie didn't want to do this, I was more than ready, willing, and able to take her place. It appeared to be a win-win all the way around.

"Jackie," I said, "when you resign from this position, would you mind recommending me to the major?"

She smiled and slightly tilted her head. I could tell that she didn't know whether to believe me or not. I returned her quizzical expression with a steady stare into her eyes, hoping to answer her unasked question.

Her facial muscles relaxed. "Sure. I'd be glad to recommend you."

I smiled. "Thanks. So tell me more about this task force."

When Jackie explained the details, I became even more intrigued. It consisted of two squads with a total of eight males and two females. One squad worked for a week while the other team went back to their patrol squad. The next week, the squads switched roles.

Ironically, I had left the DUI Task Force to be home more with my children. Now I strived desperately to get selected for a spot on a task force that would take me out of town two weeks out of the month. Those two weeks would require me to be gone from my family from Tuesday morning through Friday evening.

Before seriously considering the opportunity, though, I needed to think about whether it could and would work with my family. My youngest daughter was in middle school, and my older daughter was about to graduate from high school. My husband's schedule consisted of very long workdays with a few meetings in the evenings.

Fortunately my wonderful friend with two girls offered to help out with some transportation needs. She and her husband had helped with my girls while

I was at the academy, and they said they could also keep my younger daughter at their house when my husband worked late. In addition, my mother was still available and offered to pitch in with dinner and transportation as well. I felt satisfied that I had solutions to meet the physical needs of my children should I get selected for this task force.

I knew this assignment was important for my career goals. If I got the position, I would make it work.

As it turned out, I got the chance to make good on my promise to myself. Jackie did a great job convincing the major that I was a good candidate for the task force.

One morning while I was on patrol, the dispatcher contacted me. She said, "Trooper Turner, a major from Tallahassee wants to get a hold of you. He needs a phone number where he can reach you."

Although the dispatcher didn't tell me why this major was trying to contact me, I already knew it had to do with the task force. Since I was near my house, I gave the dispatcher my home number. That was before cell phones, so if someone needed to call us, we had to go to a payphone, our home, or a police station, and then wait for the call.

My heart pounded with excitement, and I didn't think I could get home fast enough. I was almost tempted to put on the lights and sirens but decided against it. I didn't want to bring about that kind of attention from my neighbors as I pulled into my driveway.

I barely got my car parked before jumping out and almost running into my house. As soon as I walked inside, there was instant silence. I tried to wait for the call by sitting down. I had too much pent-up energy, so I decided to stand by the phone. I eyed it, willing it to ring.

Finally it did, and its ringer was the most beautiful sound. My heart pounded with exhilaration.

I picked up the receiver and forced myself to remain calm. "Hello?"

"Trooper Floy Turner?" a male voice asked and paused. He sounded very professional and busy. "This is Major Sims. You need to report to Tallahassee for training in one week."

After this phone call, I gently laid the receiver back in its cradle. I felt an involuntarily sigh of relief escape my lungs. Evidently I had been holding my breath, and now that I got the orders, I could let it out and relax.

I sat down on my couch and stared. My feelings jumped from sheer excitement to concern about my family and how they would adjust to my absences. Then logic set in, confirming that this was the chance of a lifetime, at least for the time being.

That evening, I announced the opportunity to my family for the first time, so I knew they would need to get used to the idea. Their initial smiles of support faded with pensive looks as I explained I would have to be away from home some of the time. I could only imagine what they were thinking. I needed their blessing, and finally they gave it to me.

So the following week, I drove to Tallahassee to embark on one of the most interesting and exciting times in my career with the Florida Highway Patrol.

CHAPTER 7

Undercover with Rest-Area Comprehensive Enforcement

Training for my first undercover assignment turned out to be so much fun, and yes, it turned out to be exceptionally educational as well.

Undercover detectives from the Gainesville Police Department came to Tallahassee's Florida Highway Patrol Academy. They educated us with the slang terms used by prostitutes, the johns, and the truck drivers on the CB (Citizen's band) radios. We also received legal training, which consisted of entrapment issues that could jeopardize our court cases. My mind became a sponge, eagerly receiving and learning everything. I knew that soon I'd have to apply these lessons in the field.

Also while at the academy, the major in charge of this operation introduced me to Lenny Powell, the lieutenant over my squad and an amazing man. Lt. Powell had worked for years as an undercover operative on a federal auto-theft task force with the FBI, infiltrating a large criminal ring. His undercover work led to the dismantling of a multistate network of thieves.

After his undercover assignment, Lenny became an investigator for the highway patrol and never worked in a uniform again. Hailing from Florida's cowboy country near Sebring, he talked slow and wore alligator boots, plaid cowboy shirts, and blue jeans with a big brass buckle on his belt.

His fit and trim frame stood about six feet two inches, and his dark-brown eyes enhanced his macho image. The grey hair around his temples made me think that he may be in his late forties. His ruggedly handsome face contained a few scars that were allegedly put there during a knife fight while working on the federal task force.

Lenny's experience, cool demeanor, and good looks impressed me, and I was quite taken with him. We hit it off from the get go.

I thought him to be the total package of a sexy man, and I felt like he admired my eagerness to learn the ropes of working undercover. His approval fueled my desire to become an excellent undercover operative.

After training, I returned to Miami with enthusiasm about my new assignment. Then my emotions bounced back and forth like a ball in a fast and furious game of tennis. Guilt set in about possessing such an intense focus on my job. I knew I'd miss my daughters and wondered for the hundredth time if they would be able to adjust to my absence. Then I thought about how I just couldn't pass up this assignment and the positive long-term effect it would have on my career. Then I thought about how I may miss out on some of my girls' important activities, such as dance or music events.

The tennis match still continued during my drive from Miami to Gainesville where I would start putting my training into action. I couldn't get my daughters out of my mind. As a result, my woven nylon tactical bag wasn't the only kind of baggage I had in the car with me. My emotional baggage seemed so much more heavy and burdensome.

Finally, I arrived in Gainesville about three o'clock in the afternoon. Stepping outside, I could feel my hair wilting. I blamed the moisture from the overcast sky that increased the humidity level.

While checking into an old Holiday Inn, I recognized a tall and overweight trooper from Crystal River named Benny Dean in the hotel lobby. We greeted each other and made some small talk. Just before leaving to find my room, he and I agreed to meet for an early dinner before the five o'clock briefing.

I then walked to my room. A concrete walkway functioned as a hallway that fed into the rooms' entrances. The openness forced me to hear the constant hum of the I-75 traffic.

Stepping inside, I noted its cleanliness despite its worn appearance. I began the task of unpacking my sparse wardrobe.

Throughout my undercover training, the highway patrol stressed what we should and shouldn't wear for this assignment. They wanted their undercover officers, or UCs as we were called, to dress conservatively. They prohibited low-plunging necklines or short shorts.

I took the pink high-top sneakers that I borrowed from my daughter, some old *Bike Week* t-shirts, and loose-fitting jeans out of my bag. I also packed a blue denim work shirt to hide my gun that I'd keep in the back of my jean's waistband. The entire wardrobe made for easy packing within my small duffle bag.

I worried that my white teeth and well-cut hair might cause me to look too clean cut and not credible. To try and "correct" this concern, I took a bottle of baby oil and used it as hair grease and applied darker makeup to my face.

Pulling out my training notes, I started pouring over them. I reminded myself that rest areas were referred to as the pickle park or lizard lot on the CB radio. The working girls were called lot lizards.

I wore my working-girl attire when I met Benny in the lobby. We located a Perkins restaurant near the motel to eat our dinner and talk.

I learned that Benny had been a trooper for few years longer than me. He also saw this as an opportunity to learn about investigations. He was married and had a baby at home.

After dinner, we stopped at a gas station market to pick up drinks and snacks for our shift. We then drove to the rear of the motel parking lot far away from any cars or buildings to ensure privacy for our first briefing.

Lt. Powell had already arrived. Soon afterward, the rest of the task force members started to join us. One other female stood in the midst of this testosterone-fueled group. We contrasted with our appearance, and I was a few years older than her. She stood about five feet four inches and wore her long dark hair in a ponytail. Her dark eyes seemed to smile even when her mouth didn't.

Lenny introduced her to me as Ann Morgan from St. Augustine. I got the sense that we would get along very well.

During our briefing, I glanced over at Ann a few times from the corner of my eye. Her smile never seemed to leave her face. I suspected that she was just as excited as me.

Lt. Powell then introduced both Ann and me to the group. "These ladies are our decoys. They'll be wired and have a battery case, a mike, and an antenna that'll be taped to their persons. They'll take turns standing outside the maintenance room behind the walkway that leads to the men's room. Entrapment's going to be hard to prove in court if the johns put forth the effort to walk off the sidewalk to where they are."

He then emphasized safety. "It's extremely important you keep all of your activities as low-key as possible. Ann, Floy, you'll drive to the rest area in that BMW over there and park it in the rear." He pointed to an older model BMW mixed in with the other hotel patron's cars. "Yeah," he said, "thanks to the Florida Highway Patrol. They seized it in a drug case, and we get to use it."

"Okay, ladies. Once the john offers to pay for sex, try to lead them from the sidewalk behind the maintenance area through the picnic area and then near the BMW."

He then assigned four men to the takedown team. "You'll hide behind the trees or cars near the BMW," he told them.

"Once we hear the offer, two takedown members will walk up from the rear. One's going to come from the john's left, and another will come from the right. I need the other two of you to stand close-by and off to the side in case we need you.

"After you make the arrest, you'll put the john in the station wagon, and the decoy will get in the BMW. You'll all drive to the next exit. A trooper in a marked patrol car will be waiting for you in the gas station parking lot. While there, pictures need to be taken of the decoy with the john for court purposes. The decoy will then need to fill out the booking paperwork, and the marked unit will take the john to the local jail for booking.

"Floy and Ann," he continued, "repeat everything the johns say. We have to record the conversation, so we want to make sure it's clear. Make sure the rest of the team can hear you in case you need to use any established emergency codes.

"If you see a gun or knife, mention the item. Say, 'That's a big knife,' or 'What are you doing with that gun?'

"If you run into another emergency, again state the problem. Say something like, 'Why are you trying to pull me?' If you can't explain something, yell some kind of code word."

Benny said, "What about using *snake* for the code word?"

We all got a chuckle out of that suggestion because this rest area had signs posted throughout it warning visitors to watch out for rattlesnakes inhabiting this area.

Lt. Powell said, "Okay. Be safe out there. And Floy, I'm going to have you start the activities by going first."

Then he, Ann, and I walked to my room to put the wire equipment on us. He showed us each of the recording components and then suggested that we tape the antennae to one side of our bra strap and the mike to the other side. At that time, this recording system was considered high-tech, but now it's rather antiquated.

He said, "A trooper will be in the van monitoring the device, and I'll be with him. I'll let everyone know when to take down the john, and if I see danger, I'll abort it. If you're not outside, you'll be in the van with us."

While he talked to us, Ann and I discreetly taped the devices onto our bra as he had instructed. Since I was very thin, I placed the battery container with a 9-volt battery between my breasts inside my bra. This worked, except the battery heated up so much that it felt like it was burning me.

We then left for the rest area. Ann sat in the passenger seat of the BMW, and I drove. Once we arrived, I pulled into the parking lot and drove around to the back. My eyes immediately scanned for an isolated spot.

Half of the guys on the team drove to the rest area in an older station wagon that looked like a family car complete with camping gear strapped to its roof. The other half rode in a nondescript white van. Its interior had been designed and altered to accommodate this detail. A curtain separated the front seats from the rear compartment, ensuring privacy from passersby. The whole back part of the van contained a monitoring and recording area that could hold a couple of people and a work desk.

Both the van and the station wagon parked in front of the plaza and mingled among the other cars while keeping their distance from each other. All of the units dispersed throughout the parking lot and blended in with the tourists and travelers.

Ann and I walked to the van and got in the back. I was nervous and excited and raring to go. Lt. Powell must have noticed my high level of energy. "Okay, Floy. Ready?" he asked.

I nodded and climbed out of the van. A slight drizzle patted my face.

I walked to the rear of the building that contained the restrooms. About fifteen feet from the sidewalk stood a large oak tree with Spanish moss dripping off of its branches. I decided to go over and stand under its clusters of leaves because they made a great umbrella.

In the southbound rest area, a sidewalk led up a hill from where the trucks were parked and to the building containing the restrooms. My post was in a dark area off to the side, and I hoped my team was going to be diligent in their surveillance of my activities. I felt comfort in knowing my gun was tucked inside the back of my belt.

I stood at my assigned post for about thirty minutes when a man walked up from the truck parking lot. The first thing that caught my attention was his huge belly pouring over his dirty jeans and stretching a black t-shirt full of holes.

A mental image formed in my mind. If he stooped over, his jeans would show the plumber's crack. I had to force myself not to shake my head at the thought.

He also wore a greasy yellow hat over his greasy brown hair. Embroidered on the hat's bill were the words *Diane's Produce* and images of some vegetables. I wondered if the hair made the hat greasy, or if the hat made the hair greasy. Either way, one looked as if it fed off of the other.

When this man got within a few feet of me, I smelled his body odor. Instinctively, I took a couple of steps backward.

He asked, "Are you working?"

I learned in my training class that "Are you working" actually meant "Are you a prostitute?"

I responded in all honesty, "Yeah, I'm working." After all, I was *on the job*, which is a slang term for being a cop. I then said, "What are you doing?"

He said, "I want a BJ."

I knew BJ stood for blow job. I had to appreciate his desire to push past the small talk and get down to business.

I remembered that I needed to repeat everything he said for the sake of the recorder. Every word must be clear. The team members also needed to be sure of what was said.

I tilted my chin upward and asked in an almost haughty voice, "You want a BJ from *me*?"

"Yep, that's what I want." He licked his lips as his staring eyes fixed on my breasts. There was even a bit of drool escaping from his mouth.

"You want a BJ from me? What's it worth to you?"

I had to phrase my question like that. Telling the john a dollar amount could be deemed entrapment in court.

The trucker responded, "Twenty dollars." The licking of his lips was becoming more apparent.

Well, now I felt completely insulted. This guy thought I was only worth twenty bucks!

The offer was what it was, and I wasn't in the position to negotiate. I looked at him square in the eyes and said, "Twenty bucks? Okay. My car's parked over in the back. We can go there."

He dug his hands in his pocket and looked down a moment. When he looked back up, his hungry eyes went back to my breasts, and I think he started to pant.

"Why don't we just go to my truck, Sugar?" he asked in a flippant tone.

"No way," I said. "The cops hang out looking for working girls in the trucks."

He bought this excuse and shrugged. "Alright," he said with a grin.

I turned toward the BMW, and I could hear his heavy breathing as he followed behind me. Once we got near the car, the arrest team walked over to us, showed him their badges, and arrested him.

I then rode with the takedown team and the john to meet the transport units in a gas station parking lot. One of the troopers took a picture of me and the prisoner together. These pictures would be shown to any possible juries to prove that I wasn't wearing suggestive attire.

By five o'clock, I had made it through my first night on the task force. We all drove to Shirley's Diner to eat breakfast.

When I finally got back to the hotel, I was so tired. We all dispersed to our respective rooms where we hung the "Do Not Disturb" signs on the outside of our door handles.

We soon learned that the maids at this hotel didn't heed the signs. I think we were awakened every morning by the maids knocking and "double checking" to make sure we didn't want our rooms cleaned. Toward the end of this detail, one ingenious trooper took all of our "Do Not Disturb" signs and taped them to the outside of his door to make a statement.

It still didn't make a difference. The maids then had the desk call the trooper's room, waking him up, to verify that he didn't need them to clean his room.

The first week on the task force was the toughest. I experienced some trepidation with most of my thoughts centered on my family. A chill ran down my spine when I thought about what my girls would think of their mom if they saw me working and playing the role of a prostitute. I also worried if my absence would become burdensome to my husband's career as he tried to juggle the role of a single parent with ambition.

With each passing day, though, my apprehensions lessened. I managed to play my role with much more ease and so did each of the team members, especially as we became closer. We learned the good, the bad, and the ugly of each other's personalities and what to anticipate from everyone.

We all took the job seriously, but we also had fun with each other, taking every opportunity to laugh. The team dynamics stayed consistent, except for the role of one of the men.

One night while working, Benny went into the men's restroom to take care of personal business. A few minutes later, he came back out with a man in handcuffs.

Even though we all knew that Benny was a real cutie, we were still surprised to learn why he made this arrest. It turned out that the man had stood next to Benny while he used the urinal. Just as soon as he finished his business, his neighbor grabbed his genitals, or as Benny preferred to call them, his prized possessions.

Once Benny relayed this information to the task force members, his fate was doomed. He became the third decoy on our task force.

Not long after this unexpected change, a potential john approached me. After talking with him for about twenty minutes and trying to get him to finalize the "deal," I started to get frustrated. Then Benny walked by us.

The man's eyes immediately left me and fell onto Benny. He turned on his heels and followed after Benny like a puppy dog, dropping me like a hot potato. The next time I saw him was a few minutes later in handcuffs and being escorted by Benny.

The task force also used Benny to patrol the men's restrooms. Some johns picked up other males and took them into the stalls for their sexual encounter.

We learned about the stall "bag trick." In these situations, a paper grocery bag or a shopping bag was placed in front of the stall's toilet to hide the extra pair of feet.

We experienced other strange occurrences as well. For instance, during the early months of summer, we arrested a lot of watermelon truck drivers. I don't know why they were so horny. I haven't enjoyed watermelon since. I was also surprised at the types of men who were our johns. We arrested preachers, doctors, corrections officers, and college students.

To add to the mixture in the perv pool, Gainesville and Ocala were both in close proximity to a lot of the Florida prisons, including Starke, the famous Florida death-row prison. As a result, we arrested a few newly released men for solicitation [for prostitution]. I'm glad we made these arrests. If these released prisoners didn't change their behaviors after serving time, they needed to be back in the prison system.

As the task force progressed, we moved to rest areas all over Florida. We also worked in the Ocala I-75 rest area because a number of men had been murdered. A female prostitute was the suspect. We kept hoping to come across her. Who knows but we could have been in the same locations as her and not known it.

Later on, the serial killer was identified as Aileen Wuornos. Years down the road, I would get to know Aileen. I have often thought about her victims and her sad life.

Regardless of our level of naivety when we arrived on the task force, though, we all acquired quite an education to the world of illicit sex. A person couldn't work undercover on that task force without being changed. I had to confront those breaking the law from a different angle. I realized what it felt like to offer myself up to do despicable acts with strangers, and then thanking God that I didn't have to follow through with them.

Along with the creepy guys wanting to do god-awful things to me and other working girls, our setting intensified the mood. Dark skies, lingering fog, and dripping Spanish moss hung from large oak trees. It got even more eerie when the wind or a slight breeze blew, causing the moss to swing back and forth like vines in a dark jungle. Of course no jungle would be complete without hungry lions and lionesses. They prowled the rest-area jungle looking for their next meal.

One night, some members of our team unexpectedly confronted one of those hungry lionesses in our white van. A trooper had been sitting in the driver's seat when a "real" working girl opened the unlocked passenger's door and jumped in uninvited. She asked if he wanted her to perform oral sex on him for thirty dollars.

The trooper noticed that the dividing curtain was halfway open. He quickly closed it while repeating her offer, hoping the monitor recorded the conversation. Fortunately, Lt. Powell had been sitting in the back and had turned on the tape recorder. Enough of her proposal had been captured for evidence.

Undoubtedly, this jungle had its share of hungry lions. Another time, a small man wearing a pink dancer's tutu and thumb cuffs approached Benny. He offered Benny money for a sexual encounter. The "dancer" was arrested, but he soon made bail.

Several days later, some of us decided to join Lt. Powell at the Waffle Hut. Evidently he liked the food because he had been eating there all week. I sat across from him with my back to the kitchen.

His seat allowed him a clear view of the opening between the kitchen and the bar. All of a sudden, Lt. Powell's face went white. His mouth froze in mid-chew, and then he dropped his fork on his plate.

I turned around to see what had caused him to react so drastically. I also stopped in mid-chew when I saw the focus of his attention. Reading an order on the other side of that kitchen opening stood Benny's "dancer" now wearing the uniform of the Waffle Hut cook. It appeared that he had been cooking Lt. Powell's food all along.

Lt. Powell jumped up out of his seat, threw some money on the table, and charged toward the door. He couldn't get out of there fast enough. As far as I know, Lt. Powell never ate at another Waffle Hut again.

On another night, a very short man walked up to me while I worked. He never said a word but just grabbed my left breast and pinched it through my bra, battery case, and wires.

The first thought that crossed my mind was *He now knows I'm a cop.* Whether or not he knew, it surely didn't phase him one bit nor did it deter his intentions. This pervert also began to pinch my right breast really hard.

I went nuts. I wrapped my right arm around his neck in a choke hold and worked my body around to his back. I tried to kick his legs out from under him, but I couldn't knock him off balance. The pervert was built like a fireplug, and I couldn't get him to the ground.

So I did the only thing I could—hung onto him so he wouldn't get away from me. I didn't have any handcuffs with me, just my gun.

He started to run down the hill with me attached to his neck ready to strangle him. I started yelling to the arrest team, "Get over here and help me take down this guy!" I didn't want to go with him to the truck area, but I refused to let go. I needed my team to help me get this guy into custody.

I kept yelling, knowing that everything that came out of my mouth was transmitting into my mike. Of course, they would have heard me better if I just talked in a normal voice and didn't scream, but I was so angry.

Finally out of the corner of my left eye, I saw all six guys charging down the hill after us. As they got closer, another concern leapt into my mind. I didn't want to be on the bottom of that pile when this all came to a screeching halt. I was afraid I would really get hurt if those guys all landed on the pervert with me still attached to his neck.

Just before my team jumped on this guy, I made the smart decision to let go. It was at that time when I realized I had never told this pervert I was a cop.

I found out later that one of the troopers who came to help me had run into a low-hanging oak branch just above his eye level. He saw stars, and unfortunately, he needed a couple of stitches above his eyebrow. This incident was a great example of how circumstances can lead to hazards when running through a rest area at night while working undercover. By the way, the pervert went to jail for battery.

The fact that I had never told this perv I was a cop was inconsequential. Some of the johns found out too late that they had been mistaken about this preconceived notion they shared. They thought that by asking a working girl three times if she was a cop, and she denied it each time, then she could not be a police officer.

I always answered their questions by saying, "No, but I think you're a cop."

I relished in their efforts when they tried to convince me that they were not cops. Nevertheless, I still might get asked two more times if I was a cop.

Sometimes I couldn't get rid of a driver who just kept talking without wanting to pay for a sexual encounter. When that happened, I then asked him if he had any beer.

I soon realized that I had opened a gateway for narcotic arrests. Many times, the driver didn't have a beer but promised to retrieve some cocaine, bennies (amphetamines), or weed out of his vehicle. Sure enough, they fast walked back to me with their drug of choice and offered me a hit.

On another night, I noticed a man approaching me. He had walked by earlier with an attractive and slightly overweight gal wearing a tank top, blue-jean shorts, and flip flops.

As they walked by me, I observed her face framed with brown bangs and shoulder-length brown hair. She wouldn't make eye contact with me.

The man wore a dark t-shirt, jeans, and a baseball cap. Since the temperature was in the upper sixties, I immediately pegged them as tourists. No Floridian would be dressed like that on such a cool night. I was shivering in a sweat shirt worn over a long sleeve Bike Week t-shirt.

The woman stayed near a picnic table as her companion neared my location. I wondered if he wanted a threesome, or as the French would discreetly call it, a ménage à trois. If so, I had never encountered this proposition.

The man continued to shuffle toward me at turtle speed with his head hanging down. I thought, *What is he so reluctant about?*

When he finally got within arm's length, he said, "My wife and I are broke. We're trying to get to Daytona, and I wondered if you would mind her hanging around here to prostitute."

Oh my, now I had heard it all. Well, I didn't want to arrest her, but I would love to bless him with a night in jail and all of the frills that went with it.

I thought of the opportunity he presented. "Okay, if you give me a beer."

My tactics worked. He replied, "I don't have beer, but I have a couple of crack rocks in my pocket, and we can share them."

Oh yeah, he was going to be taking a vacation in the Alachua County Jail. On the other hand, I felt really sorry for his wife. I offered her some information on the local domestic violence shelter, just in case she wanted some help. What a nice husband he was, wanting his wife to turn tricks in the rest area.

Then there was my best-known case that involved a driver of a produce truck loaded with pole beans. These are big, flat green beans grown in Florida.

We were working near central Florida during the winter months. On this particular night, Ann and Benny made arrests, but I couldn't make even one.

Finally a trucker, another dirty, smelly guy, approached me. He said, "I want to fuck you."

I repeated his lewd comment for the wire. "You wanna fuck me? What's it worth to you?"

He said, "I ain't got no money, but what about a bushel of pole beans?"

I thought about how I really wanted this case and that for court purposes, an offer of a product for payment could probably replace money. I agreed to the deal and got my bushel of beans.

When the takedown team tried to arrest this guy, all hell broke loose. He fought harder than any arrestee we had ever had on the detail.

I lived to regret this arrest for more reasons than one. It haunted me for awhile as word of my pole beans spread throughout a lot of law enforcement agencies.

Although we experienced some comical situations, this world was miserable and destructive. All of these people were the creatures of the night, so to speak. The more I worked throughout these hours of darkness, though, the easier I found myself adapting to this every-other-week habitat. While most people slept in their comfortable beds, my team and I whisked away sexual deviants. Sadly, some had a family at home waiting expectantly to see them again, yet they came to places like the rest area, betraying the very ones who loved them the most.

The Tiffany Sessions Case

The task force changed motels again, and this time to a recently built Cabot Hotel. I always exercised by running in the mornings after waking up. Some of the back roads and trails near this hotel provided ample area for me to run.

About a year after I ran on these trails, a twenty-year-old University of Florida student named Tiffany Sessions disappeared in February 1989. She had told her roommate that she was going for a power walk and was believed to have disappeared from the same area where I ran. She was considered missing for the next twenty-five years.

During that time, I came to know her mother Hillary Sessions. As a result of this tragic incident with her daughter, Hillary has become a national champion for child safety.

The FDLE investigator assigned to Tiffany's case has since retired. He's still in touch with Hillary. I suspect he had spent some of his personal time looking for her daughter.

Then during the early part of 2014, Tiffany was deemed deceased, even though her body has never been found. She possessed a lot of potential and would have excelled in her endeavors. Some monster had robbed this beautiful young woman of her life and robbed the world of what she would have contributed to it.

Although the system got closure on this case, I'm quite sure Tiffany's loved ones never will. In addition to never finding her body, no one has officially been held accountable and brought to justice for her abduction and murder. However, authorities feel they have an overwhelming amount of circumstantial evidence that led them to a prime suspect, a convicted sexual predator who died in prison in 2013.

Still, the family hopes that one day soon, a small piece of evidence will surface, and this case will be closed and Tiffany's body discovered. Maybe then, they can finally put Tiffany to rest.

A Newfound Passion

Everyone on the task force used jokes as his or her own way of finding release from these bizarre sexual incidents.

Looking back, I smile when I realize just how much fun the team had with me repeating all of this vile talk. Many times, they were entertained at my expense.

However by the time the detail ended, that modesty ended as well. My teammates could hear everything through my mike, so I always made a point to turn it off when I went into the rest-area bathroom. I then turned it back on when I flushed the toilet so that they heard the loud swooshing noise.

I admit that I had a blast working undercover on this task force and delving into this seedy life, confronting guys with deviant sexual undercurrents, and getting them off the streets. But then every other week, I'd go home. I preferred not to talk about any of my job with my husband or friends. In the midst of my home environment, my work seemed nasty, and I felt tainted and dirty. Can you imagine the small talk in church on Sundays over what you did last week?

I lived one life at work and another at home. I realized that my double life was a natural consequence from working undercover. I have never shared these details with my daughters. I realize that if they choose to read this book, they'll now know these stories. I can't imagine my precious grandchildren knowing about my undercover days.

I did reap some benefits from being exposed to this type of life. I gathered an understanding of how victims of sex trafficking could be seduced into captivity through drug addiction, exploitation, manipulation, and the promise of a better life.

I learned that the police need to focus on the pimps and johns. They're the evil ones who maintain the supply and demand. Law enforcement needs to realize these underage girls and many of these women need to be labeled and treated as victims. Arresting them for prostitution only exacerbates their victimization.

The laws are now very clear in defining sex trafficking. It's the recruitment, harboring, transportation, provision, or obtaining of a person to perform labor or a commercial sex act through force, fraud, or coercion.

Any commercial sex act performed by a person under the age or eighteen is considered human (sex) trafficking, regardless of whether force, fraud, or coercion was involved. But in the 1980s, we didn't realize that many prostitutes were in fact sex slaves. Modern-day slavery had yet to be termed *human trafficking*.

I now know that a higher calling drew me into this sleazy realm of existence. For some reason, my path in life led me in this direction. The knowledge, understanding, and insight I gained through this unique exposure by working a few years in this undercover detail became a stepping stone in my career. I now possessed the discernment and instinct I needed to recognize and communicate with both suspects and victims alike of human trafficking.

Just as important, I garnered a valuable awareness that an ongoing injustice and basic human-rights violations were being committed against women and children. They were controlled by pimps and purchased by johns.

This squalid life never left my conscious or semiconscious being. As my career progressed, so did my interest in and righteous anger against the adult sex industry.

Consequently, my compassion for the women and children who were chewed up and eventually spit out compelled me to champion for them. True victory, though, would come from taking down the pimps, both male and female, who freely exploited them and seeing the justice that would be meted upon them as a result.

The Miami Riots of 1989

In January 1989, a black man on a motorcycle was being chased by the police when a Miami police officer shot and killed him.

The historical Miami Overtown district became a riot zone for days. The police were attacked, buildings were burned, and cars were both burned and stoned.

At the onset of this civil unrest, I was back in Miami on patrol because it was an off week from the RACE. I was dispatched to an area where I-95 crossed Overtown. My assigned post was near a ramp.

I listened to my radio to keep up with the situation as the city and county officers attempted to control this lawlessness. I heard yelling from the north-end troopers assigned to maintain control of the interstate.

They shouted second-by-second updates on the surge of rioters running up the interstate and throwing rocks and bottles. Their high-pitch screams conveyed panic about being overtaken as they cried out for immediate backup. My heart raced as their words of urgency blasted through the radio frequency at a much faster pace than normal.

When dispatch gave me the call to respond, my heart beat even faster. I must say I felt terrified. From what I heard, it sounded like a war was being fought.

I checked to ensure that I had supplies and my gear intact. My equipment consisted of an old riot helmet that looked like a baseball helmet, my service weapon, and my five-shot Smith and Wesson revolver that I wore in my ankle holster. I then placed my shotgun on my front seat and headed north at probably about a hundred miles per hour.

When I got close to the scene, other troopers had already arrived, so the incident commander gave me another assignment. I drove to my assigned post, which was on the overpass where I-95 crossed Overtown. I got out of my car to look at the burning city below. The billowing thick, black clouds of smoke prevented me from clearly seeing the intensity of the flames that literally engulfed buildings. I could make out crowds creating fires in dumpsters and feeding them with mattresses. They then moved these large burning trash receptacles into the streets, using them as colossal-sized Molotov cocktails.

I began coughing and sneezing. If the smoke overwhelmed me where I stood, I couldn't even imagine what those in the city were actually enduring.

I could feel the heat from the fires, even at my distance and wondered why my assignment included standing. I knew I was exposed to danger where I could be hurt or killed. I felt like an easy target for any possible gunfire. My adrenalin kicked in, causing my senses to become ultrasensitive.

I focused on the crowd and the possibilities. A lot of the activity seemed to move in slow motion.

In case the crowd tried to overtake me or if gunfire erupted in my direction, I planned to get in my car and get out of there. Knowing I had a way out gave me a much-needed surge of strength.

Tear gas had been expelled and mixed with the black smoke. Nobody had given me a proper gasmask. My eyes watered. Endurance became my only immediate plan to overcome this complication.

Then the rocks and bottles started to land near my location as the frenzy of rioters neared. I felt as if I was in a horror movie with the zombies staggering up the embankment toward me.

Furthermore, the black smoke started getting thicker. I decided to move close to the ramp where some of the other troopers and city officers had gathered.

We just about lost control of the interstate a few times that night. Admittedly, it was terrifying for us, but we felt a duty not to retreat, although we knew we could have been overpowered.

Thank God that a team of SWAT members responded to our cries for help. They drove a bulletproof armored vehicle that looked like an army tank. They used it to further block off the ramp.

My lungs ached so much at one point from breathing in the smoke that I needed to urinate. I knew I had to find a safe area to relieve myself.

A car filled with another SWAT team drove by and stopped to ask how I was holding up. I asked those macho guys to give me a ride off the interstate so that I could find some kind of bathroom.

They laughed, but I hopped into their car anyway. We exited close to Biscayne Bay and located an abandoned gas station with an outside bathroom door.

One of the SWAT guys kicked the door in for me, and I entered a stinky, filthy bathroom, but I didn't care. I was just glad I wasn't made to go behind a building or dumpster.

My predicament didn't embarrass me at all. I figured these guys probably had to urinate too, so they shouldn't be shocked at my need. The only difference was that they could turn their backs and relieve themselves while standing.

They then took me back to my car, and the night turned into morning. I was never so glad to see the dayshift replacements so that I could finally go home.

After showering off the grime, I got some sleep. I then went back out the next evening for day two. I survived three days of this riot and was glad to come out unscathed in the end.

The Miami Riot of 1989 turned out to be a very sad time in Miami's history.

Life after the RACE

Sooner or later, some details and task force assignments come to an end. The rest-area detail was no exception.

Not long after the riot in the early part of 1989, the team members all celebrated and said our farewells over a few beers after working together as a unit for the last time. Some of us, though, would cross paths again.

I felt sad to see that our crazy and weird time together was over, and I felt relieved that I would be home more. Even though I had adapted to the double life and really enjoyed working undercover, I was ready to go back to a somewhat normal life with a somewhat normal schedule.

When I returned back fulltime to what I considered my home squad, we were down one member. Jackie had received a promotion to sergeant and moved to Tampa after marrying her boyfriend. So now my squad consisted of Jenny, Jacob, Dean, and me.

The hours were better for my family life. However, I now had to face monsters of a different kind and deal with the loss of innocent lives who happened to be in the wrong place at the wrong time.

During one of our afternoon shifts, I received a radio dispatch to a fatality of a pedestrian within a few miles of my home. Once I arrived at the scene, I discovered that the victim was a teenage girl who had been hit by a car while crossing the highway.

When I saw the victim's face, I realized that I knew her. She was part of my older daughter's high school class. The fact that she was my daughter's age, and they were friendly with each other literally hit home.

I notified the sergeant that I needed a traffic homicide investigator (THI). In turn, he contacted the on-call trooper to respond.

Once her body was released for transportation to the Medical Examiner's Office, it was my responsibility to make the death notification to the family. As a trooper, I have had to make dozens of death notifications. It's the most gut-wrenching task we were given. Most of the time when a trooper rang a doorbell, the person who answered got a look of dread on his or her face. They knew why the trooper was standing at their front door—to deliver tragic news.

Miami had an ample number of troopers, so when conducting this mission, we requested a second trooper to accompany us. For this notification, Jenny responded. We met each other a couple of blocks away and then went to the family's home.

Before arriving, I wanted to know as much about the family's circumstances as possible. I located a neighbor and talked to her. She agreed to go to the family's house after we spoke to them.

Having to tell a parent that his or her cherished child was dead is difficult. Telling a parent of a child who you personally know and who is your own daughter's classmate is even more difficult since you feel a more personal connection. Furthermore, I had seen the parents at school functions. We'd speak and greet each other.

I held myself together as best as I could when I pushed the doorbell button. I didn't know if I wanted to throw up, cry, or run. One thing I did know was that I'd rather be anywhere but here waiting for a family member to answer their door.

My heart pounded hard in my chest. The seconds seemed to creep by, yet by the time someone responded to the ringing doorbell, it would be too soon.

A middle-aged woman answered the door. Her initial smile disappeared as she saw two uniformed law enforcement officers standing in front of her. Confusion replaced hospitality as her eyes narrowed, and her eyebrows pushed together. Then her eyes widened and her trembling hand involuntarily jerked to her mouth. She stepped back, trying to increase the distance from us.

I kept the announcement as monotone and professional as possible, but I felt my eyes water and heard a slight crack in my voice. The words forced their way out of my lips, words that no mother wants to hear.

She collapsed to the floor, screaming *no* over and over again. I bent down, not to help her up, but to gently touch her arm. My cop mode changed to mother mode. I empathized with her pain, mother-to-mother.

Dealing with as much death and carnage as law enforcement officers do, you learn to compartmentalize while on the job. It's not easy to work in this field for years without coming out somewhat tainted.

Law enforcement needs to be a calling, not just a job. As for me, I released my feelings through physical exercise, and I processed them through my faith and prayer.

Never a Chance at Life

The heavy rain calmed down the summer night's heat. Once it stopped, the steam from the road rose up into a cloud of vapor.

I carefully drove my patrol car through the wet streets of the small town called Naranja. Around eleven o'clock, I noticed a gray van speeding in front of me. Its hazard flashers blinked, creating a red glow onto the thin layer of water.

I signaled for the van to pull over onto the side of the road, and it complied without delay. An elderly short woman dressed in a pink flowered robe with matching scuff slippers and wearing pink foam hair rollers jumped out of the van. She screamed at me for help.

I immediately radioed Jacob to let him know my location. I told him that he should head my way because I wasn't sure what was going on with this situation.

The incoherent woman ran in my direction. When she got to the back of the van, she threw open its two back doors.

My heart skipped a beat or two. I drew my gun and ducked for cover behind my car trunk in case a hail of bullets started coming my way. I envisioned armed men jumping out and shooting me.

I quickly darted my head around the side of my car and back as I tried to assess the situation. Something either had happened or was happening in the rear of that van. At the time, I didn't know whether or not it presented a danger.

The woman waved her hands over her head and yelled, "Baby is coming! Baby is coming!"

I suddenly realized what was going on. Glancing into the rear of her van, I could see a pair of legs bent, spread, and facing me.

When I moved forward, I heard a female voice from behind the legs screaming in agony. The elderly woman must have been driving the screamer to the hospital because a baby was about to be born.

I rushed to the van's rear doors. Jacob arrived and ran up behind me. He and I looked between the legs when another scream occurred.

I radioed to the dispatcher. "We need fire rescue at our location, and we need them now!"

As soon as I leaned in the van near the legs, a baby emerged. I held out my arms and grabbed this very small bundle.

Immediately, I knew something was terribly wrong. The placenta was still wrapped around the fetus. A strange smell floated in the air. The baby had been stillborn.

The mother screamed and cried. She kept asking to see her baby.

I wrapped the tiny infant in a yellow plastic emergency blanket. As a mother, I felt an intense grief for this tragic little bundle that I still held in my arms. Jacob attempted to comfort the young mother. When fire rescue arrived, they took her and her baby to the hospital.

Jacob and I cleaned ourselves up as best as we could and drove to the hospital to talk to the young woman. We learned that she was a prostitute. She disclosed that she was an intravenous drug user of heroin and smoked crack and that she had gonorrhea and hepatitis. Throughout the whole interview, I found her calmness very strange. But what I found more disconcerting was the fact that not once did she ask about her baby.

Such mixed feelings about this entire situation overcame me. I was mad at the girl but also felt sorry for her.

Jacob and I realized we needed to document our body fluids contamination with a First Report of Injury form. Our sergeant demanded we be checked out at the emergency room.

When we saw the doctor, he said we both needed gamma globulin shots to ensure that we didn't receive any infections. After Jacob and I received our injections, we left the hospital about three thirty in the morning and went to an all-night coffee shop.

I tried to choke down a donut with my coffee but was only half successful. About an hour later, I arrived at my house and went to bed, but I couldn't sleep.

I kept watching the clock, and the minutes crept by. The tick-tick-ticking of the second hand resounded throughout my bedroom like thunder in a storm. When a couple of hours had passed, I got up and called Jacob. He said he couldn't sleep either. I realized this event had deeply moved him too.

After that night, we never spoke of this incident again. We just buried our thoughts, our grief, and our tears. It brought home to me just how much misery is caused by the use of illegal drugs.

I thought about this young mother's sad life as a drug-dependant prostitute and the baby who never had a chance to live. I began to wonder what I could do to combat this situation.

I contemplated and prayed about where I needed to focus my career. I realized that God had to be the One to guide my life. I knew that in order to find my way, I needed to surrender to His will.

As it turned out, my career would lead me to combat the flow of narcotics for a season. It would be there in the Felony Drug Interdiction Team where I would find myself battling many more demons.

CHAPTER 8

The Beginning of the Felony Drug Interdiction Team

I didn't have to wait long before I was given the chance to dive headfirst into the world of drugs.

In the spring of 1989, Jacob told me that he had heard rumors of a unit being formed to combat the flow of narcotics across the Florida highways. The rumor turned into a reality called the Felony Drug Interdiction Team, which would consist of fifteen units and thirty teams statewide. Each team would be comprised of two troopers and a dog.

Once the openings were formally announced, Jacob applied for the felony K-9 handler position, and I applied for the felony officer position, but we weren't the only ones throwing our names into the hat. Troopers all over the state submitted their applications for this highly coveted opportunity.

When the selections were announced, Jacob got chosen, but I was disappointed to discover that I had not been. Jacob subsequently attended K-9 school with his new partner Sniffer who came from Germany with an impressive resume. Allegedly, he had been an East Border German Sheppard.

Simply put, Sniffer was beautiful with big, loving, brown eyes, perky ears, and a shiny black and tan coat with a touch of gray. However, his adorability belied his fierceness.

As a result, Sniffer quickly developed quite the reputation. On the upside, his best attribute was his ability to adapt well to sharing Jacob's house with Sandy, the Golden Retriever. On the downside, Sniffer was well-adept at clawing, eating, and destroying all furniture padding and items, such as Jacob's beeper and leather accessories. He proved to be a challenge for Jacob in other areas as well. On his first visit to the state veterinarian, Sniffer took a small bite out of her leg, destroying her pants in the process. Jacob soon purchased a muzzle to avoid any future Sniffer vet attacks.

Amazingly, though, Sniffer and Jacob did graduate from K-9 school. They then began working with a felony officer who was also on the SWAT team.

Jacob and his human partner came across a situation where Sniffer located a kilo of cocaine under a vehicle's bumper. Jacob then placed Sniffer back into his cage inside his car. When they started the process of arresting the owners, he and his partner found themselves in an intense struggle with the dopers.

Both troopers had been badly injured and had to be taken to the emergency room for medical treatment. Jacob's partner almost lost this fight. He decided to leave the unit as a result of that incident. This opened up a spot on Jacob's team, and I was ecstatic to be offered it.

At the time I was the only female felony trooper in the state. Once again, this role clearly added a lot of responsibility for me. I needed to prove that I could handle myself as well as any other male trooper.

When Jacob and I spoke about my selection to be his partner, he expressed some concerns over my physical strength. The recent event with his previous partner made him rightfully wary.

All I could do was promise Jacob that I would do my best. With this pledge, I began a very exciting and dangerous undertaking.

Since I hadn't had the advantage of receiving the formal training in Tallahassee, Jacob and I started working together to get me up to speed. We decided I needed to know how to handle Sniffer to a limited degree. I've never been afraid of dogs, but I am cautious with them. I was extra cautious with

Sniffer due to his reputation of attacking the vet. Since he was known to bite, we thought it important that he recognize me as the good guy.

We began slow and easy, allowing me to walk Sniffer so that he could get used to me. Next, we bumped up the intensity of our drills. Jacob and I took Sniffer to an area far from suburban Miami. This time when I held Sniffer's leash and walked him, Jacob performed a different activity, like looking into a car. We wanted Sniffer to be comfortable with me should Jacob need to be involved in something at a distance from him.

Another time, Jacob ran off as if he was chasing a person. I sprinted over to Sniffer's door. This was before K-9 vehicles had remote-door openers. As soon as I opened it, Sniffer jumped out, passed me, and ran after Jacob. Once I saw his backside, I could let out a big sigh of relief, knowing that I had made it through another exercise without me getting bit.

We also created codes to cue the other one when certain situations presented themselves. For instance, we decided upon the code *hot day* when Sniffer pawed at an area. Pawing was how he was trained to alert his handler when he detected narcotics. Using the code *I'm having company later today* would cue the other that we needed a back-up officer.

One morning a week, our team of three joined the Miami Troop E K-9 squad for training. My first time with the K-9 squad took place in a training area west of Miami. This field contained a few trees and a lot of vegetation and palms.

The K-9 boss, Sergeant Miller, assigned me to be the bad guy since I was dogless. He instructed me to wear a hidden sleeve and run the track and hide. Then the dog would be released and follow my scent to my hiding place.

He said, "When the dog finds you, extend your arm out far so the dog'll bite the sleeve instead of your face."

Initially that seemed like a simple enough concept, but looking back, I think someone set me up. I wasn't familiar with the different kinds of hidden sleeves, and so I accepted the one given me without question. The cop who told me to wear it must have realized that I didn't have a lot of time to inspect its synthetic material with thin padding. He must have taken a guess that I didn't know there were sleeves reinforced with sturdy wire or a handle made of wrapped wire. He must not have considered that my thin frame didn't allow much natural padding on my wrist or hand to bear the strong crushing pressure of a big dog's jaw.

I took off running and made it around the track one lap before seeing a large bush. I dove into it. Within a second's time, I heard heavy breathing and a deep barking that got louder as some creature came closer to my hiding place.

I froze when I peeked through the leaves and saw the chosen dog charging in my direction, a monstrous Rottweiler named Bear. I broke out in a sweat, not from an external heat caused by the sun's strong rays but from an internal fear. Bear leaped through the air and descended upon my hideout. He bore down on me with wild eyes and foaming mouth that showed off what seemed like the largest and sharpest teeth I had ever seen. I turned my head in the opposite direction and just stuck out my hand and wrist.

Big, big mistake! I felt intense pain. Despite the fact that my hand and wrist were covered with the sleeve, I still had the sensation of being in a vise grip. I could feel Bear's teeth clamping down on me. I was worried that I might pass out.

Finally, Bear's handler pulled him off me. When I realized it was safe, I crawled out from the bush using only my unhurt hand to balance me. My wrist and other hand throbbed so much, but I tried to act tough in front of this group. I couldn't show any hint of how much I hurt.

So I sucked it up and continued with the mornings activities, but I learned from that painful experience. That was the last time I wore what was referred to as the "hidden sleeve." From that day on, I wore the heavier wire-enforced sleeve with a built-in handle.

All in all, the day was good, though. I had accomplished one of my initial goals: I had been accepted by the guys of the K-9 squad.

DEA Trained and Ready

As a trooper with the Felony Drug Interdiction Team (FDIT), I was issued a Beretta semi-automatic 9-mm pistol. I needed to complete a week of qualification at the academy before I could carry it. So a few days later, I was sent to Tallahassee to receive training for it.

The range was located on acreage outside the small town of Quincy, Florida. Once there, I received my new gun and holster.

The range instructor said, "Before you begin shooting the gun, you need to practice drawing it from the holster a hundred times."

This holster had a built-in safety feature to keep others from pulling out your gun. The person wearing the holster had to press down and back. This motion released the gun as it was being drawn.

The brand-new leather caused the holster to be extremely stiff. Pressing the gun in or getting it out wasn't easy. My right hand was still bruised and my wrist was very sore from my encounter with Bear. Every time I took that gun in and out of my holster, I gritted my teeth from the intense pain. I swallowed a couple of aspirins, but they didn't provide much relief. This was going to be a long week. Wimps were not accepted, and I knew this was too important for my career. I must succeed.

At least the weather cooperated with nice, cool days, and I persevered. By the end of the week, my hand and wrist felt better. I learned how to field strip my gun, shoot on a combat course, and on Friday morning, I qualified. I held back my sighs of relief until after I got into my car for the five-hundred-fifty-mile drive to Homestead.

All in all, the week was well worth the pain. I had succeeded and overcame the final hurdle.

I couldn't wait for Monday when Jacob and I would begin to hit the highways looking for narcotics. We decided to use the first week after my training as a fishing expedition. The waters were full of all sizes of fish, and we knew we needed to figure out where they were biting and the type of bait needed.

Jacob and I created a strategy. Since I was the trooper without the K-9, it was easier for me to put the "pedal to the metal" and take the lead. A lot of quick starts and stops would throw Sniffer around in the rear cage of Jacob's car. Therefore, I would make the traffic stops, and he would pull up behind me.

Next we needed to determine where. We knew we had several places from which to choose. Miami possessed the reputation as being one of the destination areas for transferring drugs that came from South America. Then once in Miami, the drugs were dispersed to states north of Florida.

Since motorists used I-95 to enter and leave Miami, we decided to work the north side of the interstate around the Golden Glades Interchange. We settled on the strong likelihood that more drugs left Miami than entered it.

After that first week of fishing, Jacob and I patrolled I-95. The weather gave Miami a perfect day, balmy and cloudy with a nice breeze. Then about ten thirty in the morning, I observed a small white hatchback car speeding with two men in it.

I put on my lights and sirens to signal to the driver to stop. He complied, and Jacob pulled up behind me. Jacob approached the passenger side while I approached the driver's side.

The young driver appeared nervous. He seemed to be in his early twenties and was casually dressed in a blue t-shirt and jeans. His dark eyes kept darting back and forth from the rearview mirror to the passenger and then back to the rearview mirror.

Jacob told the passenger to step out of the car. When he did, I saw that he wore an expensive designer-looking silk shirt and tan pants with a beautiful leather belt. He looked exceptionally well-groomed. I noticed his fingernails appeared to be manicured, and he smelled like he wore expensive cologne. He looked much older than the driver, about forty years of age, and had a stocky build. His dark eyes complemented his well-cut black hair.

As the passenger and Jacob talked, I placed my attention onto the young driver and talked through his rolled-down window. "Your driver's license please."

He swallowed hard and stared straight ahead. "I don't have one."

I asked, "Can I have the vehicle registration and proof of insurance?"

"I don't have those either. The car belongs to my friend. He just let me borrow it."

"What's your friend's name?"

He murmured, "I don't remember. We just met last night."

"Please step out of the car," I said with no emotion.

The driver obeyed and followed me to the left taillight. Jacob made sure the passenger stayed near the right front side of the car. We kept them separated so they wouldn't have a chance to get their stories straight. We then had them both sit down so that Jacob and I could meet halfway between them and exchange stories.

Jacob said, "My guy told me he's been unemployed for a long time and was looking for work. He said the driver's his cousin."

"Well, that's not what my guy told me," I said. "According to him, he just gave your guy a ride and that they had just met last night."

I glanced over at Jacob's suspect. "No way has that man been unemployed unless he's very wealthy and doesn't need a job. Look at his expensive haircut, manicured nails, and expensive-looking clothes."

At that point, I walked back over to the driver. "Can I could look through your car?"

"Sure. Go ahead."

I opened the hatchback and looked into a brown zippered tote bag. I immediately spotted a black subcompact machine pistol with a silencer attached to the barrel.

I used the code word *scarlet* to indicate I had discovered contraband. I grabbed the driver and began to handcuff him.

The passenger knew we were onto them. Jacob lunged at him but not before he could jump up and take off running to a canal bank that could be seen from the shoulder of the road.

To my right, I saw a turnpike trooper on the side of the highway. I radioed for his assistance while I put the driver in my backseat. In the meantime, Jacob ran over to his car to get Sniffer.

The trooper arrived immediately and agreed to watch my perp. I started running to the embankment. This all happened so quickly that somehow I managed to get ahead of Jacob and Sniffer. All of a sudden my heart felt as if it was in my throat, not so much because of the foot pursuit but because I heard Sniffer running up behind me.

As Sniffer neared me, I feared this crazed attack dog might not know the difference between me and the bad guy. At that moment, my mind became consumed at the prospect of him making that mistake and biting me. I was thankful when he passed me by and kept running.

When Sniffer reached the canal bank, Jacob yelled for him to stop. When I got close to its edge, I considered going into the water. I then reconsidered that decision when I thought about my heavy bulletproof vest and my heavy guns, one on my gun belt and another on my ankle. Most importantly, I didn't want to get into a fight in that murky water. So I stopped and contemplated what my next action should be.

Suddenly, a man ran up to us from the highway area. He said, "I saw him dive into the water. I'm an off-duty marine patrol officer," and he proceeded to dive into the canal.

By the time the marine patrol officer hit the water, the passenger had swam to the bank on the other side and then disappeared behind a row of townhouses. Unfortunately, the marine patrol officer had to come back to our side of the shore empty-handed.

We walked back to our patrol cars and thanked the marine patrol officer and turnpike trooper. I placed the recovered gun in my trunk, making sure that any possible fingerprints wouldn't be smudged or removed. We then searched their car thoroughly to ensure there wasn't any more contraband. When we were done, the tow company towed the car to its lot.

We spent a few hours interviewing the driver at the highway patrol station. He restated that the car belonged to the passenger. I felt he was forthcoming and that he really didn't know where the passenger had gotten the car. He was probably paid to drive the passenger somewhere.

We only charged the driver with the misdemeanor traffic offense of driving without a valid driver's license. We took him to the identification department to ensure he had provided us with his correct name and date of birth. We then booked him into the jail.

Afterward, we took the Mac-11 gun with the attached silencer to the Miami-Dade Police Department's crime lab for processing. They examined the fingerprints on it and tested the gun to make sure it was functional.

The fingerprints provided us with the passenger's name and then some. It appeared that our runaway perp was Mario Lopez, who was wanted for numerous weapon violations and an attempted murder charge.

We eventually sent the gun and our reports to the local Miami office of the Bureau of Alcohol, Tobacco, and Firearms (ATF). They took the ball and ran with it now that they knew Mr. Lopez was in Miami. Because of our lead, the ATF was able to successfully arrest and prosecute this felon.

Our felony team days were off to a great start. Several months later, Jacob and I were proud recipients of a prestigious ATF award and recognized at a formal ceremony in Miami.

When asked whether I was in fear during this situation, I had to say no. The entire episode happened so quickly. Frankly, my only fearful thought was about my second partner, Sniffer, and that he'd mistake me for the perp during the chase. As it turned out, Sniffer and my relationship evolved into a mutual respect for each other. We ended up getting along very well.

With that in mind, I totally respected Sniffer's dual personality and was smart enough to never challenge my furry friend. A lot of trained attack dogs become loyal and friendly family members when off duty. They can even interact with and protect the police officer's children. However once on duty, they will attack a bad guy with a fierce aggression.

This case also brought Jacob and I very close. It changed the dynamics of our working relationship and Jacob's trust and comfort level when working with a female. He told me he now understood how I brought qualities other than physical strength to our partnership.

When we discussed the way this case unfolded, Jacob gave me the credit. He pointed out that I recognized the red flags, such as Lopez's expensive clothing and grooming and the contradictory statements given by the driver and Lopez, all of which didn't add up. Maybe we could pass that off as woman's intuition, or maybe it could merely be attributed to our different interests. What we both realized was that we complemented each other in this partnership.

After our first case, I decided I needed more training on narcotics. I aspired to excel in my new position.

I desperately wanted to attend the two-week DEA Narcotic School, so I drove to the Miami DEA compound to obtain an application. A young man greeted me upon arrival and directed me to where I needed to go. I walked down a short institutional-green hallway until I arrived at a wall plaque that said "Training." A list was taped to the wall next it showing the dates for narcotics classes for the upcoming quarter.

The door was open, and I saw Agent Rios sitting at the desk reading some papers. I tapped on the doorframe. He didn't look up but murmured, "Come in" in a distracted tone.

I walked in front of his desk, wearing my uniform that clearly identified me as a highway patrol trooper. He looked up at me, and his half-smile vanished.

Oh, boy, I thought. I forced myself to push past his glare and address the reason I was there.

"Special Agent Rios? I'm Trooper Floy Turner. I heard your presentation to my academy class in Tallahassee, and I really enjoyed it."

He wasn't impressed with my compliment. "Yeah, well, I was thrown out of the academy's training program. I'm no longer allowed to train the highway patrol recruits."

His eyes narrowed, and he didn't mince words as he continued. "Do you have any idea how much grief your academy major gave me?"

"I'm sorry about that," I responded. "However, I do want to develop my career further. I respect your knowledge, and I'm here to get an application. I hope you won't harbor any feelings of ill will against me. Please understand, I had nothing to do with the major's decisions."

He gruffly handed me a packet and said, "Good day." He then looked back down at what he had been previously reading.

Feeling as if he had just dismissed me, I turned and left his office, a small knot twisting in my stomach. This meeting did not go well, but I refused to allow it to keep me from pursuing the training.

I immediately took the application back to the highway patrol station, filled it out, and mailed it back to DEA. I prayed I'd be accepted to one of the next classes.

I never heard back from the DEA. I suspect my application was trashed. I kept calling and speaking to Agent Rios' staff assistant. In fact, I got to know her on a first-name basis.

She repeatedly told me that the classes were filled. To say I felt disheartened would be an understatement.

After not being accepted for three classes, I told my husband over dinner about how I wanted to attend the DEA Narcotics School and the challenges I faced. "I'm so disappointed," I said. "I think Rios threw my application in the trash."

My venting came from a perspective of hoping my husband had some words of advice since he knew a thing or two about the DEA. At the time, he worked as a police chief, and he had been involved in a case with the DEA that resulted in a major shootout in South Miami. A notorious narcotic trafficker shot at the cops and was finally killed after about sixty rounds of ammunition were exchanged.

My husband squinted his eyes as he studied my face. "So you really want to attend the DEA class, Floy?"

I looked up at him and took a deep breath. "Yeah, but I don't know what to do now." I shrugged. "I've tried to follow up, but I feel I'm getting the run around."

After dinner, I started clearing away the table. My husband picked up our kitchen phone and made a call. I then overheard him address the Special Agent in Charge (SAC) of the DEA Miami Division by his first name.

I didn't have any idea that he even had the SAC's personal phone number. This event amazed me, but I found the lack of communication between my husband and me amusing. He didn't seem to know about my aspirations in narcotics and desire to attend this school, and this was the first I knew of his personal relationship with the DEA SAC.

My stomach flipped and flopped as I listened to his side of the conversation and watched his relaxed body language. He said "My wife Floy applied for your narcotics school, but she wasn't selected. She's a great cop and would be an excellent candidate."

Once off the phone, he smiled. "You've got your seat in the next class in Miami." He walked away, his steps light and confident.

A few weeks later, I checked into the Marriott Hotel located on Biscayne Bay for the DEA training. About ten minutes before the class started, I walked inside the large training room and found a seat at one of the cloth-covered tables near the middle of the room. A notepad and pen, both carrying the hotel's logo, sat on the table in front of each chair.

I looked around and saw that the room held two rows of four tables and that the floor was covered with typical hotel carpet. The front of the room held a podium and another table with flip charts for exhibits.

The room filled up quickly. After all of the participants were seated, Agent Rios walked over to the front rows and scanned the room. The first words out of his mouth were "Which student is Turner?"

I raised my hand. "I'm Turner."

He then addressed the class. "Trooper Turner went over my head to get herself in this class at the last minute."

I felt so embarrassed and hoped that the earth would come to my rescue by opening up at that very moment and mercifully swallowing me.

Agent Rios then addressed me and said, "You've caused me a lot of trouble. I don't appreciate being pushed around by the SAC and told I had to put you in my class."

My embarrassment escalated to outright humiliation. My cheeks burned as heat radiated throughout my body. I now knew without a doubt that I needed to excel in this training since I was such a pain in Rios' backside.

Actually, I ended up finding Rios to be one of the best instructors I've ever had. Throughout this class, I respected his abilities to successfully captivate a classroom full of students. He engaged us with excitement through a fascinating exchange of information. Despite his unorthodox language and stories, he always pulled an over-the-top delivery. Many years later after I retired from the FDLE, I became an instructor. I modeled some of my presentations after his unique style minus the crude language and stories.

During this two-week course, I never went out to dinner or to the bar with any of the participants. I stayed in my hotel room, ordered room service, and worked on my notebook, which would be graded.

I studied and achieved success. In fact, I had the second-highest grade in the class. Not too bad for a trooper!

Another highlight of taking this class was a luncheon where a graduation ceremony was held. Broward County Sheriff Nick Navarro requested twenty-five Colombian police officers join us and hold the graduations together. These officers had just completed a narcotics investigative course through his agency.

His request was granted, and in the summer of 1989, we had the honor of sharing our graduation with these brave officers. I remember looking at them and wondering how many would be murdered upon returning to Colombia.

That period was the height of the Colombian drug wars. Powerful drug cartels initiated bounties on law enforcement resulting in the murderous assassinations of way too many brave Colombian officers.

When Sheriff Navarro presented this courageous group, every American cop in attendance stood up and applauded our South American colleagues. We knew they would be facing extreme and unimaginable brutal violence upon returning to their country.

I didn't see Agent Rios in person again, but about six months after graduating from his school, I did see his picture on television and in the newspapers. During the U.S. invasion of Panama, he escorted the ruthless Panamanian military leader Manuel Noriega onto a U.S. military plane bound for Miami.

Noriega was tried and found guilty on eight counts of drug trafficking, racketeering, and money laundering. He remained in the South Dade Prison until 2007. He was then extradited to France where he served seven years in their prison for murder and money laundering. Afterward, he returned back to Panama to serve another twenty years for the murders of Panamanian military Commander Moisés Giroldi Vera and political opponent Hugo Spadafora Franco as well as the death of troops who aided one of his opponents in a rebellion.

Yet Fighting for Acceptance

Since I didn't have the responsibility of handling a dog with the Felony Drug Interdiction Team, I became the team coordinator. My job description involved marketing the felony squad by making initial contact with other agencies and fulfilling their requests.

At the time, Major Wilson had been overseeing the investigative unit at the FHP headquarters and the activities of all of the statewide felony teams. He wanted to use my newly acquired credentials of graduating from the prestigious DEA Narcotic School to promote his felony teams.

He called me one morning and said, "Trooper Turner, go on over to the DEA and introduce yourself and Jacob to the supervisors and agents. I want you to start working with them."

Easier said than done. He made this order sound as uncomplicated as going into a diner and ordering coffee and a piece of pie. At the time, I had a big wall to contend with called Agent Rios. I soon came to realize that Major Wilson really didn't grasp the working dynamics of Miami, which were completely different than those in Tallahassee. I figured he was probably clueless as to what had transpired with DEA Agent Rios at the FHP Academy.

When I told Jacob what Major Wilson had ordered and the way in which he ordered it, we both laughed. I said, "Yep, I'll just take myself on over to DEA headquarters and say 'Hi, I'm Trooper Floy Turner. I'm here to help you.' Yeah, right. Like that's going to do anything."

Unless we could come up with a way to be an asset to the DEA, they were never going to be interested in working with us. They just weren't going to embrace us showing up on their doorstep. They were the big dogs of the Miami narcotics world, and they would never accept two rankless troopers into their cases that easily. Our mission wasn't going to work with just a meet and a greet.

Jacob and I both needed a way to prove to the DEA that we could be beneficial to *their* mission. We brainstormed and came up with some solutions.

At the very least, we three had acquired an impressive resume with training and skills that would behoove the DEA. While I had attended the DEA Narcotic School, Jacob and Sniffer attended the K-9 Narcotics Detection School offered by the Miami Police Department. In fact, they graduated in the number-one spot from that school.

Our most obvious advantage, though, was Sniffer. We then began our own mini-investigation. We drove to the DEA offices and spoke to the agents to inquire if they had access to K-9s twenty-four hours a day, seven days a week. We discovered what we had suspected, that the Miami DEA office didn't have its own K-9s.

Furthermore, I had been given some valuable intel that the DEA would want and need. A friend in the medical profession had told me that a doctor in Cutler Ridge had been providing narcotic pain medication to anyone who came in for an office visit. The doctor operated one of the early "pill mills."

These clinics turned out to be very popular throughout Florida in the 1990s. They led to an enormous flow of traffic in and out of Florida from the Midwest and East Coast states. All sorts of addicts came here to acquire their legal "fix."

I consulted with another doctor about this clinic. In addition, Jacob and I had developed some informants from arrests made by law enforcement officers who knew we were working drug interdiction. These arrestees were willing to give us information about doctors selling scripts to addicts in exchange for decreased sentences. We had methodically placed our ducks in a row, so to speak, and I knew the DEA could not pass up what we had to tell them.

We also knew that the DEA had a special drug diversion group that monitored all scheduled prescription medicines known to be used by addicts. Armed with our information, Jacob and I began our pursuit of this group. We called a meeting to offer up this information about the pill mill.

As expected, they were interested, so we met the diversion group at the DEA headquarters in Miami. We then provided them with our knowledge of this doctor's set up. We told them about our potential sources who could provide more information about the doctor's exchange of money for drug prescriptions.

According to these former addicts who had visited the clinic, the doctor never examined them. They just walked into his office and received a prescription. Then the doctor charged them for an office visit.

One of the agents asked, "Floy, will you go into that clinic as an undercover and wear a wire?"

"Sure," I said. "That sounds okay to me, but I've got to run it through my chain of command."

I submitted the request to my lieutenant to go undercover in this operation. He approved it and told me to call Major Wilson for the final approval.

Although we were entering somewhat unchartered territory with the highway patrol, I felt this case with the doctor could pave the way for our mission of working with the DEA as well as give kudos to the FHP. I just knew the major would approve it. After all, he was the very same major who had told us to work with the DEA. I figured it was a done deal.

Unfortunately, I was sadly mistaken.

Major Wilson denied my request. He said, "I can't justify your undercover role because it doesn't relate to the highways."

I said, "Almost all of the addicts drove to this doctor's office."

Major Wilson didn't buy into my justification. In fact, he acted very annoyed with me for expressing my opinion.

Now we needed to shift gears somewhat and fine-tune our strategy on how to get accepted by the DEA. Sniffer may very well be our golden ticket, our only ticket, and so we planned to make him our focus. I prayed that he would be able to demonstrate how he, Jacob, and I were a force to be reckoned with.

We then decided to avail ourselves to the local Homestead Police Department (HPD). We had provided back up for them and worked their traffic crashes in the past.

I called their narcotics lieutenant and told him what we could offer his squad. I said, "We're available and want to work with you." To give him more confidence in our abilities, I told him about the trainings that Jacob, Sniffer, and I had gone through.

The lieutenant was receptive to my proposal for a variety of reasons. He knew we could help with jurisdictional issues. He was also interested in Sniffer because the HPD had K-9s, but at the time, none of their dogs were trained to seek narcotics.

Fortunately in working with the HPD, we wouldn't be required to contend with the red tape that temporarily kept us from working with the DEA. The truth was, we needed the DEA, and more importantly, they needed us. In the meantime, though, we'd gain some valuable experience in the world of drugs while working with the HPD.

CHAPTER 9

Shifting Gears

In 1990, I ran into Drew Milton from the Miami FDLE office.

He advised me to finish my college degree so that I could apply to become an FDLE agent. On the surface, that idea seemed quiet doable since state employees could attend any state college without paying for tuition.

But underneath that semblance, I found that taking advantage of this benefit wasn't so easy. I learned from colleagues that many of the classes they needed to take were filled and thus unavailable. So I decided to enroll in a local private university where I felt I could earn my degree much faster. This meant that in deviating from the state's designated schools, I would need to pay for my own education.

Up until then, the focus on college had been reserved for my daughters. My husband and I always stressed the importance for them to obtain a higher education. We realized that to send them to college, though, we'd need extra money for their tuition. Now that I intended to go back to school, we'd need even more money to pay for my classes too.

As a trooper, I always worked extra jobs to supplement my families' income for this reason as well as pay for my daughters' extracurricular activities. My all-time-favorite off-duty job was working at the Miami Federal Courthouse for the U. S. Marshals Service. It was an extremely busy place due to all of the narcotics cases, and consequently, the Marshals were always in need of supplemental law enforcement officers.

The job offered many other advantages. For instance, working in a suit allowed me to feel a little more feminine than the tactical gear I wore day in and day out as a trooper.

Many times my days off would be during the week. This was a perfect fit with the Marshals' duties. Often I drove my personal car to the Dadeland Metro Station and rode the monorail train into the heart of Miami.

I partnered with an amazing and beautiful marshal named Maria, who hailed from Puerto Rico. Her dark-green eyes augmented her blond hair, and she always dressed her curvy figure to perfection.

On the other hand, Maria was tough as nails, even though her nails stayed perfectly manicured. She took her job seriously by keeping in shape and strategically staying on top of her game.

Her agency assigned her to the Marshals fugitive team, which was known in law-enforcement circles as the top-fugitive hunters in the U.S. Although younger than me, Maria's maturity level matched my own. To me she represented the total package of a young, self-assured woman who had obtained a meaningful career.

She also knew the locations of all of the good small Cuban restaurants in the vicinity. During our lunchtime, she and I enjoyed walking along the sidewalks surrounding the courthouse. Sometimes we simply grabbed a cup of coffee as an excuse to take advantage of this fascinating area. It made me feel as if I had somehow been teleported to a street in Central or South America or in Haiti because the shops catered to the Latin and Haitian community. I just loved the ambiance and embraced the diversity of the colorful wares they proudly displayed.

Another reason I liked this job was because it gave me the opportunity to participate in the courthouse setting. I never got tired of watching and listening to the interaction between the lawyers, witnesses, and judges. This was a classroom within itself and a show of the criminal justice system in progress.

The courtroom, especially in violent criminal cases, brought excitement and drama to its forefront. I saw defendants rolling in wheelchairs for the sole purpose of acquiring sympathy from the jury, yet I knew they could walk just as well as I could. Others brought in elderly family members and ministers as another sympathy ploy. I was curious as to what excuses they intended to use to justify their criminal behavior. Regardless, I always rooted for the victims and the prosecution.

Listening to the trials of some of Miami's highest-profile drug cases intrigued me. While moving these defendants in and out of the courthouse, we took extra precaution to monitor the security as well as thwart any attempts of escaping. Designated cars led and followed the transport buses due to the high risk and propensity of an ambush involving the drug dealers.

When transporting prisoners with the Marshals, I either boarded the buses or drove behind them from the Miami Federal Courthouse to the South Dade Correctional Center in the evening, which was about an hour's drive. I always preferred to follow, though. I never got mentally comfortable being enclosed with a busload of dangerous federal prisoners in the heavy stop-and-go traffic of Miami's busy roadways.

During those times when I had no other choice but to ride the bus, I stood in the front below the main platform on the steps near the door. My eyes perpetually darted in a panoramic mode, searching for any hovering helicopters. After all, this was Miami.

For long-distance transports throughout the United States, the Marshals used their own fleet of passenger jets. None of these types of aircraft had any markings to reveal that they belonged to the U.S. Marshals Service. For security reasons, prisoners never knew when they would be moved or to what destination.

One early morning, Maria and I travelled to one of the state-prison facilities located near Opa-locka. We were assigned to transfer a female prisoner to a Marshals' flight scheduled to depart from Homestead Air Force Base.

Maria and I told the prisoner we needed to conduct a body search. We then proceeded to methodically pat down every inch of her person, making sure we didn't miss anything. A prisoner can use something as simple as a hairpin to escape from handcuffs. We then placed a waist chain on her to secure her handcuffed wrists and leg cuffs to her waist.

We transported the prisoner to the airbase. By the time the commuter flight arrived on the tarmac, Marshals were positioned on roofs and in buildings with automatic weapons to guard against any threats or escapes.

We took our prisoner out of our car and placed her in a line with other prisoners who were also going to board the flights. They all wore the same prison jumpsuits, slip-on sneakers, and their cuffs and chains adorned their prison garb.

Since these fights don't have typical flight attendants, each passenger is given a bagged meal as they walk up the stairs of the plane to board. Of course, my curiosity compelled me to glance into one of the bags to see the type of food offered. On this particular flight, the prisoners got to anticipate a meal consisting of a baloney sandwich with white bread, crackers, a piece of dried fruit, and a drink in a small box minus the plastic straw.

I walked the prisoners up the steps and into the plane. Although it still sat on the ground, I surprised myself to discover how exceptionally uncomfortable I felt just being inside. Its interior actually looked like a regular plane but without the first-class section.

I imagined a long flight where the travelling marshals were tense and on edge the entire time. The math seemed a little off-balance: two hundred prisoners to two brave marshals. I knew I would never want to partake in this type of a detail.

A few years later, I saw the movie *Con Air* that starred Nicholas Cage. As I watched the story unfold, I almost experienced a déjà-vu moment of being back inside that plane loaded with convicts.

I admire the U.S. Marshals Service and all that they do to keep us safe from violent criminals. At the time I worked with them, the marshal in charge of the Southern District of Florida owned a large collection of official police hats. One day I happened to be in uniform when I stopped by his office. During a casual conversation, he told me that he had always wanted a Florida Highway Patrol

Stetson. Sadly, he never could acquire one. When I left his office that afternoon, I was hatless. Fortunately for me, the "statute of limitations" has long passed for leaving behind my FHP-issued Stetson hat in his office.

I considered my "forgetfulness" as my parting gift to the feds. Strangely enough and later on, he and I would find ourselves collaborating on a possible trip to Italy for my very first FDLE homicide case.

When One of Our Own Commits the Despicable

I worked another part-time job for years. I taught driving classes at the Dade County Citizens Safety Council off of LeJuene Road near the Miami International Airport. The old two-story building had been revamped into an institutionalized government setting with large classrooms.

As a certified instructor in Defensive Driving and Advanced Driver Improvement courses, I taught drivers who wanted relief from the points system. A ticket or citation for a traffic infraction could result in points getting assessed on their driving record. This, in turn, could increase their cost for car insurance. After receiving a minor traffic violation, a driver could request to attend the school for a fee in lieu of receiving the points. Hundreds of motorists took advantage of this opportunity and attended this driving school all throughout the day and night.

In addition, I oversaw the council's security department. The extremely large parking lot required a full-fledged security detail to patrol the area. The high visibility helped to detour any crimes, such as breaking into cars or robbing students.

Security officers also monitored those students who were court-ordered to attend. They kept an eye on their activities and behaviors for court-reporting purposes as well as to intervene should the need arise.

I also taught the Driver Improvement Course. The students who enrolled in this class happened to be near and dear to my trooper heart—habitual traffic offenders. Most of them confronted more issues with the court system than just a revocation of their driver's license. They were hardcore felons, and most hated cops and any other types of authority.

The very strict requirements enabled me to control the class. It was based on transactional analysis to affect behavior modification. Tardiness to class or failure to return after a break resulted in some tough consequences, such as being kicked out of the course. However, they still needed to take the program, so they would have to reenroll, pay additional fees, and attend all of the classes all over again, not just the ones they missed. Thus the security department was needed just in case the student took this message really hard and needed to be escorted out of the building.

My normal routine consisted of arriving an hour ahead of time to set up my classroom. Therefore when my students walked in, everything was ready and in place, enabling me to stand in front of the room to observe them as they arrived.

One night in 1990, I immediately recognized one of my new students. Lenny Soto, a well-dressed young man in his thirties with dark hair and dark eyes, strutted into my classroom about a minute late.

However, he didn't show any sign that he knew who I was. He probably didn't pay any attention to the instructor, and therefore me. I suspected ignoring me played a role in his game.

Mr. Soto continued strolling to the front row where he selected a seat. He took his desk and turned it in such a fashion that it faced the rear of the classroom. Then he sat down with his back to me.

Before I go further, I need to explain how I knew Mr. Soto.

About a year earlier on a rainy spring night, I received a call to assist in the initial investigation of a pedestrian who was killed in a hit-and-run incident in Cutler Ridge. I only briefly saw the victim's slight body lying crumpled in a fetal position on the road. Her long red hair seemed to be strewn in several directions. Even the visible abrasions didn't detract from her beauty. I shook my head, thinking about another wasted life.

The investigation revealed that on the night of the victim's death, she had engaged in a heated argument with her boyfriend Lenny Soto. Allegedly, he waited in his car close to where the altercation took place so that he could run her down. Then he left the scene of the "accident." Shortly afterward, Lenny reported his car stolen.

Two witnesses gave their testimonies to this horrible event, and Lenny Soto was charged with vehicular homicide. He hired a great defense attorney, and the witnesses recanted their testimony. Since the trial couldn't go forth, I didn't get a chance to testify, and Lenny ended up beating the charges before the case ever went to trial.

Rumor had it that Soto was a midlevel cocaine dealer. I didn't know about his drug involvement, but I heard on the street that he was an overall badass.

But that was then, and now he was disrupting my class. I calmly informed Mr. Soto that I needed to converse with him in the hallway.

He followed me out of the room. I spotted one of the security troopers, Bradley Peters, and motioned for him to join me.

I faced Lenny and stood as tall as I could as I looked into his dark eyes. I squared my shoulders, and didn't waver my stare. "Mr. Soto, you can't attend my class anymore. There's a conflict of interest. I was involved in your vehicular-homicide case. Also, when you take this class in the future with another instructor, I suggest you improve your classroom demeanor."

I saw Lenny's eyes squint as the smirk disappeared from his face. He clenched his jaw as Bradley said, "You need to leave now. I'll escort you out of the building and off the property. Let's go."

The next morning I called Betty, the council's executive director, and explained what had transpired. I liked Betty and the council's manager Jeanne. These classy ladies were intelligent, competent, and beautiful, always dressing in stylish suits and driving cool Corvettes.

Betty later informed me that Soto had filed a complaint with the judge saying he wasn't allowed in my classroom. All I know is that afterward, I didn't hear another word about Soto from anyone at the council or in court system. I hoped I never had an occasion to cross paths again with that thug. I believed he was responsible for his girlfriend's brutal death.

I never asked Bradley what happened with Soto after they left me. In fact, I didn't give it another thought. I had worked with Bradley at the U.S. Marshals Service and considered him to be capable enough to handle someone like Soto.

Even though Bradley was competent in his job, he didn't seem to care about his appearance and hygiene. His overweight physique created a double chin and heavy cheeks that minimized his light blue eyes. It also seemed that his shiny reddish hair always needed a good shampoo.

Even though I had felt relieved to have Bradley there during the unexpected Soto incident, I preferred to keep my distance from him. I found him totally disgusting with the weird comments he insisted on making to me. He enlightened me about how he slept naked when he attended training sessions at the academy. He also told me that after he finished his shift, he always stopped by the Green Dumpster Inn, a name we had affectionately given the local liquor store in the hood. After picking up some beer, he liked to go home and sit naked in his living room and drink.

I mentioned these comments to Jacob. I wanted to know if Bradley spoke to the guys in the same way.

Jacob agreed that Bradley was strange, but he never recalled hearing him talk about his nudist fetish. One thing I knew with certainty—never would I even consider visiting Bradley in his living room and sitting on his sofa.

A few weeks after the Soto incident, I interviewed a vehicle-accident victim in the emergency room at Baptist Hospital Kendall. After finishing my report, I grabbed my belongings to leave. I walked through the large corridor, making my way to the exit signs.

Up ahead I saw Bradley in the hallway. He stood outside a cream-colored curtain that provided an element of privacy to a small area. I had been on the other side of those curtains more times than I care to admit, standing beside a gurney that held someone who had been injured in a vehicle accident.

Out of obligation, I walked over to him to greet him. I noticed that his eyebrows were pushed slightly together, and his hands were crammed in his front pockets.

I said, "Hi, Bradley. What brings you here?"

"Me and my wife had to bring her teenage daughter to the emergency room because she has a stomach virus or something."

About that same time, Bradley's wife appeared from behind the curtain. I tried to hide my surprise at seeing such a pretty, slim woman with a healthy tan, vibrant blue eyes, and long blond hair. A large, lovely brown belt with matching sandals adorned her floral-print, knee-length skirt and peasant blouse. She wore large-hooped gold earrings that looked very fashionable.

A soft shade of pink lipstick covered her full lips. The corners were turned down, though, and she seemed stiff. I sensed she was stressed; any mother would be understandably anxious if her child was ill.

She left a slight opening in the curtain, and my eyes automatically peered through it. A young girl lay sleeping on the gurney. She looked like a fourteen-year-old version of her mother.

I spoke to Bradley's wife for a few moments. I didn't want to intrude. They were there to seek medical services for a sick child, and I wanted to respect their time and their privacy.

I wondered if this lovely lady had any idea as to the idiot she married. The image of her tubby hubby sitting stark naked in her living room flashed before my eyes. Then I wondered about her daughter. What if she walked into the living room and saw that hideous sight? I then wondered how this beautiful, clean, and fashionable woman ended up with someone like him.

Several months went by without a thought of Bradley, his sick step-daughter, and his pretty wife. For some reason, I never noticed him at the driving school again.

Then without warning, the memory of seeing him in the hospital forced its way back into my psyche in a nightmarish manner, ruining what had started off to be a promising day. I had just gone for my morning run, and the weather couldn't have been more perfect. The low humidity and slight breeze offered the ideal running conditions, causing my endorphins to run rampant.

After turning the last leg of my run, I rounded the corner of my street. I sprinted, breathing hard and pushing my body to the point of exhaustion. I came up to my driveway at full speed and propelled myself over my chain-link fence.

After slowing down through the pool and patio area, I came to a complete stop before opening the back door to my home. I quickly walked from the family room to my kitchen and grabbed a drink of cold water.

While taking a big gulp, my phone rang. I picked it up and heard Jacob on the other end.

"Floy, the MDPD arrested Bradley last night."

I felt a bit lost for a moment and tried to process what I heard. "Wait a minute. What are you talking about?" I then sat down on a stool in my kitchen.

"The MDPD arrested Bradley while he was working at the Marshals' office. He had supposedly sexually molested his fourteen-year-old stepdaughter."

Realizing what this child must have endured sickened me. What's worst, knowing that I didn't say anything to Bradley's wife about her husband's strange comments when I saw her provoked feelings of regret and guilt.

I was upset with myself that I didn't see Bradley as a perverted child sex offender. He had fooled me as well as all of my colleagues. How could we have missed the monster lurking beneath the badge of protector?

Child sex predators function successfully in all occupations. They can be ministers, priests, doctors, lawyers, elected officials, educators, and scout leaders. In other words, individuals who prey on children come from all walks of life. They're manipulators. They hone their skills on acquiring the confidence of unsuspecting and vulnerable members of the community. Their ultimate goal is to gain access to children.

I learned that the MDPD chose to arrest Bradley in the cell block area of the Marshals' office. The arresting officer knew Bradley wouldn't have his gun on him since officers were required to lock their firearms in a safe box if they were going to be around prisoners. This was a very smart tactical move because most cops have an arsenal of guns on their person and at their disposal.

Bradley was booked into the Miami jail. He was then housed in the protected area reserved for law enforcement, cooperating witnesses, and snitches.

Rumor had it that Bradley spent his remaining finances to hire an attorney. He took a plea agreement of guilty and was sentenced to spend fifteen to twenty years in prison. Also, his pretty wife married his defense attorney.

About eighteen years later, I crossed paths with Bradley in an interesting and unexpected manner. I was instructing at a law enforcement conference in the Tampa Bay area when we came face to face in the hotel lobby. He had just been released from prison and was now a registered sex offender. A psychologist, also presenting at the conference, was conducting a study about rehabilitation for sex offenders. She had him talk to law enforcement officers about how child predators think.

He didn't appear a bit hesitant on talking about this matter. In fact, he seemed quite confident. What came out of his mouth both sickened me and made me fire-hot angry.

He said, "As law enforcement officers, we all have too much stress. The pressure of the job and alcohol made me go over the edge."

I couldn't believe that he still identified himself as a cop and acted as if he was one of us.

He continued to speak in a calm tone as if speaking about a trivial situation that involved other people. He wore a smile the whole time, not one of embarrassment or shame, but a smile of enjoyment. I could see that he took great pleasure from being the center of attention.

Not once during his whole "presentation" did he admit to his crime or take any kind of responsibility. Instead he blamed his circumstance as the reason he raped his stepdaughter. He was a typical sex offender in that he only cared about his own well-being and not the emotional and physical pain he had inflicted upon his child victim. Still completely self-serving, Bradley obviously had not been rehabilitated.

I had no time to listen to his lies and no patience for his sad story and litany of justifications. I eyed him and felt a sarcastic smile emerge on my face. I just wanted to leave.

Even if he didn't think about the beautiful young life he violated, I did. I continued to think about her and pray to God that she has healed and is now living a good life.

Unfortunately, we don't always get the monsters before they inflict damage upon their victims. You can rest assured, though, that we try out best. The only recourse or closure we can offer in the aftermath is justice for the victim and his or her family. And sometimes, justice can be a powerful thing.

Working with the Undercover Narcs

Predators came in all shapes, sizes, and types. Some preyed upon children for a perverted self-gratification. Some preyed upon the public by peddling drugs to try and fulfill a perverted sense of greed.

Drug trafficking was still alive and well in Miami, Florida. I was more motivated than ever to do my part to stop the flow, and I didn't have to wait long for the opportunity.

On a Saturday morning in early January 1990, while getting ready for my five-mile run, Detective Scott Adams from the Homestead Police Department Narcotics Team called me. "Floy," he said, "I need you and Jacob to help me out. Can you two meet with my team this afternoon?"

I immediately called Jacob and woke him up. I told him about Scott's call and to meet me in the HPD parking lot at twelve o'clock. After changing into something more appropriate, I walked outside to get into my car.

I arrived at the parking lot before Jacob did. I looked around at the hub of activity along Krome Avenue, the main street in the heart of Homestead. Lots of Hispanic farm workers walked in and out of the stores as they conducted their weekend shopping activities.

Once Jacob and Sniffer showed up, we strolled into the old bank building that now housed the HPD. The former bank evidently found a better neighborhood while the HPD simply found a home. It had been there long enough to mark its territory, though. To keep in line with the décor of other police stations, its walls were painted a bland color too many years ago. The scuff marks on the floors appeared to be embedded into the speckled tile. Clearly, its institutionalized ambiance demanded that visitors and staff alike focus on the problem at hand rather than the interior design surrounding them.

The bulletproof dispatch center was located over to the left side of the front door. I happened to know the middle-aged receptionist who sat behind that glass. She smiled and waved at Jacob and me before buzzing us into the station. We signed in and proceeded up the stairs and to the rear of the second floor. When we arrived, we approached a push-button pad and a telephone mounted on the wall next to a lone door.

Someone had taped instructions beside the handset telling readers to pick up the phone and dial a code. Then it directed the reader to speak into the intercom in order to gain entry.

The phone appeared to have a few years of dirt covering the receiver. Therefore, I suggested that Jacob might want to be the one to let Scott know we were at their door.

He didn't hesitate to pick up the phone, and I got a chuckle out of him following my directions. We were immediately buzzed into the inner sanction of the police department's narcotics office.

We walked into a large open squad bay, which is basically a large room furnished and arranged to meet the functionality needs of a law enforcement squad. I noticed a walk-in safe in the corner and police memorabilia, such as police patches, hats, and gear, dispersed among the room's ten desks. I felt like an interloper in the midst of a testosterone-fueled cave surrounded by personalized wall posters exhibiting pictures of guns, knives, hunting, skulls and crossbones, and half-naked women hovering over Harley-Davidson motorcycles. One poster showed Gloria Estefan wearing a more dignified outfit than the motorcycle girls. Different strokes for different folks, I guess.

This secured section gave many of the detectives the liberty to display pictures of wives, kids, and girlfriends in the midst of their desktop sports memorabilia. If this had been an area where suspects were walked through or interviewed, these desks would have been void of anything that gave a hint of family. Most law enforcement officers carefully guard that information due to possible retaliation from the bad guys.

I saw Scott sitting on the corner of a desk sipping a cup of coffee. Several men of all shapes and sizes stood in front of him wearing jeans, t-shirts, and holsters placed in different places: inside their waistbands, outside their waistbands, and in shoulder holsters hanging against the sides of their chests. They too sipped some kind of beverage, mostly soda.

Scott welcomed us and then briefed us. "My team's working on an undercover buy-and-bust case where a CI [confidential informant] will be delivering four kilos of cocaine to a warehouse outside of Homestead. Just to let you know, but only one of those kilos is real. We seized it from one of our previous cases, so we'll be taking that out of evidence. Now the other three kilos are just dummy bricks that we made from sugar, flour, and lidocaine. My detectives packaged them up, and they look like the real deal. They even put the word HOLA on each of the cocaine bricks."

Scott smiled and shook his head. "We want your help and your marked patrol cars for the jurisdictional issues. We're going to need to use them to take down the perps, hopefully today."

He went on to explain that this deal could be a quick transaction. They had worked up most of the case, so we wouldn't need to perform any investigation.

"Not only do we get another doper off the streets," he continued, "but we also get to forfeit the money the bad guys are using to buy the four kilos. We can put the whole amount in a fund that's going to help finance other investigations and equipment.

"The CI's going to let me know when the buyer tells him he has a hundred and twenty thousand dollars and is ready to receive the goods."

I was excited to be part of this operation. We sat around the narcotic's office and waited while Scott's CI called every hour to give him updates as instructed. With each phone call, the CI assured Scott that the deal was definitely going to happen and that he was working out the last-minute details with the bad guy.

At the end of every conversation, I'd hear Scott bark the order, "Get the deal done today."

These back-and-forth conversations continued for six hours. The only entertainment we had during that time was food, so we ate just to pass the time. Believe it or not, but after all of that snacking, we still got hungry. We decided to head over to a Mexican hole-in-the-wall restaurant across from the police station to grab a meal.

When we returned, we found out that the deal was still pending, so we all gave up. We agreed to meet the next morning to see if this case had moved forward any.

That afternoon was our welcome to the cat-and-mouse game of narcotics deals. I learned that the sooner you can grasp and accept the hurry-up-and-wait motto for drug cases, the sooner you'll come to relax a bit more when involved with them.

This isn't television like the popular Miami cop shows where the police go from one exciting event to the next. These fictional cops didn't have to spend days writing reports, analyzing data, and waiting for the case to come together. Many folks say that police work is ninety percent boring and ten percent stark-raving terror. That is a philosophy with which I must agree.

The next day, Jacob and I stopped at the donut shop and picked up breakfast and coffee on our way back to the HPD. The quiet Sunday morning roadways reminded me that although another day of catching bad guys for us, most people attended church during this time. I thought about my own family and how I wish I could be with them in church. Unfortunately, the bad guys weren't going to wait until after Sunday morning services to commit crimes.

Jacob and I pulled into the HPD parking lot in hopes of a productive day. Instead, we sat again in the narcotics open squad bay. We ate and we waited as the snitch kept making promises again to Scott over the phone. He continued to assure him that this deal would surely happen that day.

About two o'clock in the afternoon when the CI called, he reported that the bad guy was encountering money problems. He then promised that his buyer would be ready to purchase the kilos the following day.

We were all disappointed, but I think I could feel the group releasing their pent-up adrenaline simultaneously. Bodies went lax, and sighs escaped lungs. We had all been on go, physically, mentally, and emotionally, and now that we knew without a doubt it just wasn't happening that day, we closed shop to go home.

Jacob and I walked out of the station, our steps a bit heavier than when we arrived earlier that morning. Giving up was not an option at this point. We both decided that we had invested too much time not to return the next day and see this case through to the end.

About midnight I heard my telephone ring. I had just fallen off to sleep, but when your phone rings at that time, it can't be ignored. I picked up the receiver and heard Scott's voice on the other end. "Floy, I just talked with my CI. He told me the deal was happening first thing in the morning. Do you have a pen and some paper?"

I grabbed a notepad from my nightstand drawer. My pencil needed sharpening, but it still worked, which was all that mattered at the time.

Scott went on to tell me that his CI had given him all of the information we would need—the location of the warehouse where the deal would happen, a description of the buyer, and a description of the car that would be used along with its license plate number. His detectives ran the CI's information through data checks, and as a result, were able to identify who they thought the buyer might be. They checked out addresses where he may be located. Scott then told me the plan, where we were supposed to meet, and our position and role in this operation. As soon as I got off the phone from Scott, I called Jacob and relayed everything to him.

I was so excited I couldn't sleep. I must have looked at the alarm clock fifty times throughout the night.

By six in the morning, I was up and out the door and drove directly to the meeting place. The Homestead detectives had already set up their surveillance on the warehouse while Scott gathered the kilo of real cocaine from the police storage and the three dummy bricks. The former would be used for testing purposes during the transaction.

Within a few minutes, Jacob and Sniffer arrived. They followed me to an empty lot behind a garage a few blocks away. Soon, the breakthrough of the sun's light would expose what could be seen, so we made sure we remained concealed in our hiding place.

Scott walked over to us and firmed up the details. He told us to remain in contact with him using HPD's handheld radios. Everyone was very cautious because these types of drug deals are not for the faint of heart. When exchanges of money and dope are conducted, not only are the bad guys always on edge, but they could be planning a rip off or con job.

Admittedly, the whole situation seemed surreal. After days of waiting, this deal was finally happening and happening fast. Scott had put a concealed monitoring transmitter on the informant. This device allowed the police to hear the conversations while taping it for evidence to corroborate criminal intent.

At the scheduled time, we saw a gray two-door rusted sedan pass us. Scott confirmed that it was indeed the car that held the buyer. We watched as it pulled behind the warehouse.

From our vantage point, we observed the CI meet with the buyer. They talked briefly before the informant took a little knife out of his pocket. He proceeded to cut a tiny flap in the real cocaine brick. He then scooped out a small amount of the white powder onto the tip of the knife and held it out toward the buyer to test.

The buyer accepted the offer. He dipped his finger in the pile and tasted it. We all held our breaths during the entire exchange.

Evidently, the buyer found the CI and the sample credible because they swapped briefcases. The buyer then got into his car and drove past our hideout. The surveillance detectives kept a continual watch on his gray sedan as it headed south.

Jacob and I stuck to the plan. I pulled behind the car, turned on my blue lights, and hit the siren. Jacob pulled behind me. We knew that the person in the vehicle just committed a felony and that he knew he faced a lengthy prison sentence if arrested. The chances were great that he could be armed, so we knew we'd have to conduct a felony stop.

All car stops have the potential to be dangerous for the police, but a felony car stop was treated with even more severe caution. When conducting one, we kept our guns aimed at the driver and any occupants throughout the whole process. First, we ordered them to keep their hands in view and to get out of the car. We then told them to walk backward and kneel down with their hands on their head.

So after this bad guy pulled over to the side of the road, I used my PA system to order him to step out of his vehicle. The suspect complied, and we saw a little guy about five feet five inches, wiry, and balding emerging from the driver's side.

He asked, "Is there something wrong, Officer?" He spoke with a heavy Spanish accent.

I then had him go through the drill that ended with him kneeling on the ground. I stood next to him while Jacob took Sniffer out of his car and walked him around the suspect's vehicle. Sniffer started barking and pawing in the air at the back door on the driver's side. Jacob shone his flashlight into backseat area and onto a blanket that had been thrown haphazardly onto the floorboard. He opened the back door, and when he removed the blanket, he saw four packaged bricks with HOLA marked on them.

He yelled, "Got it."

I grabbed the bad guy's hands from behind his head and handcuffed him. We then took possession of the drugs, put the suspect in the backseat of a HPD detective's unmarked car, attended the debriefing, and went home. Jacob and I both finished our reports the following day. We were very pleased with the way this case had "gone down."

The Lure of Money

A few days later, one of the Homestead detectives told me about a Miami-Dade detective named Juan Perez who had a knack for spotting money launderers. One of the most difficult tasks for the flourishing drug dealers was "cleaning" their money. They possessed millions of dollars in illegal cash in all dominations, which became a burden. The money must be smuggled out of the U.S. or legitimized through investments.

In 1980, Florida had enacted the Contraband Forfeiture Act as the answer to separating drug kingpins from their assets. By the mid-80s, the criminal justice system watched for large cash flows.

Additionally, the Internal Revenue Service ended up partnering with Florida law enforcement agencies on a large scale. They discovered that within our beautiful state, drug kingpins had been evading taxes on their illegal money gains.

I wanted to talk with Juan Perez, a Cuban who had honed his skills of observing the Colombian drug gangs. As a result, he knew all of their hangouts. Maybe I could get him to share with me some of his knowledge of locating these criminals.

I called Juan, and he seemed downright friendly. He gave me a warm greeting, and then he talked a lot. He told me that he had actively seized thousands of dollars by following Colombians in West Kendall. He described how he watched them go from payphone to payphone to get their instructions for laundering money. (Of course, this occurred before cell phones.) They found the payphones safer and a lot more private since the police could easily obtain personal and business telephone records that pinpointed calls and callers more accurately. Once told where to send the money, they went to the wire services to forward it.

Juan offered to let me ride undercover with him to gain insight into how to spot the Colombians moving drug money. Fortunately, Major Wilson saw the benefit for the Florida Highway Patrol with my participating in this hands-on training experience. If I could learn how to identify money launderers, then I would possess the skills needed for developing probable cause for a traffic stop where large amounts of cash and vehicles could be seized.

One morning about ten o'clock, I met Juan at a Latin shopping center off of Bird Road and SW 135 Street. I borrowed an undercover car from my lieutenant and parked it in the rear of the shopping center. I got into the passenger's seat of Juan's unmarked gray Chevy Monte Carlo.

He said, "The money launderers don't start until about now."

He pointed to a typical Cuban coffee window in the shopping center. "A lot of people here start their workday by having a Cuban breakfast of café cubano or a café con leche and a tostado or croquette. Most dress for work. On the other hand, the drug dealers wear guayabera men's shirts." (This also happens to be the favorite shirt of most cops in Miami.)

I sucked in every detail he cared to teach me. I wanted to know everything about money laundering.

Juan said, "The men wear expensive leather shoes without socks. They all have beepers attached to their waists. The Colombian women are all well-manicured, well-dressed, and favor large leather shoulder bags with fringe.

"If we can spot these people, then we watch to see if they use the payphones after getting beeped and getting a message. If we see them drive to banks or money-wiring services, then they're probably laundering money for the drug cartels."

I applied the valuable information that Juan had given me as we drove around all of the Latin shopping centers and restaurants in the area. We drove for hours until I proved to Juan that I could identify this activity.

However, I felt uneasy using this type of profiling. I didn't want anyone assuming that I discriminated against a person based on his or her culture or national origin. As a law enforcement officer, I didn't want to be challenged in court over the profile I used. To prevent this would require careful documentation of the suspicious behavior as well as the need to look at the totality of the circumstances.

I decided I wasn't interested in becoming involved with Juan. I must admit, though, that the day was interesting and educational, and I ate a lot of great Cuban food.

I didn't think much about Juan until a few months later when watching the local news broadcast. I learned that the Integrity Squad from Miami-Dade Police Department had arrested one of their own for stealing money from smugglers.

Smack in the middle of the television screen was Juan being escorted into the Dade County Jail. It turned out that he had been ripping off large sums of cash from the money launders to fill his own pockets.

He wasn't the only cop lured by drug money. Unfortunately, this amount of cash enticed many vulnerable cops. As police officers, we all swore to uphold the law, yet sadly some fall into temptation and evil. One of the female troopers who I didn't know very well was arrested for trafficking narcotics from Overtown and Liberty City to locations in North Florida. She used her patrol car for her dirty deed, figuring she would never be stopped and searched in a marked police car. Guess she never figured that one of the dopers would snitch her out to avoid a hefty prison sentence. The criminal justice system threw the book at her, and she went to prison for many years.

Unfortunately, the attraction to acquire more money continued up the chain of command. Homestead's mayor was arrested and sentenced to the federal penitentiary for drug smuggling. Almost every line of profession was approached by drug dealers, and some fell into the grasp of greed. This happened all over South Florida.

Even my husband and I experienced a close call when a couple invited us to a party in the Redland area outside of Homestead. We accepted because we assumed they were upstanding business owners in our community.

After we arrived, I overheard that some of the guests were getting high in the upstairs bedroom. We immediately left the party and never associated with this family again.

I was surprised, but mostly I was disappointed. My children had played with their children. Afterward, I had to tell my girls that they couldn't go back over to their home. I explained to them that their friends' parents didn't share our family values of God and country.

Of course, they weren't happy with me. They insisted that their friends had really nice parents. I let them know that I expected them to greet their friends and be nice to them. What I didn't tell them was that the real victims in this situation were their friends, the children.

As it later turned out, that family experienced an armed home invasion by two men. These robbers were their business associates looking for drugs and money. Their young children saw these men standing over their parents holding guns to their heads. This was an image that will forever be imprinted upon their minds.

Finally Working with the DEA

Jacob and I had just finished a cup of morning coffee when my beeper went off. I looked down and recognized the number belonged to Sergeant Miller, a.k.a. Sarge, who oversaw Miami's FHP K-9 squad.

I walked to the payphone in the diner, digging into my pocket for a quarter along the way. I called the number and only heard one ring before hearing a gruff voice on the other end. "Sergeant Miller."

"Hi Sarge, this is Trooper Turner. You just beeped me?"

"Yeah, I did, Floy. Hey, I'm about to head over to DEA headquarters. They're requesting assistance with a narcotics case. Would you and Jacob mind meeting me and the other K-9 squad members there?"

My answer was short and to the point. "We'll be there within the hour."

Jacob and I ran out to our patrol cars. He had kept the air conditioner running while Sniffer waited in the backseat. It appeared that Sniffer knew we had a mission. I heard him bark excitedly through the vehicle's windows.

We immediately headed north to the Miami DEA office where a high fence surrounded the large complex, and an electronic gate was its only obvious entrance. The exterior of the buildings was unimpressive, constructed of the stereotypical government gray concrete. The only feature that stood out was the windows made of a gray reflective tint.

Sidewalks connected all of the buildings. The grounds were covered by thick Bermuda grass and palm trees.

We parked outside where we saw the other K-9 cars. We then radioed to Sarge that we were in front of the building.

He responded, telling us to go to the front door. He met us there and let us inside. We walked up a flight of stairs to an open squad bay that looked more like a meeting room with numerous chairs and a few desks. At first glance, this squad area wasn't much different than the one at HPD. It also contained the male-dominated decorum with its chick pictures. On closer inspection, though, this squad bay had two things the HPD bay didn't have—a small refrigerator tucked under a window sitting next to the largest shredder I had ever seen.

The DEA squad supervisor greeted us with a heavy Boston accent. "I'm Danny O'Leary," he said. He firmly shook my hand while smiling and staring into my eyes as if reading my thoughts. He stood tall with thick dark hair framing a knock-dead handsome face that contained expressive hazel eyes and a heavy mustache. His mature looks belied his fit and trim physique.

Wow, I knew I was going to love working with the DEA!

On the other hand, Danny's first impression of me was heavy black combat boots, a black t-shirt over a bulky bulletproof vest, black BDU military pants made of lightweight material with lots of pockets, and a gun belt with all of the necessary tools packed into pouches. I felt like I was sweating under all my equipment and gear. As if that wasn't appealing enough, the intense humidity had already performed a frizz job on my short blond hair.

Danny introduced me to the two agents in charge of this case. The shorter one, Chip Lester, wore a friendly smile and exhibited a friendly manner. When standing in front of him, I found that I hovered over him in height. The taller agent, Adam Barker, had blonde hair that complemented his lean and muscular body. Both agents were probably in their late twenties or early thirties and seemed like great guys who were serious about their line of business.

Chip conducted the briefing. He informed us that the DEA was working up the "food chain" to identify the top layers and players of drug organizations. Every activity acted as another step leading to more information on the links for the criminal enterprise. Their intentions were to completely disrupt and dismantle the organization and arrest those who ran them.

Chip had devised a ruse involving two hundred ten kilos of cocaine. The drugs had been seized from a thirty-nine-foot Midnight Express with a burned-out engine. It had washed ashore onto Pompano Beach a few months earlier.

During this time period when law enforcement was lucky enough to acquire a large amount of drugs, they would often use them in reverse undercover operations. A reverse operation involved an undercover law enforcement officer or agent, also known as a UC, who acted as a drug dealer. The UC sold contraband drugs to suspected or known drug dealers for the purposes of identifying the traffickers looking for contraband as well as to seize their assets. These types of sting operations are no longer approved by the court system.

Chip's CI, Bronco, had already met with the buyers, and he had worn a wire. Chip wanted to provide a cover for Bronco so that the CI could embed himself deeper into the criminal organization and eventually lead them to its masterminds.

The plan was that Bronco would meet the buyers. After they gave him the money, he would give them the keys to a white-paneled van parked in a nearby shopping center not far from the Redland area. This van wasn't just any van, though. Not only did it contain the narcotics, but the DEA techs had installed a kill switch in it. This device would be used to disable or stop the van through remote-controlled high-tech equipment.

The buyers would then have a couple of transporters, known as mules in the drug trade, to drive off in the van. They would get about a mile or so down the road when the DEA tech would then activate the kill switch. The van would be brought to a stop, ensuring the buyers didn't get away with the drugs.

The mules would probably think the van had become disabled due to an empty gas tank or perhaps mechanical issues. They could tell the distributor (a coconspirator higher in the organization) that they had run out of gas and had to walk away to find a gas station. While gone, a cop would find the dope "by chance," confiscate it, and take it off the street. Those within the drug organization would think the situation unfortunate. Then Bronco would be able to keep his cover, and the DEA would be able to keep the coke. The mules could be identified at a later time.

All of this would happen under DEA surveillance. Those involved in the operation would be kept informed through the DEA's radios.

Chip said, "This is where you get involved, Floy. You'll be the cop that stumbles across the dope. Once the van's stopped, you'll drive up as if you're patrolling the area, park behind it, and tell the driver and passenger to walk to a gas station or service center. Once they leave the van, DEA agents will take possession of it and the coke."

Sarge said, "Floy, Jacob will be about a quarter of a mile down the road with some of the agents, so I'm going to back you up. When you come across the stalled van and stop, I'll pull in behind you."

The plan went into gear, and the entire DEA squad (or groups as they called them) and the K-9 units drove to the Redland vicinity. The DEA chose this area because it was located in the midst of farm groves with rural roads. For the sake of public safety, they preferred to keep the operation as remote as possible. Coincidentally, we were only about four to five miles away from my home and about two miles from my daughters' school.

I parked in an area hidden by an avocado grove. When I heard our cue from Chip, I pulled out, drove about a mile, and saw the van stopped on a two-lane farm road with avocado groves on each side.

Sarge drove behind me with his K-9 Frisky in his backseat. I started to think this was going to be a cakewalk. After all, we weren't going to arrest anyone at this point, just tell them to take a walk.

The mules, however, didn't comply with our plan as hoped. They sat in the van and wouldn't move. We waited and waited but still no activity. After about fifteen frustrating minutes, Chip radioed to me to go ahead and approach them.

Sarge and I got out of our cars. We tried to act as casual as possible, as if we didn't know they had two hundred ten kilos of cocaine inside the confines of their vehicle. We didn't conduct a felony stop, but we were nonetheless cautious as we neared the van.

I approached the passenger's side, and Sarge took the driver's side. We told both men to get out, and they did without any incident.

The driver was just an old, skinny Hispanic man. He was hunched over and appeared to have some type of back issue.

The passenger, also Hispanic, was much younger, short, and very muscular as if he lifted weights. His overall appearance seemed to be clean-cut with clean jeans and a golf-style shirt.

We took them to the side of the van next to the grove. Our informant had told us that they were just paid to deliver the drugs, nothing more. Since we didn't anticipate either one of them wanting to stay with the van, we told them to walk away. The old man looked confused and neither took a step in any direction but stood in their spot as if glued to the ground.

I said, "Vamoose!"

The old man looked down and shuffled his feet in the gravel. The passenger wore a smirk on his face, and his eyes narrowed. His chin jutted upward slightly, making him look like a defiant kid. I could almost hear his brain saying, "Make me."

I told him, "Leave now, and walk to a gas station."

He stood with his chest puffed out and his head pulled back slightly. I anticipated him spitting on us at any moment.

I looked at Sarge and shrugged as if to say, *What now? This is not going as planned.*

I then made a decision that if the passenger didn't leave, then I would arrest him. I removed my newly issued hinged handcuffs from the back of my utility belt.

I told the passenger, "Turn around."

Sarge quickly moved next to me. His combat experience as a marine in Vietnam caused him to be in constant vigilant mode.

The passenger started swinging at us. I grabbed his right arm and got the handcuff locked on his right wrist. The golden rule of handcuffing is that if you get one wrist handcuffed, you never let go. I was all about the "never," determined not to loosen my hold.

Sarge gripped the passenger on the left side, but he was strong enough to knock both me and Sarge to the ground. When we went down, we took the passenger with us. Somehow he broke free with his right hand.

We still had a hold on him, albeit a slight one, so I moved up to a kneeling position to try to regain control. He moved the handcuffs out of my grip. The serrated edge tore my skin across both of my palms. I was thankful that Sarge was with me, fighting what we discovered was an underestimated miniature Hulk.

With one bracelet still attached to his right wrist, he swung the heavy and dangling cuff and walloped me on the right side of my temple. I literally saw stars before I fell unconscious on the ground. Not to sound cliché, but that was truly all that I remembered. By the time I got off of the ground a few moments later, the troops had all arrived.

Blood covered my hands and ran down my face. Trust me, I felt as bad as I looked. Jacob came and checked on my welfare. He then took off to look for the mules.

One of the DEA agents drove me in my car to the hospital to complete the First Report of Injury form. It was the state's documentation of what happened, so if it didn't get filled out and turned in, then it never happened.

Sarge later told me that after the passenger knocked me out, he took off running into the grove, and the old man had walked in the other direction. By the time Sarge had let his dog out of his cage, both passenger and driver had gotten away.

Jacob ended up finding the driver during the manhunt. He saw the old man walking as fast as he could with his head down. When he arrested him, he was compliant.

They didn't have the same success locating the passenger. Evidently, he was long gone. All of the K-9s took turns trying to find him by running scent tracks. None of them achieved any positive results.

All in all, I had taken a beating for two hundred ten kilos of cocaine. I had gotten hurt because we hadn't planned for the *what if* one or both of the occupants refused to walk away. We later learned that the mules had been promised a cut of the sale of the two hundred ten kilos of cocaine. I guess they didn't want to leave their cash cow behind. Unfortunately, the CI didn't know this crucial information.

We all learned a good lesson from this event. Rest assure, we never made that mistake again.

From that point on, the DEA accepted us. We worked with them frequently.

The next day, the passenger's attorney called to inform us that our runner wanted to turn himself in at the courthouse. Sarge and I went there and arrested Arturo Romero. He confirmed that he too couldn't walk away from the van because his payment came from a cut of the value.

I asked Arturo to return my handcuffs. He just smirked at me. I missed those handcuffs. I never received another pair of hinged handcuffs.

Eventually, Arturo received many years in prison for assault on an officer and trafficking two hundred ten kilos of cocaine, even though his trafficking expedition in this case turned out to be less than a mile.

The DEA determined that the quality and amount of this high-demand drug was valued at over five million dollars.

A few days later, Sarge, Chip, Adam, Jacob, and I had an informal ceremony in the squad bay at the DEA office. They presented me with a pair of extremely lightweight handcuffs made of aircraft aluminum. They assured me that the aluminum was so light, I couldn't be knocked out, even if I was hit on my head.

We then celebrated with the contents of that refrigerator—Corona beers with wedges of lime.

There's No Fool like an Old Fool

My next assignment with the DEA came via a phone call from Chip.

"Floy, I need your help on a case. Can you and Jacob meet me at my office around noon for a quick briefing?"

"Sure, Chip," I said, "I'll see you then."

We got to Chip's office at the DEA building a few minutes early. He said, "Go ahead to the squad bay. I'm expecting a few more people, and I'll just conduct the briefing there."

By the time the meeting started, there were a handful of us in the room. Chip stood in front of our small group with a clipboard in his hand.

"Thanks for being here. I've asked each of you to help me on this operation because of what you can bring to it. Here's the scoop. One of my informants called. He told me that he saw some men loading suspicious cargo into a Coachman trailer at a warehouse located near the County Walk Development. The CI thought the cargo was probably a large amount of cocaine. Listen, I know this CI. He always provides excellent information. I don't know when they're going to move this cargo, but as soon as I get the word, I'll let you all know. Floy, Jacob, don't forget to take a radio with you when you leave."

I didn't hear from Chip until the next day. "Floy, the cargo's on the move. The trailer is aqua-colored, and it's being pulled by a late-model yellow Ford truck. And get this—two senior citizens are driving it. They're heading north on SW 117 Avenue now. My squad's heading to the Kendall area as we speak, and I've requested air support."

"On our way," I responded, feeling that familiar surge of adrenaline kick in as I prepared myself for the unknown.

Fortunately, Jacob and I were already in that vicinity, so we also headed north on SW 117 Avenue toward Kendall Drive to meet up with them.

The DEA's helicopter flew possible routes in an effort to locate the truck and trailer from the sky, which was a different perspective than mine. Even with the traffic jams on the busy Miami corridors, I felt the pilot would still have a better chance of eyeballing a yellow truck and an aqua travel trailer.

I dodged in and out of heavy traffic in my patrol car trying to locate and catch up to this truck. I made good headway despite the fact that in Miami, if an emergency vehicle runs with overhead lights and sirens, traffic doesn't always move to the right, especially if it's a police vehicle. Most of the time, the cars just stop on the roadway, almost like deer caught in headlights. This leads to total gridlock, and clearing traffic on congested roads takes longer.

I had managed to get a mere few blocks away from Kendall Drive, which runs the length of Kendall, when Chip notified us on the DEA radio that he was also within a few blocks.

The jam-packed roadways had caused me to lose Jacob for a bit. So when I glanced over into my rearview mirror, I felt a bit of familiar comfort when I saw that he had caught up to me and now followed behind me.

Just ahead I could see the helicopter hovering over something or someone. As I got near it, I saw the aqua trailer about a block from Kendall Drive.

This scene became unreal; I felt like I wasn't just watching a movie; I felt like I was in it. The closer I got, the lower the helicopter seemed to get to the roadway. Traffic veered away to the left and stopped. I turned on my overhead lights and beeped my siren.

The truck and trailer came to a halt. All of the traffic behind us was also at a standstill as we pulled up behind the couple.

Chip and Adam arrived at the same time and in the same car. Jacob and I attempted a felony stop of the truck occupants. I used my PA system and told them to exit their vehicle. They just sat there and didn't move.

I got frustrated, and I was concerned about my safety. I carefully walked to the driver's side with my gun drawn and at ready, which is both hands holding my gun at waist level and pointing it down. I held my body at an angle with my back to the suspect's vehicle to make myself a more challenging target in case they had guns. Jacob followed the same procedure on the passenger's side.

Adam and Chip were behind us, crouched behind my car in case all hell broke loose. I pulled the driver out of the truck, and Jacob pulled out the passenger. Adam and Chip covered us. None of us knew what to expect. After realizing that neither the driver nor passenger possessed guns, we holstered our own.

They looked to be in their seventies, and both wore huge glasses that overwhelmed their faces. When the man stood, he stooped over at the waist. The woman looked frumpy with her faded pink muumuu house dress and steel-gray hair shaped into tight curls. They appeared confused and acted as if they didn't understand what was happening, but then again, they could have been playing dumb.

We then opened the trailer to a full view of a lot of cocaine, about three hundred thirty-five kilos to be exact.

This scene had developed into a major traffic backup. The possibility existed that the product's owner may be conducting countersurveillance. We certainly didn't want to risk a gunfight on the busy streets of Miami.

I put the woman in my car, and Chip and Adam put the male driver in their vehicle. One of the DEA squad members quickly got into the driver's seat of the truck. We then drove to the DEA office in a caravan while other agents protected the rear. The helicopter flew over us for as long as it could before breaking off due to entering the flight path from the Miami Airport.

When we questioned the couple, the old adage there's no fool like an old fool showed itself loud and clear with these seventy-plus senior citizens. They both admitted there was something odd about this opportunity. After all, it's not every day a woman approaches you while shopping in a grocery store with an offer to drive a truck and trailer for a thousand dollars. Since they had been living on a sparse social-security income, this gig made them feel like they had won the lottery.

When the woman asked where they lived, they provided their address. She showed up at their house a few days later with five-hundred dollars. She then gave them the warehouse address. There they would find the truck that they were supposed to drive with the trailer attached. They would receive the rest of their money after they dropped the truck and trailer off at a condominium parking lot in Hollywood, Florida.

They accepted the first installment. On the designated date and time, they drove their old, beat-up car to the warehouse and around to the rear. They saw that the trailer had already been loaded. They claimed they didn't know anything about the dope and of course where the dealers had kept it prior to placing it in the trailer. They swore they never saw the warehouse doors open.

From our investigation, we couldn't dispute their story. When we searched the warehouse, it was empty. The drugs were never in that location but were transferred behind it. We also found that the warehouse owner was legit and that the condominium's large, unsecured parking lot was filled with cars belonging to retirees from New York.

The yellow truck was stolen from a car lot in Pompano Beach. The tags on the truck and trailer were stolen in North Miami Beach. We could never establish the origin of the trailer due to its age and condition.

We all agreed the chances were slim-to-none that these "mules" would be convicted of a crime. As far as we could determine, a law against stupidity didn't exist.

The DEA's Tow-Truck Delivery

A few weeks later, we had another opportunity to work with the DEA.

In the spring of 1990, Chip and Adam were investigating a marijuana case. They summoned us to their DEA office where we all met to learn the plan.

Chip had seized twenty-five hundred pounds of marijuana from a tractor trailer that had crossed from Mexico, into Texas, and then travelled east across I-10. The weed now sat in a truck that Adam had driven from the DEA warehouse to our briefing location.

He planned to conduct a controlled delivery to the drug dealer who had ordered the product. Adam would be the undercover agent making the trade. As soon as he completed the exchange and left the park, we were assigned to drive into the park and intercept them head on.

After the briefing, Adam got into the truck to move it near the delivery location at a gas station located on Krome Avenue and Tamiami Trail. When he turned the ignition key, all we heard was a grinding noise.

The truck also had a kill switch that had been installed by a DEA technician. We suspected this might be causing an issue. Kill switches are great when they work, but when they experience a technical failure by prematurely activating on their own, it can really cause havoc on a well-laid plan.

Adam became very creative. He called for a large wrecker to tow the truck to the handoff point. We thought it comical that the elite DEA needed to hire a tow truck to haul twenty-five hundred pounds of marijuana. I wondered if its driver ever knew exactly what he had towed.

A smile crept on my face when I envisioned the bad guys hopping into the truck after the exchange with the hope of driving off into the sunset with their dope. Then I pictured the expression on their faces when they realized the truck that held their dope wouldn't work.

Since the meeting time wasn't scheduled for a few more hours, Jacob and I decided to grab a quick lunch at Rio Crystal on Bird Road. It was one of our favorite Cuban cafes. The DEA team decided to stay and wait for the tow truck.

Finally, the time had come to meet at the agreed-upon staging area. When we arrived, the DEA group and the truck were already there in position. However, I noted that the tow-truck driver had dropped the truck off in a small turnaround just large enough to accommodate it.

Jacob and I were somewhat troubled with this takedown. For one thing, we didn't have many places to park our cars as we waited for the buyers. To make matters more precarious, we didn't know if the bad guys were armed and might start shooting when they couldn't start the truck, especially if they thought they had been set up.

We preferred a better tactical advantage. We would have liked to conduct an initial traffic stop where we could come up from behind the suspects. Unfortunately, though, our options were limited at this location. Our only choice was to drive head on into a possible violent situation where we could be easy targets.

Regardless, we still agreed to go with the plan as is and pray. We knew that if we didn't do this, someone else would, and we were better trained and more experienced to handle such an encounter.

These were dangerous situations where a lot can go downhill quickly, and it can lead to injury and even death. One of the DEA agents working with us had a nasty scar as the result of losing a few inches of muscle on his upper arm during a previous gunfight. The drug dealers had tried to rip off the cocaine from an undercover case in a warehouse. His informant was killed in the gunfight.

The bottom line was that we all wanted to go home at the end of the day to our families. Nevertheless, we had a job to do, even though our job was an inherent danger.

The Lord protected us during that operation. After the delivery, we approached the bad guys and made the arrests without a hitch. Afterward, we all had a really fun time talking about the truck with the dope that had to be towed for the delivery.

CHAPTER 10

Cocaine Wars

I had been working with a Hispanic female informant who had been providing me with information about some narcotic dealers.

This informant always treated me with respect. She was attractive with "big" brown 1980s hair and beautiful eyes. I appreciated her colorful personality that she supplemented with colorful makeup. Every time I saw her, she wore tight jeans, low-cut tops, and lots of bracelets and necklaces.

Her recent break up with her dope-dealing boyfriend motivated her to let narcotics officers know about his activities as well. I don't think the boyfriend treated her properly, and I suspected she provided me with this information as a means to seek revenge.

Her boyfriend owned an armor-plated Ford Bronco. These were the type of vehicles that drug kingpins owned, but they owned them and drove them in South America. Owning one, let alone having one in the United States, definitely raised a red flag because it was very rare and usually meant only one thing. Where there's smoke, there's fire, so I just knew his bullet-proof SUV was somehow involved with drugs.

He parked his vehicle in an abandoned storage unit located near Carol City not far from the Opa-locka Airport. Supposedly it had sat in storage for years because it guzzled way too much gas to make it practical for any type of use.

He planned to ship this vehicle to Columbia, but thanks to her detailed information, I found it beforehand. I noticed that all of the VINs (Vehicle

Identification Number) had been removed, including the VINs that are hidden, which is a crime within itself. I seized the vehicle in hopes that our highway patrol's S.W.A.T. team could find a use for it.

All of a sudden this woman disappeared, and I wondered where she had gone. About a week or more after our last meeting, a Miami-Dade police officer discovered a pickup truck in a Latin shopping center in Southwest Miami.

Evidently, the truck had sat abandoned in the shopping center for a few days. Its bed contained a lot palm fronds. Between the commonality of abandoned vehicles in Miami parking lots and its appearance of being a truck merely toting away yard trimmings, I'm sure the cop didn't consider looking through the fronds before he had it towed to a wrecker yard.

While the truck sat in the wrecker yard, the hot Florida sun continued to bore down upon it, baking it and thus its contents a few more days. When one of the yard's employee walked by it, he noticed a stench and some seepage leaking onto the ground from under the truck's bed.

This employee decided to investigate to see what caused the foul odor and leakage. He discovered the decomposing bodies of two females under the palm fronds.

I had been very worried about my snitch, so that night when the news made the announcement of two women found dead in the back of a truck, I got a knot in my stomach. I waited for the story to air and saw my snitch's picture on the screen. The other woman was the missing informant's cousin. I felt absolutely terrible about their murders.

The next day, I talked to the homicide detective to verify that the woman was indeed my snitch. I needed to make sure with a proper police identification and police report. He showed me the crime scene photos that included her picture, and I recognized the butterfly tattoo on her right shoulder. I knew that was her. He told me they had been shot execution-style. Later on, her identification was confirmed through her fingerprints.

Tragically, these women had become two more victims in the Miami cocaine wars.

The Weed and Seed Program

During the 1990s, crack cocaine came on the scene and became quite the force with which to reckon. Its potency and highly addictive nature combined with its low price created a popular and lucrative market, even in poor communities across America. It was cheaply and easily made and even easier to sell on the streets.

While patrolling Miami's inner-city area known as Overtown in my marked patrol car, I heard the street dope dealers yelling "Five-O, Five-O." This was a street term yelled out as a warning to the dealers and buyers to cease business. It came from the popular '70s police television series "Hawaii Five-O" and meant *police*. So in the "hood," catching dealers was difficult unless you *fit* into the neighborhood.

As a result, I was excited when Chip and Adam contacted us after getting assigned to the newly developed national Department of Justice Weed and Seed Program in 1991. It was designed to control drug trafficking, drug-related crime, and violent crime, all of which seemed to go hand in and. The intended end results were to provide a safe environment where residents could live, work, and raise their families.

The program consisted of three different yet relevant prongs. The first prong was fighting drug dealing. The second was providing social services, and the third prong was developing community policing.

The DEA had rented an upper apartment in a new and vacant high-rise apartment building across the street from the Miami Arena. The agents used high-powered binoculars to monitor the drug activity on the streets.

Those assigned to surveillance in the apartment radioed descriptions to Jacob and me while we waited in our patrol units a few blocks away. We then stopped the described buyers who had purchased crack cocaine from the street dealers.

Instead of seizing millions of dollars worth of narcotics, we were now involved in street sales. We made a lot of arrests—as many as six within a few hours. Since this high-crime area was located near the Dade County Jail, we had a quick turnaround time.

We appreciated the results this exercise produced. The buyers snitched on the sellers who snitched on the transporters who in turn snitched on the producers making the crack. The chain of snitching worked its way up the criminal enterprise.

Jacob and I worked this detail on and off during the course of its investigation. Our efforts not only took the small-time buyers and sellers off the street, but they eventually led to seizing bank and property records and the identification of the big-time key players.

After about a year, Chip and Adam had gathered enough evidence to dismantle and collapse this entire crack distribution network. They asked Jacob and me to help arrest those processing, manufacturing, transporting, and selling the drugs.

So one early spring morning, we joined the DEA and other federal and local agencies at a four-thirty in-the-morning briefing to proceed with the takedowns. Afterward, we conducted raids and executed search warrants and arrest warrants.

Throughout the process, we followed the legalities that required us to knock on the doors first. We knocked softly, and then we kicked in doors. We ended up entering a lot of apartment homes in Overtown and searching those premises. I was amazed at how many children slept in dirty clothes or underwear on sofas, chairs, and floors in roach-infested, dirty homes. So many of them didn't have bedrooms or regular beds; they just plopped down anywhere they could for bedtime.

The children pay a high price for the drug use in our communities. These are God's children, yet we fail to recognize the neglect, abuse, and danger taking place in our own cities.

My heart broke at seeing what these children endured and suffered due to the sins of the fathers and mothers.

You Put the Drugs *Where?*

Jacob and I also spent a lot of time in North Miami at the turnpike interchange. One day I stopped a speeding new Chevrolet with a Georgia license plate and three occupants.

We went through our normal drill of separating everyone and asking them where they had been and where they were going. We also asked each person to provide us with the names of the other people in the car.

We received three different stories about their activities. No one knew the correct names of the others.

Jacob took Sniffer out of his car. He sniffed here and there, but the front passenger door got his attention. We directed the occupants to sit on the curb and called for another trooper to watch them. After he arrived, we began to search the car since Sniffer's actions gave us probable cause.

Jacob used a tool to remove the interior portion of the door. We then saw a kilo-sized package sitting in the interior framework.

Just like in the movies, he cut a small window in the parcel to remove a miniscule amount of the white powder and ran the sample through our test kit. The results revealed the substance was cocaine.

We arrested the driver. He only made one statement: "The kilo must have been put in there at the factory."

This comment made Jacob and me speechless. I thought it was one of the most creative excuses I had ever heard. The perfect "loaded" car for Miami comes off the assembly line with a kilo of coke. I wonder how much one of those cars cost.

This area of Miami became our target-rich environment for locating contraband. After that arrest, Jacob and I frequently drove through this vicinity searching for those committing traffic infractions. You'd be surprised at the number of them who carried contraband. You'd think they would want to keep a low profile and not bring attention to themselves.

On another occasion, we pulled over a black Camaro for speeding. Jacob walked to the driver's side while I approached the passenger's side. Jacob asked the male driver a few routine questions, like where they were going and where they had been.

My eyes darted between the driver and the passenger, a young, thin female with dirty blond hair. For some reason, she acted extremely nervous, and her hands shook and twitched. She either looked down or straight ahead, anywhere but at me.

We ordered the two occupants to exit the car and told them to sit on the curb. I then walked over to Jacob to suggest he retrieve Sniffer. That way, Sniffer could walk around the vehicle to see if he could detect the smell of any narcotics coming from it.

I watched the reactions of the occupants when Jacob brought Sniffer out of his car. As Sniffer came closer, the female's eyes widened and froze. Her tan face lost all color and seemed paralyzed. She stood and then wrapped her arms around her waist and crossed her legs. Clearly she was terrorized, but I realized that some people are frightened of dogs, so this fear didn't lead me to suspect that she may be hiding drugs.

All of a sudden she pleaded, "Please help me. I need to tell you something in private."

I said, "Okay. We'll walk over here away from the others."

By the time we reached the rear side of my car, she was trembling and looked like she would faint. Then she looked me in the eyes, shaking her head she back and forth. "I'm holding the dope."

I said, "Alright, hand it to me."

She said, "I can't. I can't take it out here cause it's in my snatch."

Now I was the one close to fainting. I recovered and asked, "Why did you put it there?"

"My boyfriend told me to hide it there when he saw you were going to stop us."

Okay, this made sense. That would probably be the last place I would ever think to find their dope.

Then she said, "I knew that dog would bite me there."

Now I shook my head in disbelief. I gave Jacob the code word to arrest the driver.

Once Jacob had the driver in handcuffs, I told him where the dope was hidden. Now Jacob looked like the one who would faint.

We called another trooper to transport the male driver to the Florida Highway Patrol headquarters, and I drove the female passenger. Once there, I marched "little Miss Snatch" into the ladies restroom. I put on my gloves.

"I need you to retrieve your package."

She asked, "Is it okay if I turn around with my back to you?"

For safety reasons, I said, "No. Just reach up under your skirt and take it out."

She did and within a moment's time, she produced over four grams of crack cocaine wrapped in plastic.

After booking both subjects, Jacob and I went into the lieutenant's office. We told him we had made an arrest.

Wearing another glove, I pulled the cellophane bag containing the crack out of a brown evidence bag. I told the lieutenant exactly where we had found the dope.

I placed the bag on his desk. He turned a shade of green and yelled, "Get out of my office! Now!"

We left, taking our evidence with us. I was thankful he couldn't see the grin on my face.

We gained something of value with this incident. We learned that desperation can cause people to do the craziest things, and that a search of body orifices to recover evidence was not out of the question.

The quirks of this job and the potential dangers involved caused my appreciation, love, and respect for Sniffer to grow every day. As we battled an unending barrage of demons, I felt comfort in knowing that my furry and courageous friend would fight with us every step of the way without thinking twice about his own safety, welfare, and life.

Drug Adventures with the DEA, FBI, and FDLE

In 1991, FBI agent Buddy Hank called me.

I had previously stopped by the Florida Department of Law Enforcement (FDLE) a few times and offered my assistance. They ended up telling Buddy about Jacob, Sniffer, and me and that we were available to assist with highway drug interdiction. They suggested that we might be useful with their investigation since they needed someone to perform traffic stops to identify the criminals. The FDLE also let them know about our experience of working in the federal system with the DEA.

Buddy asked me, "Trooper Turner, can you meet with me? I want to talk to you about helping my narcotics squad with a case we're working with the FDLE."

Thus began our adventure with the FBI and FDLE joint investigations. I was thrilled. My aspirations of becoming a FDLE special agent still remained with me and stronger than ever.

Jacob and I drove to the North Miami FBI office located near the Golden Glades Interchange. This neighborhood had seen better days, and the FBI building looked like a stereotypical low-budget, gray-concrete government building. Although functional, the drab and worn dark interior offered limited space that allowed for quick overcrowding.

Despite the poor aesthetics, Buddy and I hit it off right away. We both came from neighboring states: he from East Tennessee and me from Eastern Kentucky. We shared the same slow accent.

When Buddy spoke about the case, I became intrigued. This investigation involved a high-tech method for concealing cocaine through a process that involved two chemicals. It transformed cocaine into what looked like a plastic object and then back into cocaine.

According to Buddy, K-9s were unable to detect the smell of cocaine when in plastic form. The FBI laboratory in Quantico, Virginia, experimented with a machine that determined if a piece of plastic contained any cocaine. This machine looked like a small vacuum cleaner.

Buddy said, "Once we confiscate this plastic, we'll use this machine to determine its parts are cocaine. A chemist applies a solvent to convert the plastic back to cocaine.

"This is where you and your team come in." he continued. "You'll ride with one of my agents in an unmarked car to surveil suspects smuggling in the plastics made up of cocaine. You'll also be trying to identify those transporting, storing, and possibly selling the product. We need Jacob and Sniffer to conduct the car stops in his marked patrol car."

I thought, *This is out of a science-fiction novel.* I was very excited to be involved with this ground-breaking case.

Another enticing component of working this assignment was that some of the members of this FBI narcotics squad were survivors of the Bloodiest Day in FBI History. I really respected these amazing men.

When we met for our first briefing, I saw the obvious physical scars they had obtained from the gun wounds; however, I knew they kept the emotional scars well-hidden. I also saw that this time around, the FBI agents came armed with impressive firepower. They carried full-automatic weapons while I only carried a shotgun, 9-mm Berretta pistol, and a five-shot snub-nosed Smith and Wesson revolver. They had been extensively trained at Quantico and were clearly an elite squad, well-prepared for the cocaine wars. I felt a whole lot better knowing they were on my side.

I was honored to be partnered with an agent named Fernando, another Bloodiest Day survivor. Part of our assignment included conducting car stops in my marked patrol car to identify some of the unknown drug transporters in Miami. After the identification was made, we let them go. We needed to build our case, and this involved identifying the entire network. Their freedom wouldn't last for long, however. At the conclusion of the investigation, they would be arrested as coconspirators.

Fernando and I set up our posts in public parking lots. The surveillance team relayed information to us, such as descriptions and travel routes of cars they had seen driven or occupied by known traffickers. We then stopped the described vehicles and identified the drivers and any occupants.

One afternoon, Fernando and I stopped a driver who was so nervous he fainted. During another time, a driver who had been identified as a suspect parked and jumped on a city bus before we had the chance to approach him. I had to navigate ahead of it to the next stop so that Fernando could get on the bus and closely watch the suspect. I ended up driving behind this slow-moving bus through multiple stops.

Although we didn't have enough probable cause to arrest our suspect that day, his activities were well-documented. We also covertly took his picture for possible identification later.

A scientist from Colombia turned into a cooperating witness for this investigation. We later learned that the drug cartel in Colombia murdered the scientist's sister and little niece. We were all devastated that a little child was murdered by the evil and ruthless cartel members.

One night, Jacob and I worked with the FDLE narcotics squad on a typical hurry-up-and-wait case that took place in Homestead. The CI happened to be with us when the bad guy assured him over the phone that this exchange of money for drugs would still take place. As it got later, we concluded that no more activity would occur that evening.

We were all exhausted. I lived nearby, so I told everyone they could come to my house to get some sleep while waiting for telephone calls from the doper.

Everyone appreciated having a place to relax. The guys turned off the lights, spread across the floor of my family room, and took naps.

My husband worked late that night, and I fell asleep before informing him about our house guests. He arrived home, opened the door, and walked in on six men he didn't know or recognize sleeping in his house.

I heard him blurt out, "What the hell is going on here?"

In fact, I heard him all the way in my bedroom. At first, the sleep kept me from comprehending the reason for his rant. Then boom, the memory of the six agents in my house forced me to jump up out of bed and run into my family room.

I yelled, "They're FDLE! They're FDLE!"

I was a little worried since everyone was armed. I'm glad a gunfight didn't ensue.

As it turned out, this drug deal went on for a few more days, but that night was the only night they slept at my house. When the case concluded, we took eight hundred fifty-five pounds of marijuana off the streets. I'm still in contact with some of these FDLE agents who are now retired. Even to this day, we enjoy telling that story about my husband's surprise at coming home at two in the morning to a house full of strange men.

The Glades and a Massive Find

Although we enjoyed working with the feds, some of the assignments that Jacob and I worked took us in other directions.

During the summer of 1991, we attended training in Tallahassee to learn how to search and identify marijuana fields. While there, we met Alan, a six-foot-five-inch airplane pilot for the Florida Highway Patrol. He shared his passion for finding areas that grew marijuana. Flying in an airplane provided a tremendous advantage for spotting this leafy plant. Its vibrant green color differed from the normal plant life, making the task of spotting them much easier.

When the training ended, Alan invited me to fly back with him to Homestead in the highway patrol aircraft. This saved me from the long ride home in Jacob's car. Additionally, it provided an opportunity for us to discuss how we could work together.

Despite the positives, I felt a little trepidation about flying in a private plane. The last and only time I flew in one was in high school with my dad and brother. We had travelled from Ashland, Kentucky, to the Indy 500 in Indianapolis, Indiana. I wondered how that bumpy ride would compare to flying in the FHP Cessna aircraft. I had seen this plane before, and it looked tiny, so I could only imagine how much more rough the flight would be.

Alan picked me up from my hotel, and we drove together to the airport. Once there, I followed behind him to the hangar, carrying my suitcase and duffle bag. The closer I got to the plane, the smaller it looked. I didn't know if my bags would fit, let alone me. I hoped Alan didn't think I had packed too much.

I placed both bags behind the front seats. Alan never commented on the little bit of room I left for him to put his small tote bag. Once aboard the plane, I found the interior even smaller and more compact than I could have ever imagined. Thank goodness I didn't suffer from claustrophobia.

Alan handed me a headset. "Here, put these on. You can listen to my conversations with the towers, and it'll allow us to talk as well."

We then took off into the wild blue yonder. Alan spent most of the time communicating with the air traffic controllers. Every once in awhile, he'd ask if I was comfortable, but we really didn't talk much shop.

Our southbound plane flew south over the Ocala horse farms. Gazing through the windows, I thought about the beauty displayed by the countryside, even from the sky.

Alan said, "Floy, we're about to hit some turbulence," and then the plane popped up and down and up and down. The windy and stormy weather conditions didn't help. Thank goodness I didn't suffer from motion sickness either.

As we continued to fly south, the weather calmed down. In what seemed like a short time, I could see Fort Lauderdale and Miami before us. My elevation allowed me to admire the picturesque magnificence and compare the topographies offered. Although the colorful plant life covering central Florida's countryside was beautiful, I garnered a new appreciation for the beauty of South Florida. I saw miles and miles of white sandy beaches and clear, turquoise-colored ocean waters stretched out below me.

However, the closer I got to Homestead, the less significant the scenery became. My eagerness to see my family trumped any beach or countryside. I thanked God under my breath for giving me the opportunity to arrive home earlier than originally expected.

A few weeks later, Alan called Sarge. He told him that while flying over the Everglades, he spotted an area that could possibly contain marijuana. He then asked for our assistance.

This type of operation required several troopers for safety reasons. Police have been known to get hurt when entering marijuana grows, so a team is needed for security reasons. Also, a squad can help should one of us get overheated or injured while struggling through the thick foliage.

When Sarge asked all of the K-9 handlers to participate in this mission, I immediately agreed. I guess I got carried away with the ideology of another new adventure without taking into account the reality of foraging deep into the Everglades. I didn't think about the rough terrain and steamy-hot jungle inherent of this environment.

Jacob and Sniffer, the K-9s and their handlers, and I rallied together at a fruit stand in Florida City on the scheduled date of our expedition. We then all drove southwest in our individual patrol cars and entered into a field from a dusty dirt road.

The field led to woods that we needed to penetrate to reach our destination. I recalled the training instructors' warning about how some dopers protected their marijuana fields by setting booby traps. They strung out tripwires with guns and spring-loaded traps with nails. They dug holes in the ground and spread brush or palms leaves over them. Once the unsuspecting person stepped onto the vegetation, it would give way, and they would fall onto rows of sharpened spikes. These dope dealers were no doubt territorial about their marijuana, so much so that human life was inconsequential compared to growing and selling their product and making a whole lot of money.

However, dopers weren't the only territorial creatures of the Glades. Hideous forms of wildlife hid in the thick tangled brush, also waiting to ambush the first intruder who had the audacity to invade their turf. They didn't need to create booby traps; their venom, claws, and sharp teeth accomplished the job quite well.

I must admit that I didn't want to cross paths with any of the slithering reptiles known to live and frequent this area. When some owners of exotic large snakes got tired of feeding and caring for them, they've been known to take them to these kinds of environments and let them loose. As a result, the Burmese pythons have multiplied exponentially over the years. Since they're not natural to this region, this overabundance has now damaged the ecosystem.

Alligators didn't concern me at this point. They usually didn't hang out in dry places.

Alan flew overhead and watched our group from the air. He provided directions as to where to proceed through the dense foliage. A few of our team members brought machetes, which were Miami's favorite weapon for knifing and slashing. For now, they became our favorite weapon for knifing and slashing our way through the thick overgrowth of vines. Without them, we could have only gotten so far, and we didn't want to leave empty-handed.

I've shared my fear of snakes with you, but thankfully, I have absolutely no fear of spiders. In the Everglades, they hung from every appendage of greenery. I encountered several big, furry, and cute eight-legged guys that reminded me of *Charlotte's Web*, one of my favorite childhood stories. A few "Charlottes" tickled my neck, but none decided to bite.

We all had compasses on our watches, but I felt better knowing that we had a set of eyes on us from the air, especially as we kept getting further from the road and deeper into the "jungle." Finally, we arrived at the grow site. We cautiously entered the area, looking more intensely for any booby traps before taking each step. Thank God, the area seemed free of any hazards.

When I got a moment to take in what grew before me, my mind could only register a portion of what my eyes saw—hundreds of marijuana plants. I couldn't comprehend its vastness, just that it looked massive.

I shook my head as I pondered how we would even start this mammoth task. I thought fighting the elements to get this far was tough enough, but that was a child's play compared to what we now faced.

Someone yelled, "Let's start pulling them up by the roots and bagging them."

No one disputed this strategy. Instead, we all stood in a line, side by side, and pulled up one plant after another.

The work proved to be tedious. Sweat rolled off my forehead and stung my eyes. I think I lost five pounds in water weight. In reality, it wasn't much different from going to a day spa and sitting in the sauna, except for the bugs.

The latex gloves I wore quickly filled with puddles of sweat. After discarding them, I donned a pair of thin, lightly woven cotton evidence gloves. I made a mental note to take my heavy-duty work gloves with me when I went into the Glades again.

After more than an hour of pulling, tugging, sweating, and basically feeling miserable, we had the plants bagged and ready to be hauled out of this marijuana-infested area. We looked around at a job well-done and shared the immense satisfaction of knowing that we had disrupted a doper's efforts. In fact, we were thoughtful enough to leave the grower a note saying that the highway patrol had taken the crop, which we planned to incinerate.

Marijuana, such as the kind we confiscated, grows in the wild. In order to catch the owner or responsible party, we'd have to invest in a lot of expensive surveillance equipment. With that said, our interest could only go as far as interrupting the owners' endeavors instead of pursuing an in-depth investigation.

Jacob and Sniffer led the way as we all trudged back out with our booty, retracing our steps along the same path we had already cleared. Unfortunately, this would not be the last time I ventured into this no-man's zone of harsh, unmerciful land.

We threw the bags of marijuana into the trunks of our patrol cars. I climbed into the driver seat, feeling sweaty, dirty, and prickly. I couldn't wait to get to the ladies' restroom to wash the plants' green stains off of my hands.

The marijuana fumes escaped the confines of the trunk and made their way into the interior of my car. I had no choice but to take in a whiff of the sweet odor. I started sneezing, and my eyes itched and watered all the way to FHP headquarters. Admittedly, I felt lightheaded.

I knew we still had a few hours of work ahead of us before turning the marijuana over to the evidence vault at the FHP Headquarters in Miami. It needed to be weighed for security verification. Reports had to be written as to the location from where we took it.

The day had taken its toll on me physically, and I couldn't help but think about jumping into my cold pool when I could finally make it home. In the meantime, though, and with some luck, maybe we could locate a Cuban coffee window and get a high-test jolt to finish out this wretched hot day.

Fire It Up!

Occasionally, Jacob and I were called to the Miami Highway Patrol Station after the evidence custodian obtained a court order to destroy drugs no longer needed for evidence.

We got assigned to assist with guarding the convoy trucks transporting vast amounts of marijuana from Miami to Palm Beach County for incineration. This might sound like a mundane task, but the products were worth millions of dollars.

Given the climate in Miami where the bad guys also had snitches on the inside of the courts and police stations, we always stayed vigilant in our efforts. Once the drugs were placed into the incinerator, we couldn't leave until they completely burned.

I had heard that this incinerator didn't emit organic pollutants, but whoever asserted those claims must not have visited the facility when it was in full swing. When it fired up, I swear I could smell the marijuana burning in the air.

Driving School

Before that summer was over, Lt. Fagan, asked Jacob and I to meet him at the Florida Highway Patrol's Miami Investigative Unit.

The lieutenant was assigned to the investigative troop and worked directly under Tallahassee on cases for internal investigations like those involving the Division of Drivers Licenses. He had been working an investigation of an examiner assigned to the driver license office in North Miami. This state employee was suspected of taking bribes from people who either failed the driver's test or didn't have proper identification to obtain a license.

Also under investigation was the sole instructor from Bernie's Driving School. He allegedly accepted bribes from drivers and then passed the money onto the examiner. Of course, he kept a portion of the cash for himself.

Lt. Fagan said, "Floy, I want you to go undercover as someone who needs to get her driver's license. You're going to need to act like you don't know how to drive and take driving lessons from Bernie. You're going to give them fake identification, and I want you to fail the test and offer him a bribe."

"Sure, Lieu," I said, a bit unsure. "The only problem is, I don't know how well I can pretend like I don't know how to drive."

Jacob said, "I think that should be easy for you. I've seen better drivers."

They both laughed. My pensiveness quickly turned into perplexity, wondering if they really thought I was a bad driver.

Nevertheless, I received an undercover learner's permit from Tallahassee with a fictitious address and two hundred dollars for driving school. Jacob's job was fairly simple. He just needed to sit in a white van and film me running stop signs, jumping curbs, and parking incorrectly.

First, though, I needed driving lessons, so I called Bernie's Driving School. Bernie and I arranged to meet early that evening in the parking lot of the driver license office.

I arrived first and waited on my new instructor. I wore a wire underneath my shirt so that my conversations with Bernie could be transmitted, monitored, and recorded.

A few minutes later, a small faded-green Toyota drove up and parked. Magnetic signs broadcasting "Bernie's Driving School" adhered to each of the front doors. A large sign that read "Student Driver" sat on top of the car.

A wormy little guy stepped out of that funky-looking car. When he stood, he only reached about five feet six inches. I noted that he looked greasy and unkempt.

He walked over to me and said, "Hi. I'm Bernie. I'll be your driving instructor."

He held out his hand to shake mine. Once he exposed his sweat-stained armpit, the trail of released stench overtook the fresh scent of the nice breeze as well as my nostrils.

It didn't get any better either. He turned slightly and motioned toward his car with his right hand. He said, "Go ahead and get into the driver's seat."

I plodded to his car, afraid of what I may find in it. Since the driver's door was still open, I could see the front section of its interior. Worn and dirty beige seats waited for me to sink into them. A greasy steering wheel glistened in the Miami sun, and the inside of his car had the same stinking smell as its owner.

I thought, *How am I going to make it through this ordeal?* To make matters worse, I was scheduled for three driving lessons with this weasel.

I slid into the driver's seat. Bernie jumped into the passenger's seat. I looked over and noticed that his floorboard had a hole in it.

My academy-award-winning performance began by grinding the ignition when starting his car. I then pretended not to know how to shift the gear into drive.

Bernie kept leaning over toward me and placing his arm on the back of my seat. This invasion of my space made me feel real uncomfortable, not to mention how much his body odor and up-close garlic breath made me feel nauseous.

Once I got the car in gear, I followed Bernie's instructions and slowly drove forward. I decided to hit the brakes really hard, just to annoy my new friend. It worked. He rolled his eyes and shook his head.

Then I planned my next move. I hit the curb with the right front wheel, and we lunged up a bit. Now Bernie got mad, so I stopped being such a pain.

Bernie said, "Now, try to parallel park."

I pulled up at an angle that decreased the parking space, prohibiting me or anyone else from parking the car.

My last attempt for the night resulted in running over the plastic pole that bore a red triangle flag. Bernie wasn't happy with my lesson, and I wasn't happy with being subjected to this crude creature. Nonetheless, we arranged to have another lesson the following evening.

That next night, I arrived at the same location. There sat Bernie in his faded-green car. I walked over to him, and he told me to sit in the passenger's seat.

He drove me around, describing his proper driving techniques. Then he turned to me and said, "We need to swap places so that you can take another try at driving."

I got into the driver's seat. After putting the car in drive, I repeated my cycle of turning too wide, hitting curbs, and running over the pole markers for the parallel parking test.

While making these driving "mistakes," Bernie leaned over in my direction. I wore a blouse and skirt, and Bernie let his left hand drift onto my knee.

Since I was being recorded and monitored, I asked, "Why is your hand on my knee?"

His eyebrows rose up in surprise, and he recoiled backward like he had just touched a hot stove. He mumbled, "Sorry."

A few minutes later, he casually placed his hand on my right shoulder. I asked, "Why are you putting your hand on my back?"

I fumed with anger. I suspected Jacob, Lt. Fagan, and a couple of other troopers who heard these transmissions all had a hilarious time and laughed at my expense. Bernie removed his arm, but he kept touching my leg and rubbing it. I wanted to sock him right on his greasy face.

Angie Dickinson in the *Police Woman* series never experienced vile and disgusting roles like my assignments. How did I get so lucky? I wanted to puke.

The lesson's hour had finally come to an end, and I couldn't leave fast enough. I intended to go home and submerge myself into a hot, hot bath with lots of soap.

I still had more work with Bernie, though. I needed to approach him with my "concerns" of not being able to pass the driver's license test.

The next night, I gave Bernie my cover story. I told him that I used to live in New York City where I never had the opportunity to drive. After my recent divorce, I decided to move to Miami. Once here, I realized I needed to drive to get to work and get around for daily activities. I started my new job in a few days, and I really needed to get this test behind me.

I told Bernie I had taken a lot of my ex-husband's cash, which enabled me to purchase a new Dodge car that I wanted to use for the test. In actuality, my new car belonged to the state of Florida. Because it was an undercover car, it came complete with an undercover license plate.

While telling Bernie about my need to get a license quickly and my frustration about the difficulties of driving, I could see his interest perking up. My voracious little Bernie was not one to pass up an opportunity. I could almost hear his brain clicking as greed took over all of his thoughts.

I knew he would never give one iota of concern about putting me behind a wheel and unleashing me and my unsafe driving on the motoring public. Bernie's DNA didn't possess this kind of care or trepidation.

He said, "Don't you worry your pretty little head. I'll make sure you pass that test."

I forced my eyes to open wide. "How can this happen?"

He gave a slight smile. "For one thousand dollars, I can make sure you get your driver's license."

I wrinkled my nose and scratched my head. "I don't understand how money can make me a better driver. Are you talking about giving me more lessons?"

Now Bernie was hooked. He explained how the wheel was to be greased, pardon the pun. He would give the money to the examiner, who upon receipt would provide me with my license. He forgot to mention his take in the bribe, though.

He thought I had taken his bait, but soon he'd find out that he was actually both the bait and the catch.

The next morning when I showed up at the driver license office, I saw Bernie in the crowd of a few hundred Florida citizens waiting for the doors to open. The thousand dollars in my purse had been photocopied to record the serial numbers.

Bernie instructed me to meet him in his stinky Toyota for the exchange. When I got into the passenger's seat, he leaned over to me and bent his head toward my breast. Oh, I wanted to kick him in the, well, right on that part of his body where he sat.

I pushed him back by placing my hand against his shoulder. I couldn't help but grin like a cat that was about to pounce on a dirty rat. Whereas Bernie saw dollar bills, I saw handcuffs.

I gave Bernie ten one-hundred-dollar bills. His eyes lit up, and the corners of his mouth stretched almost from one ear to the other.

He reached over and offended me yet again with a pat on my shoulder. I decided that if he went any lower with his hand, I would deck him right there on the spot. I realized that I wanted to arrest Bernie more than the state employee who betrayed the public's trust.

He then got out of his Toyota and told me to pull my car up to the parking spaces reserved for the applicants waiting to take their test. I swear I saw Bernie licking and sucking on his lips.

I watched him walk into the driver license office. Another trooper had it under surveillance. He observed Bernie hand off the money to the driver license examiner.

A few minutes later, a dark, swarthy, heavyset male wearing a rumpled shirt bearing the state insignia appeared at my passenger's door. The insignia revealed that he was the examiner.

I remained in the driver's seat. He got into the passenger's seat, and we were off. I ran the stop sign that led from the parking lot to the road; I didn't even slow down. This was my first clear-cut violation. I also struck the curb two times.

Then for my grand finale, I attempted to parallel park. In the process, I ran over the front and rear plastic poles, which was another clear-cut violation for failure.

All along, the examiner only gave me verbal instructions about each maneuver. He never engaged in any other conversation until he informed me to park and follow him into the office.

I walked behind him. Once inside, he turned to face me. His face possessed no emotion, so unless you knew he was on the take, you may truly wonder the results of your test.

His voice remained monotonous as he said, "You passed."

When I walked out of the office with my new driver's license in hand, I finally received my reward for this whole stinky venture. I cuffed Bernie with Jacob laughing at my side. Lt. Fagan and the other troopers made a big show of walking my examiner out of the office handcuffed in full view of all of the other employees.

I later found out that Bernie had charged me double the normal price for purchasing a driver's license. The little slime took advantage of a recently divorced woman on her own.

Bernie pled guilty, but the examiner decided to hire a well-known expensive defense attorney to represent him. Eventually, though, he pled guilty too.

Not long afterward, Lt. Fagan called me again. He wanted me to meet him in Fort Peirce at the accident records office. He asked me to purchase a traffic crash report from a female highway patrol clerk who worked there. She was suspected of pocketing about half of the money she received from these transactions. People amaze me.

The clerk didn't make a lot of money, but her state job gave her great health insurance and retirement benefits. Plus she worked for the police. What made her think she could get away with this thievery?

Since this sting operation didn't include any driving instructors, I agreed to participate. Lt. Fagan and I met in a hotel room in a nearby location. He gave me some marked and recorded bills to purchase these documents.

As soon as I made the purchase, one of my academy classmates assigned to that office as a traffic homicide investigator walked through the room. I hadn't seen him in years, but he could have identified me. Good thing I saw him first.

I looked around and spotted a display rack containing Florida maps and some information pamphlets about wearing seatbelts. I stepped next to it and turned slightly, hiding myself from his line of vision. It worked.

Before leaving the Ft. Pierce office, I wrote a quick report to Lt. Fagan of what transpired between the clerk and me, glancing up frequently to see if anyone else who knew me happened to drop by. I then drove a few hours to get home. Thankfully, this assignment was not nearly as offensive as my Bernie assignment.

Round Two of the Glades

During the fall of 1991, I enrolled in Barry University to finish college and obtain my bachelor's degree. I enjoyed life as a trooper, but my goal was still to become an FDLE agent. Possessing a four-year degree was one of the stringent qualifications to becoming one.

So I juggled a full-time job, school, and a family. It took some effort to adapt, but my motivation pushed me when I honestly didn't think I had anything left to give. In the meantime, I was determined to exceed the expectations of both the FHP and myself as far as performance. Of course, opportunities always presented themselves, and of course I always embraced them gladly.

Not long after starting classes, I suffered from an ingrown toenail. This medical nuisance got on my nerves, so I stopped in my favorite podiatrist's office and asked him to relieve me of this nagging situation. Although Jacob and I were on the clock, we had nothing scheduled for our midmorning, so I took an early lunch break to address my toe issue.

Doc fixed me up good. He gave me a big numbing shot, cut out the embedded side of my left big toenail, placed a bandage on it to accommodate my tactical boots, and put me back on the road with Jacob.

A few hours later, we were called to a section on the north end of Krome Avenue. An ATF Special Agent had just been shot at that location by some home invaders.

Thank God, the ATF agent eventually recovered. Because the shooter had run into the heavy saw grass of the Glades, K-9s had been requested to search for him.

As a result, Jacob, Sniffer, and I once again ended up with a mission that would take place in the Glades. When we arrived at the staging site, we were given an assigned grid to search.

Upon entering the area, we found ourselves confronting six-foot-tall sharp-edged saw grass. With the foliage so thick, we decided to have poor Sniffer lead the search, followed by Jacob, and I brought up the rear. If that wasn't overbearing enough, the intense sun beat down upon us, making the already-hot day feel even hotter.

I worried about Sniffer's long fur coat getting tangled in the thick blades covering the ground. In fact, the thickness made it almost impossible for Jacob and me to walk, so we had to crawl on all fours.

We moved deeper into dense brush. Soon we continued crawling through very shallow water. We decided to give Sniffer a break from taking the lead, especially since he wasn't following a scent for a track.

I then forged ahead and led the search. I wasn't worried about coming nose to nose with the shooter. My concern came from the possibility of looking into the reptilian eyes belonging to my most dreaded species—snakes.

The spiders in this grid seemed to grow much larger than the others in my previous jungle quest. Hello to many Charlottes.

I started experiencing a burning itch on the back of my neck, and that annoyed me the most. I didn't stop to think about what it could be. I just covered my hair with the same black bandana I always used in these types of situations.

We searched the Glades for hours. By the time we came out of them, daylight had faded to the close of day. We were also starved, yet our furry companion never complained.

Jacob and I agreed that we'd meet up at his house to first take care of Sniffer. Between needing to change out of my itchy shirt and needing to go to the bathroom, I stopped at a gas station and used their restroom facilities to take care of both issues. I then drove to Jacob's place where I helped him hose off Sniffer. Jacob then fed Sniffer before we headed off to eat dinner at our favorite restaurant, The Capri, located in Florida City.

I didn't care what I looked like. At least my shirt was clean, but my hair held no hope. I just covered it with the same black bandana I wore during the search.

We enjoyed the cool from the air-conditioned restaurant as we ate, but the itching persisted. I didn't say anything; I just thought that once I took a shower, it would go away.

I noticed Jacob scratching his neck too. At one point, he said, "My neck keeps itching." He then shrugged and continued eating a delicious meal.

By the time we finished dinner, we looked at each other from across the table. Our eyes met, and we shared a simultaneous epiphany as to why our necks itched. We remembered that along with the reptiles and "Charlottes," invisible red bugs similar to chiggers were known to hang in the Everglades. Since neither of us had covered our necks while in there, we realized these bugs had embedded themselves into our skin, which now turned red. Ugh.

We knew that calamine lotion was the best way to treat this miserable condition. We couldn't get to a drugstore quick enough to purchase a couple of bottles of the pink liquid.

(By the way, the shooter was spotted walking on Krome Avenue while Jacob and I enjoyed our dinner and scratched out necks.)

I learned an important lesson that evening. When crawling through the Everglades, always protect your neck with a scarf.

The next morning I learned another important lesson. Never crawl through the Everglades with an open wound, even if that open wound is wrapped by a bandage and encased in a pair of sturdy boots. Water can seep into boots as demonstrated by the terrible infection acquired by my big toe. I ended up on antibiotics and elevating my foot for a couple of days.

Despite the lessons I learned the hard way, the day ended on a high note. Law enforcement experienced two major victories: a cop survived a shooting, and a bad guy was caught and arrested. Comparably, the physical ailments I suffered were inconsequential. After all, I would sacrifice my neck to invisible red bugs and my big toe to another infection any day to see results like this.

You Can't Catch Them All

Crack might have evolved into a huge market, but marijuana still poured heavily into our area.

Jacob and I returned from the U.S. Department of Transportation (DOT) Commercial Carrier training in Tallahassee. We decided to concentrate on tractor trailers in the vicinity of Okeechobee Road near the Everglades.

After weeks of looking into trucks and lifting Sniffer into the trailers, I came to the conclusion that we needed a Beagle-sized dog for this exercise. When I told Sarge about my idea, he walked away without saying a word.

One afternoon, I had stopped a trailer for speeding, and Jacob pulled up behind me. We told the driver, who went by the name of Julio Lopez, to step out of his truck and sit on the shoulder of the road. After climbing down out of his cab, I noticed he was short with nice features and wore clean jeans and a collared shirt.

We started talking with him and discovered that Julio had come all the way from Mexico and was heading to Miami. What I found interesting was how calm, cool, and collected he seemed.

I said, "We're going to need to see your log."

He said, "I don't have it."

"Then you understand we'll going to need to take your truck to the DOT yard and search it?"

He shrugged. "Okay." He didn't appear agitated that we would search his vehicle and that we would cause him to be delayed in his trip.

We summoned a trooper with a CDL license that's required for driving trucks. He climbed into Julio's truck and drove it to the yard a few miles away. We had no idea what we would find and confront once we opened it up and searched it.

Jacob brought Sniffer over to the trailer and lifted him up to the back of it. He barely squeezed inside because of all of the boxes packed so tightly together.

Then Sniffer went to work and did what he did best—sniffed. It wasn't long before he started digging aggressively at some of the boxes to alert us.

Julio sat nearby and watched as a DOT forklift driver removed all of the contents of the truck. He gave no objection to us searching every box and carton for the next eight hours. They contained products made in South America such as canned goods, coffee, and grooming products. We could find nothing illegal.

After we felt there was nothing left to search, we tried to fit all of the contents back inside the trailer, but we just couldn't make it work. We soon realized that we lacked proficiency in loading trailers.

Julio walked over to us as we tried to push and tug on the boxes to get them to fit. He said, "I'll just take what you were able to load."

His attitude surprised me. If he was on the up and up, he would have complained. He seemed like he just wanted to get away from us.

We provided him with a receipt for the pallets that we couldn't fit back into the trailer and subsequently took them to the DOT where they were stored.

We never saw Julio again nor did we receive a complaint from the trucking company. About a year later, we learned that New Jersey State Troopers arrested Julio for transporting hundreds of kilos of cocaine inside a commercial trailer. Maybe Sniffer alerted us about past contents, and we just happened to search his trailer at a time when he wasn't moving contraband, or maybe we missed a hidden compartment. Regardless, he did get caught in the end.

Julio's truck turned out to be the first of many trucks and vehicles that we weren't able to put back together again after dismantling them. We went through a similar experience on another occasion when Sniffer alerted us to the inside dashboard of a late-model Dodge SUV.

This time, Sniffer gave us a more-intense-than-usual alert. He took a big bite out of the dashboard.

I told the driver we needed to search his vehicle, and he agreed. We proceeded to take the vehicle and driver to the DOT yard. Since Sniffer had already ruined the dashboard, Jacob and I decided we might as well take apart the entire front compartment of the car.

We popped off the front interior cover without much effort. Each time I glanced over at the driver, he seemed bored. He rolled his eyes, took deep breaths, checked his watch, studied his nails, and removed nonexistent lint from his clothes.

After searching for narcotics and coming up empty-handed, the only thing we had to show for our efforts was a torn-up new car. We couldn't reassemble the dashboard properly, and we felt terrible about it. We apologized.

Jacob said, "Send your bill to the highway patrol. We'll make sure you're reimbursed for the repair."

The driver never complained. He just had his car towed to the dealer, and we never received a bill.

Another time, I had stopped a car for speeding while Jacob and I worked on the Florida Turnpike in Pompano Beach. Sniffer alerted us to the undercarriage of the car.

We had the car towed to the turnpike service center. We asked the mechanic to put the car on the lift so that we could conduct an inspection for a hidden compartment.

I remembered that one of the other K-9 officers recently discovered a hidden compartment in a gas tank. We were sure we would discover the same thing.

We then asked the mechanic to empty the tank and remove it. We didn't find contraband. Still, this driver didn't seem upset by our thorough search of his car.

Anger would have been an understandable emotion from these drivers, but the lack of it always made me suspicious. I always wondered if we had missed something during our searches.

Nevertheless, we had to recognize that we do the best we can, and at the end of the day, we had to accept that we can't catch them all.

Meeting Infamous Serial Killer Aileen Wuornos

Although Jacob, Sniffer, and I were felony troopers under the Investigative Troop in Tallahassee, Sarge and his Miami FHP K-9 squad included us on several of their trainings and assignments. Since Jacob needed to train Sniffer weekly, it was easier to join this local K-9 team. Furthermore, the well-populated area of Miami and the large amount of drugs trafficked in and out of its city limits made our working together beneficial all the way around.

I found the trainings to be the most difficult part, though. As the only trooper without a dog, I became a natural fit to take on the role of the bad guy. Needless to say, my initial episode with the hidden sleeve earned me the right to refuse to wear that type of "protection" ever again.

During the trainings, I ran from the dogs. When they caught up to me, I kept my balance by standing with my legs planted wide and then took the sleeve hits. I felt like all of the tugging and hits by the large canines abused my neck and back, so I came up with what I thought to be a brilliant solution. I suggested we conduct the trainings in the avocado groves in the Redland area. At least in the groves, I could run a scent track for the dogs to follow and then climb a tree. Fortunately for me, the K-9 unit agreed and moved to this location.

The bottom line was that whether or not we changed venues, I had to suffer through these exercises. They were crucial to maintaining my good standing in the eyes of this macho squad. Thank goodness this new location gave me the ability to endure the trainings with a lot less battering on my body while keeping my reputation intact.

Although the squad didn't tell me in so many words that they respected me, their actions did. For instance, Sarge asked Jacob and me, along with Sniffer, to present a training exercise for the DEA's Family Day in a park located in Fort Lauderdale. He provided me with the gun and blanks and told me to shoot it into the ground while running.

He had asked me not to fall down when Sniffer jumped on the sleeve. In my mind, though, I knew that was easier said than done. There was no way I could run, have Sniffer jump on me, and not go down. He weighed only about thirty pounds less than me, and when he hit me, he hit me at full speed.

But Sarge wanted more excitement, which at no time involved my balance. Unfortunately for him, I did end up on the ground, which couldn't be avoided as long as the law of physics exists. Regardless, this training scenario turned out to be a huge success with the families and especially the children.

The popularity of the K-9s and their handlers grew beyond family days. Some of the state prisons requested some of the units come and conduct searches for contraband, and in particular, drugs.

So on a clear winter day in early 1992, Jacob, Sniffer, and I responded to the Broward Correctional Institution with other members of the Miami FHP K-9 squad. The warden wanted us to conduct a search with the dogs.

This female state prison held the distinction of housing the only females on death row. At that time, only a few females sat in that separate section.

I had never been to this prison. As I approached the gray building, an icy sensation covered my whole body. Little bumps rose up on my arms, and I gave an involuntary shiver. I wasn't sure if my body was responding to the low temperatures or from the type of prisoners who resided behind those bland concrete-block walls. Undoubtedly, some of those women had performed some gruesome acts.

A brick administrative building stood in front. A small community sat to the south where the warden lived in a brick house, and other officers lived in trailers.

We walked in silence along the lengthy stretch of sidewalk behind the administrative building. We came to a series of gates where we were buzzed in and met by Prison Inspector Tom Watts.

Tom came across very personable. His overall neat appearance presented a well-organized guy, and his military-style haircut made me think he may have previously served in the armed forces. Highly polished shoes accentuated his starched shirt and creased pants, both of which fit as if tailored for his average build.

Tom welcomed us before introducing himself. "Come, follow me," he said before turning and walking away. We trailed behind him, and everywhere I looked I saw a high chain-linked fence crowned by curling razor wire.

I thought about my life, and I felt extremely blessed. I couldn't fathom how hard life must be within these confines.

Since then, my perspective on the way prisoners lived has somewhat changed. Originally, I thought them to be quieter and more reserved than what I had witnessed that day. Rather, I watched as the women gathered in groups in the courtyard. They seemed to be having a good time, laughing and talking. None of them looked depressed but instead engaged in animated conversation. If not for their prison garb, they could easily be mistaken as a normal group who had convened for some kind of social event.

I also learned that many females who start off struggling to survive in this environment end up adapting by creating a prison family. This becomes their focus and medium from which they vent their drama and excitement.

Still, there are some prisoners who retain their predatory disorder. Similar to their behaviors on the outside, they find the weakest and most vulnerable inside those walls to take advantage of and exploit.

When I learned what some of the women had done to get in here, I again felt a shiver run down my spine. This time I knew it wasn't from the temperature but from the cold blood that ran through their veins.

Jacob, Sniffer, and I finished our assignment. We didn't locate any drugs, but the K-9s did show specific interest in a few areas where drugs might have previously been hidden.

Tom Watts offered to take us on a tour of death row. We agreed and followed him into the incredibly well-guarded and dreary area. At least in the other sections, there remained some kind of hope, but not here. Even its gray concrete walls and floors seemed bleaker than the rest of the prison. The only other color was the green that covered the small, eye-level flaps on the steel doors.

I could feel this environment immediately sucking the breath out of me. It wasn't from the stagnant air heavily laden with humidity. After all, I've endured many muggy days in Miami. It was knowing that evil sins lurked behind those green flaps, evil that was capable of doing the most hideous things to another human being.

Tom rapped on one of the heavy metal doors with his knuckles, and then opened its metal flap. A set of eyes and a mouth appeared that belonged to the person who the media had dubbed "Damsel of Death."

I stood looking into those eyes, and the hair on the back of my neck rose up. I realized that at that very moment, I stood face to face with the notorious female serial killer Aileen Wuornos.

Aileen sounded curious with a hint of excitement in her voice as she asked, "What are you doing here?"

I imagined she welcomed the deviation from the boredom that her small dark cell offered her twenty-four hours a day.

I said, "We're finishing up from a detail with the K-9s, and now we're taking a tour of the prison."

When I mentioned the dogs, her eyes lit up, and the muscles in her face appeared to have relaxed some. "I love dogs," she said.

I stepped back. Jacob overheard this conversation and brought Sniffer up to the door. He then slapped his hand near the small window to signal Sniffer to stand. He did and placed his front paws high on the door so that Aileen could see him.

When she peered through the window, I saw her obvious delight at seeing this massive, beautiful animal. Her smile widened, and her eyes twinkled even more.

Meeting her brought back memories of working in the Ocala rest area. I also remembered her victims and how they had suffered at her hands.

Aileen thanked us for letting her see Sniffer. From that time on, if I had a chance to bring him into the area where Aileen existed, I did.

The other inmate sharing the death row quarters with Aileen that day was Judias Goodyear Buenoano, also known as the "Black Widow." She had been convicted of poisoning her husband with arsenic and drowning her paralyzed son.

When Tom wrapped on Judias' door flap, she just groaned, "Go away." A few years later in 1998, she was taken to the Florida State Prison in Starke to be executed. She was the first woman executed in Florida's electric chair known as "Old Sparky."

The third member of this elite group had been moved due to her appeal for her death sentence. Ana Maria Cardona was convicted in 1990, for murdering her three-year-old son Lazaro Figuero. He acquired the nickname Baby Lollipops because when his body was discovered, he wore a little t-shirt adorned with lollipops.

After twenty more years, nothing changed. In 2011, Ana Maria received her second death sentence for the same brutal murder of her son.

Unfortunately, Florida's death row will always have residents because we'll always have monsters who commit heinous crimes. But just like the Eagles' song "Hotel California," Florida's death row is one place where you can check out anytime you like, but here you can never leave…unless it's in a pine box.

Our Rewards for Fighting in the Cocaine Wars

In the summer of 1992, the DEA honored our entire Felony Drug Interdiction Team K-9 squad at a ceremony in Miami. They presented us with an award for outstanding cooperation in our working relationship in the war on drugs. We also received the International Association of Narcotic Officers Award for Outstanding Service. We were all proud of our accomplishments.

Sadly, we lost a few of our K-9s along the way, two from overheating during searches and another from strangulation as a result of getting his collar hooked on a fence. We all grieved because these K-9s became our partners, our friends, and part of our family.

When a police K-9 dies, the department or agency gives this police officer a funeral as well, either at the station or at a pet cemetery. All of the K-9 officers and their furry partners attend.

After working closely with a K-9, I experienced firsthand how crucial they are in the war against drugs and how special they are to those who have the privilege to work with them. They're courage is unmatched. Whereas man may hesitate in his or her actions when facing a bad guy, the K-9s don't think twice. They don't consider whether or not they'll get jammed up in legalities or whether they'll even lose their life. They have a mission to get bad guys off the street, and nothing is going to stop them in accomplishing that goal. They are the ultimate unsung heroes.

As a result, I can say with confidence that for those police dogs that made the ultimate sacrifice, there's a special place in heaven waiting for them.

CHAPTER 11

Heavenly Angels

W hen Jacob and I became members of the elite Felony Drug Interdiction Team, we agreed never to forget that first and foremost, we were troopers.

Our membership in the drug program didn't preclude us from working the normal duties associated with troopers assigned to a squad in a zone. For instance, if we came across any traffic accidents, and we were able to respond, we did so without hesitation.

One warm September day, we were in the vicinity of Homestead when a transmission came over our radio involving a school bus accident located south of Florida City. My heart jumped into my throat as I wondered if the children on that bus were okay.

Since Homestead bordered the south side of Florida City, we immediately notified the dispatcher that we were en route. We flipped on the lights and sirens and thankfully, the lightly populated area allowed us to put the pedal to the metal.

We sped on a long two-lane road lined by tomato fields as far as the eye could see. A crop duster worked in an adjacent field. A little further up, irrigation systems watered crops. As we drove deeper into this agricultural area, I smelled the combination of fertilizer and tomatoes.

When I arrived at the accident site, I saw two firemen kneeling over a crumpled little body in the road. The school bus was stopped about two hundred yards from it.

A blue late-model Buick was parked on the side of the road a few feet from the child. I saw the back of a woman wearing a prison guard uniform. She stood hunched over the car's hood, her elbows supporting the weight of her upper body, and her chin resting in her hands. Her short black hair acted as a privacy curtain, shielding her face from the world.

The school bus driver stood between the bus door and the edge of the road. She protectively wrapped her arms around another little boy.

I parked my car across the street to block any future traffic and hurried to the firefighters. When they saw me approaching them, one of them stood up and looked me in the eyes.

His face told me everything I needed to know. The inner corners of his eyebrows were pulled up. The corners of his mouth were turned down.

He shook his head. "The little guy's gone. No pulse or vital signs. He suffered from a traumatic head injury."

His sad eyes looked back down at the boy again for a moment and then back at me. "We're still going to transport him to the trauma unit, though."

I didn't know what to say, what not to say, so I said nothing. I just nodded my head up and down in agreement and took in a deep breath.

We all realized this child was deceased. We also knew that waiting with the body for the medical examiner to arrive could take hours, especially since we were so far south of Miami.

Jacob ran over to me. We stood next to each other and watched the firemen clear a field for the approaching life flight. I thought about how this little life had been cut short way too soon. I thought about the surviving family.

After the firemen loaded the little boy's body onto it, Jacob turned to me. "I talked with the school bus driver. The little boy she's holding is the victim's twin brother. The family lives on that dirt road over there." He pointed behind him with his thumb.

We trudged over to my car, and I got the yellow crime-scene tape out of my trunk. I began to secure the scene, including the blue Buick. Jacob took the correction officer over to his vehicle to take her statement.

I then walked over to the bus driver to get her statement. She used her head as a pointer as she nodded briefly at the child in her arms. "This child here said his brother told him he was going across the road to that field over there." She bent her head in the direction of the field. "He wanted to pick a tomato for his teacher. He must have seen my school bus coming because he ran toward it and darted right in front of that car over there." She bent her head in the direction of the Buick.

From a preliminary examination of the road and of the Buick, I felt the evidence was consistent with the child darting out into the path of the car. A traffic-homicide investigator would conduct an in-depth investigation once he arrived. Since he needed to travel from the station, he wouldn't be here for at least an hour.

Another bus was due to arrive in a few minutes. The bus driver and I strategized about how to move the children onto the other bus. I told her that more troopers were expected at any moment to divert traffic and to help move the children.

A loud wail and scream interrupted our conversation from the direction of the twins' road. I looked over and saw two women walking toward us. The groans came from the shorter, skinny one who looked to be in her mid to late twenties.

The bus driver said, "Oh, no. That one there, the one with the dark red hair, she's the boy's mother." This time, she pointed with her eyes, moving them in the direction of the two approaching women.

I immediately walked over to the mother and introduced myself. I looked into a pair of deep-set green eyes on a sunken-in face, all of which were obviously wet from crying. Thick strings of red hair looked as if she hadn't brushed it for awhile. Her threadbare, faded, and shapeless dress draped over her bony shoulders and hung loosely. Every bit of exposed skin on her skeletal frame was very white. She wore an old pair of unpolished cowboy boots that revealed years of neglect and scars.

She didn't speak. Only loud wails emitted from deep within her inner being. When she opened her mouth to cry, she didn't have any teeth.

I told her that her son had been airlifted to the Miami Children's Hospital. I offered to have a trooper drive her there if necessary.

Through her sobs and tears, she said, "My...my neigh...neighbor is try...trying to find my...my...husband. He...he got a job in the fields."

She was devastated. I held out my hands to the bus driver and motioned to her to give me the surviving twin. Her eyes looked into mine, and she gave a slow, hesitant nod as she released her hold on the child.

I took the little boy, paused, and then passed him onto his mother. "Here's your other son, ma'am."

She wrapped her arms around him tightly, and he threw his arms around her neck. She squeezed her eyes together, took a deep breath, and petted her son's head.

She looked up at me. "I gotta go back to my house. I need to get back to my other two kids. One of my neighbors is watching them for me right now."

I nodded. "Well, either my partner or I will check back to make sure you and your husband can get to the hospital."

She turned around and walked away holding her living son's hand. I didn't tell this grieving woman that her child was dead. I couldn't' because I hadn't received any official notification or authority.

But it didn't matter. She knew. From her mother's heart, she already knew her baby was gone.

I walked over to the Buick's driver. I said, "Excuse me, ma'am?"

She slowly pulled herself off of her hood and turned to face me, looking as if all color had been drained from her face. Her eyes were dry and held no expression. Her pallor and lack of emotion indicated to me that she was in a state of shock. She bent her shoulders forward and wrapped her arms around her waist.

After introducing myself, I asked, "Is that your friend or coworker over there?"

The woman's eyes quickly darted to the side of the road where a crowd of bystanders stood. "Yes," she whispered and looked down.

"Okay, well, you're free to go. The investigator will interview you in more detail later on. You may want to have the prison nurse check you out. In the meantime, the highway patrol will need to take possession of your vehicle until the investigation's complete."

She again spoke in a whisper. "I will never drive that car again."

At that time, I heard a loud and authoritative male voice behind me. "I don't care who you are. You cannot step across the tape!"

I turned around to see who spoke and to whom. A young trooper stood rigid on the inside of the "fence" of yellow tape. His right hand clenched the ribbon, and I realized he was the one who barked out the directive.

On the other side of the tape stood Miss Genevieve Chandler, the Florida City Elementary School Principal. She stood with her stout legs and feet apart in a firm and strong posture that let that trooper know she wasn't about to give in or be moved. She confirmed her intentions by having her hands on her hips and giving him a stern look by pushing her chin toward her chest and her eyebrows together over the ridge of her nose.

She wore a pair of matronly black shoes with a navy-blue cotton dress. The gray hair framing her weathered face made me think that Miss Chandler looked to be in her sixties.

With a scolding tone she said, "Young man, he is one of my children, and no one can keep me out."

I had mentioned to Jacob earlier that I needed to notify Miss Chandler that one of her students was a victim of this fatality. However, I had not yet had the chance to make that notification with all of the chaos and the many issues slamming into me simultaneously.

I sprinted full speed to the standoff. I needed to reach these two before the situation got out of hand. The trooper didn't know Miss Chandler, and things looked as if they may go downhill very quickly if I didn't intervene and intervene fast.

Before I go any further, let me introduce you to Miss Chandler. She grew up in the Florida City-Homestead community in a family of educators. My daughter's middle-school principal was Miss Chandler's brother.

Most of the local law enforcement officers in our area knew Miss Chandler. If she had a truant child, she went looking for that child. She didn't care if the child was black, Mexican, or white. She didn't think twice about marching into children's homes in the "hood," the labor camp, or an apartment complex and telling the parents she would take the child to school.

If a child needed clothes, shoes, food, or medical attention, Miss Chandler provided the need. She never had any biological children, but she had thousands of children who she considered to be hers. I always suspected she spent most of her salary on the needs of "her" children. She was a force to be reckoned with if someone stood in the way of her helping a child.

Everyone loved her. Her faculty adored her, and teachers vied for a position in her school which served one of the poorest populations in the county.

As I approached Miss Chandler, my eyes filled with tears. I couldn't keep up my tough image with her. She was just too motherly. I respected her more than any educator I have ever known.

I immediately said, "Miss Chandler, I'm so sorry. I wanted to go to the school and let you know what had happened, but I just became too busy with my responsibilities. This trooper is new to our area and didn't realize who you were." I then provided her with a full account of what had transpired, fighting hard to hold back the other tears which tried to fall.

Miss Chandler studied my face. She pursed her lips for a moment and then said, "I'll check on the family and take them to the hospital." She then patted my hand. "You know, this family just moved here. The dad lost his job in Texas, and they'll need our help with all of the arrangements. They're trying to get back on their feet."

Miss Chandler never failed to amaze me. She always knew the story of what was going on with each of "her" children and their families.

Over the next couple of days, I touched base a few times with Miss Chandler before the funeral. She took care of all of the funeral-home expenses. She purchased new clothes for the family to wear to the service. She even sent the mom to the hairdresser.

Jacob and I attended the funeral, which was outside our norm. We both felt compelled to say goodbye to this little first grader and to say some prayers for his family.

Since that tragedy, Miss Chandler has been summoned to heaven where she can be like a guardian angel for even more children. While on this earth, she was an inspiration and compassionate role model for so many people. She always championed for children.

On a positive note, I saw the surviving twin with his parents and siblings over a year later at the Homestead Rodeo. Dad worked a steady job. Mom showed a new smile with teeth. She looked lovely and like she had made peace with her devastating loss. Their darling children appeared happy. All in all, their lives seemed to be going better. Still I know they missed their angel.

More Angels

Jacob and I hadn't gotten over the emotional strain of the Florida City fatality when another school bus accident was thrust upon us. Midmorning about six weeks after the twin's death, we drove across the major East-West Expressway in Miami. Suddenly traffic came to a stop.

Since Jacob had been driving in front of me, I lost sight of his patrol car in the midst of all of the other vehicles. I heard him tell the dispatcher that he needed all available assistance. He was on the scene of a school-bus accident with multiple fatalities.

Within seconds, I arrived at the scene and jumped out of my car. I ran on the right side of the bus and saw the emergency door swung open and Jacob standing in the doorway.

He then began handing me screaming, crying children. Without saying a word, I accepted each one. When I tried to put the first child down onto the grassy area on the other side of the guardrail, she clung to me and wouldn't let go. I forced myself to loosen her grasp because I knew other children needed to be removed from the bus immediately.

Fortunately, other law enforcement, firefighters, and good Samaritans began arriving. They jumped in and helped me with the children as Jacob pushed them into my arms.

What had happened was one of those freak accidents. The bus had taken the children on a field trip. As they travelled eastbound on the expressway, a two-hundred-fifty-pound tire broke loose from a westbound truck. It rolled across the median and smashed through the school bus, killing two children and the school bus driver on impact. The fourth-grade teacher was in critical condition and later died of her injuries.

Finally, all of the surviving children were safely off the bus and on the side of the road. I cleaned them as best I could from the body matter and body fluids that had splattered onto their skin, hair, and clothes. These children had witnessed a horrific sight. I could only reassure them that they were now safe.

Complete strangers came over to offer baby wipes, towels soaked with bottled water, and anything else they had in their cars that could help. Other mothers walked from their cars to offer hugs and compassion to these little fourth graders. These people once again restored my faith in mankind.

A ring of children encircled me. I opened my arms to provide comfort. This was probably one of the few times in my career when I took on the role of a mother more so than that of a cop. These children needed assurance that they were going to be protected and not hurt.

We made the decision that all of the surviving children should be transported to Miami Children's Hospital by another bus. When it arrived, I explained that they needed to get on it so that they could see their parents at the hospital.

Most of the children began to wail and cry, tightening their grips on me. They were terrified to board another bus.

I agreed to ride the bus with them and sit up front where they could all see me. Many of the children still didn't want to get on that bus.

While I boarded it, I watched Jacob walk up to his patrol car and beat his fists on the hood. I think he dented it. I knew he felt ready to explode.

The school and media notified the children's parents to respond to the hospital's training room. During the forty-five-minute ride across town to Miami Children's Hospital, I came to a jolting realization. At the end of this reunion, two set of parents would be desperately looking for their children. Sadly, the reunion would not, could not take place for them.

Many of the children were too traumatized to provide their personal information to the authorities. They simply cried for mommy and daddy. Another trooper drove to the school and picked up the field trip roster and the principal and brought both to the hospital. This tragic event caused school policies and procedures to change nationwide. Each child was required to wear visible identification when participating in field trips.

Other troopers had gone ahead of us to the children's hospital to set up one of its large training rooms to be used for reuniting the parents with the surviving children. They also arranged to have some counselors and psychologists available to talk to the families.

Jacob drove to Jackson Memorial Hospital located across the street from the medical examiner's office. He helped to obtain a conference room for the parents who would need to identify their deceased children.

After a few hours at the children's hospital, my fears came to fruition. Two sets of parents could not reunite with their children, hug them, and take them home.

A trooper had driven my car to the hospital, so I opted to take those four parents to Jackson to identify their children. Upon leaving, I was so upset that I hit a pole that prohibited traffic from entering the parking lot. It put a slight dent in the rear fender of my car. I didn't give a damn. I just continued on with my mission.

This felt like the longest drive I had ever made. I could barely function. I felt numb and depleted by the day's events, and the constant surge of emotions drained me mentally.

Eventually, those parents and I made it to Jackson Memorial and walked to the conference room, which seemed like the longest walk I had ever made. No one ever wants to lose a child, but the reality that their children were the ones who didn't make it was beyond disappointing; it was devastating and traumatic.

Once inside the room, the two fathers consoled the two mothers despite the fact that they grieved as well. So the FHP staff, grief counselors, representatives from the M.E.'s office, and me huddled around the four parents to console all of them.

I stressed that they needed to give us an accurate description of what their children wore to school that morning. The accident had created so much disfigurement that I knew facial recognition would be difficult, if not impossible.

A brother-in-law, who happened to be a Miami police officer, was the only other family there. He relieved one of the fathers of his duty at the last minute. He volunteered to identify his nephew. The other father identified his child.

Afterward, I drove home exhausted. I felt guilty for being so tired because after all, I still had my girls. All I wanted to do was take my children into my arms and hug them tight.

A few days later, Jacob and I received an invitation to attend a "psychological" debriefing about the school bus accident with the City of Miami Fire Department. When Jacob told me he wanted to go, I was impressed. I also wanted to go because I had been experiencing some sleep deprivation.

I had never attended a debriefing such as this. I wasn't sure what to expect. After all, the cops' good-ole-boy-method for dealing with trauma was either suck it up or drink it up, meaning drink ourselves into oblivion.

With this debriefing, though, we sat in a circle with about twenty firefighters and mental health professionals. One of the firefighters spoke first, expressing his grief, and then Jacob spoke about his feelings. I initially felt hesitant to share, but eventually I did and felt better just talking about the horrible crash. It turned out to be a good experience for both of us.

I always wondered why firefighters seemed to be more on top of mental-health issues than cops. Now I know.

However, we may never understand why God allowed this tragedy. But I did know that as I closed this chapter in my life, we all had a few more angels in heaven.

CHAPTER 12

Hurricane Andrew's Colossal Blowout

Nothing stood out as different from any other hot and humid August day in Miami.

I followed my Saturday routine, leaving my house about six in the morning to drive north to Miami to teach my eight-hour class at the Safety Council. Along the way, I listened to the morning news. The reporter mentioned a tropical storm that had formed in the Atlantic Ocean. Tropical storms are common in Miami during hurricane season, so I didn't give it much thought.

Once I arrived at the council, my mind and time focused entirely on classroom preparations and teaching. I didn't even go out for lunch but instead ate the peanut-butter-and-honey sandwich I had brought with me.

At a little past five that evening, I started my drive home. I looked forward to winding down and enjoying a nice dinner with my husband and oldest daughter Kally. My youngest daughter Mary Ellen was away at college in North Florida.

I listened to the car radio and heard that the tropical storm had now been upgraded to a hurricane and that Miami might fall in its path. They projected its arrival in the early hours of Monday morning, a mere day and a half away. Now

I was getting concerned. How did this hurricane come out of nowhere? Was it even possible? So far, 1992 had seen no real storms.

After parking in my driveway, I rushed inside my house. My husband was sitting on the couch and talking on the telephone. He looked up, his eyes focusing on me, but I got the feeling his mind was elsewhere.

After hanging up, he stood, and this time I felt his mind was on me. "I just got off the phone from South Miami Police Department. There's a possible hurricane coming. We need to get our house ready in case it hits." He immediately proceeded to name several things we needed to do to start our emergency storm preparations.

I nodded and then mentally added a few extra tasks to the list. We then left to gas up our cars, buy food and supplies at the grocery store, and pull cash from the ATM.

The following morning, I knew I needed to act quickly. My husband had to leave to go to his police station. He'd be too busy reorganizing shifts for extra police coverage and everything else that could and would crop up as a result of an emergency situation. His police department kept calling him, which kept him from helping me further with our home preparations.

Since we lived in a one-story concrete-block home above sea level and several miles from the ocean, I wanted to believe that we'd be okay. Furthermore, I told myself that our Bahama awnings and steel storm shutters would provide extra protection for our windows. Still I couldn't help feeling a bit concerned about what could happen if we experienced a direct hit from a hurricane.

I went through the motions necessary to protect my property, just in case this hurricane did come our way. Since I wasn't scheduled to work until Monday morning, I was grateful that I could also put more preparations in place on Sunday.

Saturday's late-night news didn't really worry me. The meteorologists spent much of the airtime giving warnings about the dangers of not taking shelter. I think that in the beginning I watched the news more out of curiosity and with a slight just-in-case perspective. As the night wore on, though, reality started setting in as I saw the path of the hurricane heading toward us. I began to realize the severity of what was happening.

I watched the weather forecast early Sunday morning, and things were not getting any better. In fact, they appeared to be worsening. Since Kally was now living at home after serving in the Air Force in England, she offered to pitch in to help with the preparations. Fortunately, she also had the day off from her job as dispatcher for the Florida Highway Patrol.

My husband left and went to his police department. Before leaving, he helped me secure the two rear sliding-glass doors and the shutters on the windows.

My swimming pool was full of water, so I threw my patio furniture into it so that it would sink to the bottom. I thought that was better than tying it to trees. I also stacked our potted plants behind my personal car that I had parked in the garage. In preparing for a hurricane, one of the most critical needs is to ensure all of the outdoor furniture, potted plants, and any other items don't become flying missiles.

Surprisingly, no breeze blew to cool down the intense heat. I wondered how that could happen with an approaching hurricane.

I filled my bathtub, just in case we ran out of drinking water. Then I drove to my mother's house. She and I took her belongings and either tied them up, covered them up, or placed them into safe places to protect them from potential loss.

Mom had a yellow tabby cat, which I put into his carrier. She packed up her car to follow me home and spend the night.

Before we left, she remembered the feral cat she had been feeding for months. I went outside and spent an hour with cat food coaching that kitty into Mom's house. I finally got it into her bathroom and left food and water for it before closing the door and leaving the condo.

Jacob called and said he was on the way to my house with some of his personal items plus his dogs Sandy and Sniffer. He had moved out of his apartment a few months earlier and purchased a trailer. We both knew it wouldn't hold up during a hurricane.

My husband called from South Miami. He suggested I make arrangements to leave our home and go to a safer area.

I said, "I'm not worried. We're just going to stay put. The rising water shouldn't affect us. We're too far from the ocean, and our house sits too high above sea level."

Then the highway patrol station called and said, "Remain in radio contact for the duration of the storm. Furthermore, all troopers must stay in their homes or seek safe shelter. You're considered on duty during the storm. Be prepared to respond to any hazard or community need as soon as conditions clear."

Basically, we were *technically* considered on duty; however, they knew responding during a hurricane was too dangerous. This is why they inform the public that if they're on the roads in a flooded area, first responders can't do anything until after the storm has passed and it's safe.

In the meantime, my house was full. Jacob, Mom, Kally, one cat, three dogs, which included my Rottweiler Rex, and I all braced ourselves for the impending storm.

As Sunday night progressed, we heard a lot of howling wind with squalls of rain. We slept some and monitored the weather either with visual checks or by watching television for the latest updates.

By one-o'clock Monday morning, weather conditions took a drastic turn. The wind started hitting the rear of my house. I occasionally opened the front door and peered through the opening but didn't dare venture outside because of the danger of flying objects. Some of my trees were bent, and others had actually snapped in two like twigs.

The whipping winds sounded louder and louder with each passing minute. The dogs howled in distress. My ears felt pressure and popped a few times. The atmosphere became eerie and nerve-racking. Soon the lights flickered, and we lost power.

Jacob and I listened to our highway patrol radios. One of our fellow troopers trying to get home told the dispatcher that a tree fell on his car while driving in the Kendall area. He said, "I lost control of my car, and I think my shoulder may be dislocated."

The dispatcher said, "Stay put in your car and wait it out until the eye of the storm passes. I'll try to get another trooper to respond to assist you."

A female trooper who lived about five miles from my house yelled, "The front of my house is wide open because the frame fell in one piece to the ground. It sucked my cat out. I'm huddled in a closet with my dog. I've blocked my closet door from the inside."

I began to feel panicked.

Then the weather conditions got uncannily quiet. I knew the eye of the storm was in the process of passing over my home. Jacob and I took advantage of the stillness and walked in my front yard.

We then walked to my garage on the side of my house. Before the storm, we had parked our two patrol cars in front of my garage door and the four other cars next to them, forming a row that extended into my yard. We examined them and noticed some dings and scuffs, probably from broken tree branches that flew through the air.

Jacob and I discussed taking one of our patrol cars to assist the trooper in the closet, but the wind suddenly increased. We decided that trying to drive to her house would be too dangerous. We went back into my house again to seek shelter from the hurricane.

Within a few moments, the storm seemed to have resurrected, attacking our home with a vengeance. Now that the eye had passed, the howling became almost deafening and much more intense than initially.

The entire backside of my house vibrated as the wind began hitting it again. We heard loud noises banging on the metal that protected the sliders and windows.

All of a sudden I noticed water leaking from where the ceiling and walls met. Then I saw one of the strangest sights. My beautiful brass candelabra hung upside-down from the ceiling. This lovely fixture now looked like a fountain as water shot through it. The water cascaded onto my dining-room table and soaked my carpet.

An odd thought came to me. My slight compulsiveness with housekeeping caused me to vacuum my entire house late Sunday night. In an attempt to prepare for the possibility that we might not have electricity for a few days, I wanted to make sure my carpets were clean. Now the standing water ruined my carpets.

I thought, *I wasted so much time cleaning my house.*

Suddenly, a big groan came from my living room. It wasn't a human groan; instead, the groan erupted from my house as if verbalizing its pain. Then plop, my living room ceiling gave way.

At the same time, my telephone in the kitchen rang. My husband called to check on us.

I said, "We just lost the living room ceiling!"

"We what? What do you mean?"

Then I heard the same moaning noise come from the area that contained my new dining-room fountain. I yelled to everyone to go into the hallway. My mom ran for cover followed by Jacob and all of the dogs.

Then the dining room ceiling gave way.

My husband heard all of this commotion. I said to him, "We're losing all of the ceilings. I've got to get to the hallway." I could tell he didn't grasp how quick this was transpiring. "Call me back later."

As I ran from the kitchen into the hallway, all of the other ceilings in the house dropped. The hallway and bathrooms withstood the winds because the small areas allowed more support from the influx of water, and they didn't have enough of a ceiling to cave in.

Both Mom and Jacob were bleeding from some of the heavy drywall that had hit them. Fortunately, the wounds were scrapes and minor cuts.

We all sat down in the hallway with our arms covering our heads. After a few moments, I took a peek at the other rooms. I needed to assess our potential danger and see if we still had our roof. Fear grabbed me when I looked up and saw its condition. The plywood's edges lifted with the wind gusts. I knew if we lost one piece of plywood we would lose the rest of the house. Once the wind enters a building, the inner framework is at risk of collapsing.

I made a quick evaluation of the rest of the house, taking a flashlight to check on all of the windows and doors. I noticed my mom's tabby cat had somehow made his way to the top shelf of Kally's bedroom closest. I closed its door to ensure the cat would stay out of harm's way.

During my evaluation, I realized my bathroom window had shattered, leaving a wide-open space that had once held glass. Why didn't the steel awning protect it? I closed the bathroom door to prevent anymore wind blowing into my bedroom.

I made my way back to the hallway. Jacob had gathered pillows and comforters off of the beds to further protect our heads and bodies.

The dogs had stopped howling. I guess they figured it didn't help. I glanced over at them standing in the hallway. All three sat visibly trembling.

The fact that my extremely aggressive dog Rex sat next to Sniffer was a strange sight indeed. Rex hated Sniffer. Somehow, though, my dog knew that now was not the time or place to address differences and exhibit disdain. Animals seem to have a sixth sense about dangers related to severe weather.

Another female trooper came over the radio. She reported that she had been hit by a two-by-four board that had entered her home through a window.

She said, "Please send help as soon as possible. I think my shoulder's broke."

Each thrust of debris crashing into metal on the side of my house created an unbearable banging noise. I covered my ears, praying for an end to this nightmare. We should have left, and now because we didn't, my decision to stay might cost us our lives. At the very least, I should have had the foresight to send my daughter and mother to a safer location.

I kept pleading out loud, "Please God, let this end." My prayer wasn't because I feared death; I was at peace with God and my relationship with him.

However, the anguish of the loud noises, the shaking of the house, my concern for my mother and daughter, and the unknown were exceptionally overbearing.

About the time I felt my house wouldn't sustain another wind gust or object thrust into it, the wind began to dwindle. Rain poured into my home and into those areas where the ceilings had collapsed.

Interesting enough, we still had phone service, and so my telephone rang. I picked it up and heard my husband's voice on the other end.

"Floy, is everyone okay?"

"Yes. We survived. Our home is in shambles, but we're alive." Praise God!

A few minutes later, the howling winds finally stopped completely, and I knew the storm had ended. Daylight timidly seeped into my small hallway, revealing that a new day had arrived. I glanced down at my watch and let out a big sigh of relief. At around six forty-five on August 24, 1992, I realized that we had endured and survived an incredibly powerful hurricane. It was probably better that while going through it, we didn't know just how monstrous it was.

Around seven thirty that morning, Jacob and I knew we needed to get out and onto the street immediately. We learned a few more details from our FHP radios. The center of the storm hit Homestead and north of Kendall Drive. Miami seemed to have fared better. Although it had experienced its share of devastation and had lost power, its buildings were still intact.

Kally stayed behind with my mom. We discussed that she should pack up any of her personal items that were dry and salvageable. Once the roads cleared enough, she and my mom needed to drive to my in-laws house in Miami.

Jacob and I left and took Sniffer with us. My car's back window had been blown out, so we all three climbed into Jacob's car.

We found ourselves encountering road hazards and situations that caused us to be very jittery and nervous as first responders. Just in my neighborhood alone, we saw downed wires everywhere. Although we knew the electricity was out, we felt apprehensive about crossing any of these wires.

I felt like we were driving in a war zone and that a slew of mortars had exploded throughout the entire area. My heart rose in my throat when I saw the extent of the damage. I thought I was going to be sick. I couldn't believe that what took years to build was destroyed in a matter of a few hours.

Some houses were obliterated. Those that remained had windows blown out, leaving large gaping holes and no roof. People walked around dazed and in shock.

We made our way to U.S. 1 in Naranja. A car approached us. The driver lowered his window and yelled out to us that he needed help.

We pulled over to the side of the road. The driver exited his vehicle and ran over to us crying. "My dad's in the passenger seat. He was hurt real bad by a roof beam that fell on top of him."

I opened the passenger's door. A dead man sat upright. The seatbelt and shoulder harness kept his body erect, but his head bent to the side and leaned against the door frame. I saw a large gash on his head, which I assumed was the fatal wound.

Jacob walked up behind me. I turned to him and said, "There's nothing we can do."

Jacob didn't respond. He looked over at the deceased man and then stepped back so that I could go over to the son.

"Sir," I said, "I'm sorry, but you're father didn't make it. He's gone. We'll cover him with a yellow blanket. When the roads are clear, you'll need to drive him to the hospital. They'll do an official pronouncement over him there."

The feeling of helplessness overwhelmed me, helpless about the young man's father and helpless about all of the devastation. I tried to comprehend that we hadn't even begun the required confrontation with the aftermath of Andrew. We had just experienced Mother Nature's unforgiving power to nth degree, and it was much too late to make amends.

We got back in our car and drove a little further north. Jacob spotted a MDPD patrol car and drove over to their unit to consult with them.

The two female officers were both friends of mine. One lived in my neighborhood.

They told us that they drove their patrol car inside the Cutler Ridge Mall. The building began to crumble as the hurricane progressed. They left to seek shelter in a concrete car wash a block away.

They spent the hurricane on the floorboard of their patrol vehicle and felt it lifting off the concrete with the wind gusts. One of them asked, "What does our neighborhood look like?'

A tear escaped my eye. "It got hit really hard," I said, almost choking on the last word.

Both had their eyes staring wide as they tried to process the news. The other officer said, "We need to go and check on our families, especially before we start getting calls. By the way, some of the radio towers were blown down, so the police have lost their radio signals." They then drove away.

The MDPD was on a different system than the FHP. Fortunately, we still had radio signals.

About that time, a trooper new to Miami pulled up behind us. He told us that he had spent the hurricane in his bathtub as his trailer exploded. We would hear many similar stories for a long time to come.

A lot of troopers assigned to the inside of the station during the storm asked Jacob and me to check on their families. Other troopers rescued our injured colleagues and came over the radio to report their dispositions.

Remember the female trooper who had broken her shoulder? She was married to a civilian who was very intellectual and not an action-kind-of guy. We heard that her male partner burst into her home, rushed past her husband, and said over his shoulder, "You take care of the kids. I'm taking her to the hospital." He then loaded her into his car and drove off.

This story didn't surprise me. A strong connection develops between law enforcement officers. They bond through working together on a daily basis and facing life-and-death situations. They count on their partners to literally watch their back.

We tried to respond to the requests to check on families, but we couldn't find a lot of the local landmarks. I had patrolled the south area of Dade County for years, but I suddenly felt lost. Street signs were gone, business signs were missing, and we saw nothing but devastation after devastation.

I desperately wanted a cup of coffee. The rain made me cold and caused shivers to run through my body and rattle my teeth. At the time, though, drinking a cup of coffee seemed to be a luxury, one I had previously taken for granted.

My mind tried to process the wreckage, but then surrealism took over, if only temporarily. All of the destruction made me feel like I had been suddenly thrust into a new environment, not my hometown.

We continued to come across more houses without roofs. All of the power lines were down. Most of the trees, all of the road signs, and the traffic lights were scattered on the ground like a game of Pick Up Stix, except this wasn't a game. Ripped-up fences left backyards open to anyone who cared to trample through them. Trailer homes were blown into other structures or blown away altogether, while damaged cars added to the numerous piles of rubble.

Jacob and I drove to the trooper's house that had lost its front. It looked like an oversized doll house. Both she and her dog suffered a few scrapes, and I could tell that she was traumatized and understandably so. As for her missing cat, it had reappeared unscathed.

We got back on the road and resumed our first-responder duties. I saw a battered pickup truck with what looked like a SWAT team in its bed. We stopped, and I spoke with all of the officers.

A lot of their patrol cars were so damaged that they couldn't be driven. So they decided to use one of the officer's personally owned vehicle, or as we say in cop language, a POV.

We later drove south on U.S. 1 in Homestead to the large discount store. Patrol cars from Key West's Monroe County Sheriff's Office lined the streets. Evidently, deputies had driven up here to provide assistance. On one hand, we were shocked to see them guarding the stores with semi-automatic rifles strapped across their chests. On the other, we felt so pleased to see that police officers from the south came to help us quell the looting. Some of these folks looked for food and drinks, but many stole out of greed.

We continued on our self-assigned task, driving further south on the highway. The aroma of cooking hamburgers found its way to my nostrils and tickled my olfactory nerves, reminding me that I hadn't eaten all day. I looked down at my watch and realized that I had worked through breakfast and lunch without a morsel of food, and dinnertime wasn't too far away.

I saw golden arches ahead and wondered if McDonalds was open for business. As we got closer, I saw several men standing in its parking lot grilling hamburgers. We pulled over to talk to them and learned that they were also cops from the Keys and had the foresight to bring grills with them to feed a bunch of hungry officers. That McDonalds restaurant had turned their store over to them, knowing that the contents would be spoiled if not consumed. Leave it to cops to always find something to eat. They took the food from the restaurant's freezer and grilled them. They handed Jacob and I some burgers. When I bit into one of them, I was so hungry I thought those were the best burgers I had ever eaten.

This McDonalds turned out to be a new kind of Micky Ds, served up with an outdoor flavor. It became an overnight landmark for police officers who would be responding from other areas in Florida and subsequently other states.

We still needed to get to Jacob's trailer to see what he had left. When we were less than a mile away, two tires on his patrol car went flat at the same time. I could tell he was anxious to see if he could salvage anything, so he just kept going, driving on the rims. We were both just too dazed to care.

I thought about my own home, remembering the destruction I saw before leaving. It seemed to be more than I could fathom, and I just couldn't wrap my head around what I would need to do to have a normal life again. At that moment I had no idea what I faced with my house, but I needed to get back to it so that I could analyze the damage.

I saw a group of men with power saws clearing the road by cutting tree limbs and trunks. Their convoy was pointed in the direction of my house, which was about seven miles away and basically a straight shot from where we were.

When Jacob got to his gravel road, I said, "Jacob, I'm going to see if I can get a ride with these guys to take me back to my house. I need to see what I can do there. I'll come back and get you later."

"Okay. Wait til the morning, though. I'm going to grab whatever food I have left in my trailer. I'll just sleep in my patrol car. Sniffer's set, though. He's got enough food and water here."

I got out of Jacob's car and walked over to the men. "Hey, would you mind giving me a ride? I need to get home to check on my dog and my house."

"Sure," a few of the guys yelled out. "Jump in the back of that truck up there."

Any other time, a cop standing in the bed of a civilian pickup truck while wearing a black tactical uniform would have been a strange sight. However, I think the norm and status quo for most situations got blown away by Hurricane Andrew.

The convoy wasn't quick, but I knew I would make it back to my house before eight, which means I'd still have some daylight to evaluate the damage.

When I finally got home, dusk had fallen.

For the first time, I really looked at the outside of my house. A profound grief came from deep within, and I had to bend forward to rest my hands on my knees so that I could catch my breath.

My home, my beautiful refuge that I had worked so hard to maintain was in ruins. I reminded myself that my family and friends had survived, and that was most important. I reminded myself that I was alive. Undoubtedly, reconstruction would be tremendous, time-consuming, and life-changing not just for my family but for the whole community.

I walked to where the front door still stood. Kally had posted a note telling me that she had taken Rex to Miami with her. I walked around my house and got the complete picture of what had happened to my bathroom window. My next-door neighbor's roof had ripped off their house and smashed against the entire side of mine. As it slid down my walls, it took the awning with it. I shuddered to think of the consequences if their roof had actually landed on top of my house. It could have injured or killed all of us.

The shingles from my roof and other roofs nearby were strewn across my yard. The trees were stripped bare of any leaves.

The sunlight was disappearing, and I knew I was on my own for the night. I thought about where I would sleep.

I went into my house to look for some dry clothes. The ceilings now lay on the floors, and big puffs of wet insulation were dispersed from wall to wall. Water covered everything and filled every crevice. I forced myself to walk across my soaked carpet. Despair replaced grief, and I had difficulty focusing on how I would, how I could accomplish everything I needed to do for my personal life.

I opened my closet door and saw some clothes. After grabbing a pair of jeans and a highway patrol t-shirt, I was glad to learn they were only damp. I figured the hot temperature would dry them.

My next step was to go into my bathroom to see if I had any hot water. To my amazement, warm water still came out of my faucets, so I took a shower. I then found a decorative yet dry Christmas pillow high up on a shelf in the hall closet. These findings may seem small, but at the time, they were huge victories and gave me some comfort.

I needed to push aside my feelings and get some sleep. As a first responder, I needed to be alert. Plus, I couldn't do anything for my house tonight anyway.

I went to my patrol car to get some rest. I didn't care that the storm had blown out its back window. The front seat was dry, and I periodically ran the air conditioner and watched the news on a small battery-operated television on the dashboard.

I felt dazed as I stared at the footage of the monstrous ruins that continued for miles. Andrew turned out to be a category-five hurricane that slammed into my hometown of Homestead, Florida. It broke all of the wind gauges once its winds registered at one hundred sixty miles per hour. Twenty-six people died as a result of this storm.

Tomorrow would be another busy day. After eating a power bar and drinking some warm Gatorade, I fell asleep across the front seat.

The following morning I woke early and realized I needed to drive to Jacob's trailer so that we could figure out how to get him some new tires. Evidently with all of the debris littering the roadways, emergency responders were going through tires like crazy. Since the roads were now clearer, the trip to the county substation wasn't as challenging as compared to what it could have been like the previous day.

After picking up Jacob's tires, I drove my patrol car with its blown-out rear window to his trailer, well, to where his trailer used to be. Just as we expected, it was gone, just gone someplace into the Everglades. He had been unable find many of his personal items.

Sarge notified us via our radios that starting tomorrow, our shift hours would be changed to three in the afternoon to three in the morning. I didn't like it, but no one asked my opinion. The other shift would work from three in the morning to three in the afternoon. The highway patrol felt this type of "alpha-bravo" schedule gave all troopers daylight hours to take care of their homes or locate another place to live.

The next morning I drove to my mother's condominium and saw that her doors were all blown open. Some of her furniture had been pushed outside with the strong winds. Mom wouldn't return to her home for over a year. The bathroom door was still closed, though, and the feral cat inside weathered the storm quite well.

After I left my mom's condo, I drove back to my house. I still hadn't seen my husband, but we did talk thanks to the faithful phone in my kitchen that still worked. We kept our conversations limited to mostly business, such as the damages incurred, where we would sleep, and how to safeguard our house while I worked.

I couldn't do much other than take valuables small enough to go into my car's trunk. The armed vigilantes who walked through my neighborhood day and night honestly gave me some comfort. Desperate times called for desperate actions.

That afternoon, Jacob and I worked our first twelve-hour shift. They actually turned into fourteen hours by the time we could leave and go home.

Some of our diverse duties during the daylight hours included directing traffic or assisting with water and food distribution. But working during the night proved to be wild. When the dark enveloped the area, our assignments shifted drastically. Calls poured in about armed predators prowling businesses, looking for opportunities to rob and steal.

More than once, we hit the ground and took cover because of the gunshots that seemed to come out of nowhere. We could only assume the looters came armed for success in their shameless crimes of greed. However with no streetlights and the heavy cloud coverage, knowing where these rounds were coming from or going to was almost impossible.

A few days later, the cavalry in the form of the National Guard arrived as well as more cops from all over Florida and other states. We all held onto our mission to serve and protect, even in the face of our own adversity, but having a few more on our team surely did help.

I came across folks without a dry place to sleep. They didn't have any food or anything to drink and needed medical assistance. I shared whatever water Jacob and I could spare. We also radioed to the Emergency Operation Center their locations and their situations. Unfortunately for the first few days after the hurricane, the response was too overwhelming for them to get immediate help.

Friday morning, I drove my friend Linda to her medical practice so that she could get samples of baby formula. We took them to the migrant labor camp. As we got close, I could have sworn I saw monkeys frolicking on dead power lines. I wondered if I had lost my mind.

I later found out that I was quite sane. Actually, they were primates from a medical research laboratory nearby. Over two thousand had escaped during the storm. Unfortunately, a rumor circulated that the monkeys were infected with the AIDS virus. Some misinformed citizens shot more than two hundred of them.

While some folks were lawless, others helped and shared with those less fortunate. For the first time ever, neighbors in many of Miami's suburban communities got to know each other. Strange how it took a catastrophe to get this to happen.

Several days after the hurricane, South Florida was nowhere near to getting things back to normal; however, situations were not as volatile as they had been during the first few days. Once the additional troops arrived to help out, Jacob and I joined members of the K-9 team on the Turnpike. Traffic was too heavy to meet at the stationhouse, so Sarge had us park on the highway turnaround median so that he could brief us.

I faced oncoming traffic and saw a familiar car. I blinked, thinking how much it looked like my husband's unmarked police vehicle.

That car then pulled over to the side of the road near us. I saw my husband get out and walk quickly toward me. I now blinked to hold back the tears as a flood of emotions overcame me. For the first time in days, I saw my husband. We both had been busy working in the aftermath of the hurricane, and our home phone had quit working. As a result, we hadn't had a chance to speak to each other either.

Finally, he had been able to leave his police department and was driving home. He just happened to pass us on the busy Miami roadways.

We hugged each other, and I abandoned my resolve not to cry. The tears poured unashamedly as if all of the devastation from the past several days had come to a head and erupted. At the moment, I didn't care that I didn't look like a tough cop. Although I felt comfort from being in his arms, I felt sad for what he would see when he arrived home. He'd realize that our house and possessions were now trash.

For now, I allowed myself to grieve. I grieved for my losses and the losses of a whole city. I grieved for what used to be.

Our lives were completely changed now, and it was as if the hurricane not only created some of the change, but it confirmed what had been brewing beforehand in my marriage. We both worked demanding jobs, which in turn became even more demanding as a result of the storm. We were forced to put the rebuilding of our lives on hold while we worked long hours to help rebuild a city. I feared that our already untenable marriage wouldn't be able to cope with all of the additional stress.

As my husband continued to hold me, I grasped his shirt feeling as I was grasping the last threads of us. I think I knew in the back of my mind that my marriage had shifted along with the winds. We may have survived a category-five hurricane, but we might not survive as a couple.

About a week after the hurricane, my friends Betty and Jeanne from the Safety Council called my husband at work. They knew we lived in Homestead and that our community had been destroyed. They asked him if we wanted to stay in the vacation home they shared in Key Largo while our house got rebuilt.

We jumped on their offer and ended up staying in their home for the next few months. I truly appreciated them and their benevolence. Best of all, their house had electricity because the whole time we lived in Key Largo, Homestead didn't have any.

My daughter Mary Ellen called me from college in Tallahassee. She and a group of friends from Homestead wanted to drive home and help us.

I wanted to see her so much, but we weren't in Homestead, which is where she wanted to stay. Plus, I knew I would be constantly working. I suggested they all wait until Thanksgiving to come home.

The National Guard erected hundreds of army tents to provide housing for people to live. They came complete with food kitchens, medical services, and free shopping for hygiene products like soap and deodorant. I knew a few families who lived in one of the tent cities erected on U.S. 1 at Harris Field in Homestead, so I frequently stopped to check on them while at work.

Jacob and I ended up eating all of our meals together at the MDPD substation, Homestead Police Station, or the outdoor Micky Ds. At both of the police stations, large tents with tables and chairs had been set up in the parking lots. Three meals a day were served. Most of the time, we ate with the Miami FDLE agents who we had worked with on narcotic cases. However, if I missed the mealtimes at the police stations or wanted a special treat, I stopped at my friend Linda's house and opened a can of ravioli.

A host of dignitaries and celebrities arrived daily. As troopers, we were assigned details to drive them through the area. I escorted tennis star Chris Evert.

Not long after we moved to Key Largo, troopers from North Florida rotated to all of the severely damaged troopers' homes to make repairs. They arrived at my house early one morning and emptied the house of all of the wet carpet and furnishings. They also set up two generators. One provided electricity for the cleanup inside my house, and they used another small generator to clean the debris out of my yard and pool.

My brother–in–law, an emergency room doctor, came all the way from Virginia to help. He put tar paper on my roof. After he finished, he volunteered at the Homestead Hospital triage center. I knew his first patient, a police officer who had fallen off his roof and acquired a compound fracture in his leg.

The National Guard took over a lot of our traffic duties, and they manned the curfew checkpoints set in place to protect unsecured areas from looting as well as other crimes. An older-model car driven by a male passed through the checkpoint one evening. When a National Guard member peered into the car, he saw a kilo of cocaine on his front seat.

The member called Jacob and me over to assist with this situation. We were pleased to have a kilo handed to us on a silver platter, well, so to speak.

CHAPTER 13

My Final Trooper Days

A lthough it had been several months since Hurricane Andrew barreled through South Florida, the devastation it created continued to haunt us as we slowly rebuilt our community. With each day, though, hope grew as the city saw the progress being made on its behalf.

Life went on, and before we knew it, 1993 had arrived. Unfortunately, the drug trade went on as well, and even Hurricane Andrew couldn't slow down its progress.

No one knew this better than those of us in law enforcement. That spring, the Miami FBI called Jacob and me. They needed uniform police to help them with a controlled delivery of three hundred thirty-five kilos of cocaine in South Miami. A controlled delivery is the term used when the police have already confiscated drugs from a seller, and the intended purchasers are identified. In this situation, the deal had already been finalized. All that remained was for the undercover agent to deliver the coke, and the buyers to turn over the money to the UC.

We all drove to the planned location of where the transaction was to take place. As I sat waiting in my marked patrol car, I looked at the overcast skies where some parts were dark gray and the remaining was just black. I could tell that a simple spring shower wasn't coming our way; we were in for a downpour. Hopefully we could wrap up this deal before the rain started. I preferred not getting wet in the process.

The UC met with the buyers, but I couldn't see what transpired from my vantage point. We waited, our anxiety levels a bit higher during these times, and prayed the deal would go down smoothly.

The FBI surveillance agent notified us via radio once the transaction took place with the exchange. We followed the buyers' van for about a half mile before pulling them over and conducting a felony stop.

When we ordered them out of the van, they complied. In fact, they looked shock. Their faces seemed to have lost all color. I thought their eyeballs were going to pop out of their sockets. One of the dopers said, "Oh my, god. I can't believe this is happening."

Thankfully, the buyers weren't armed. Jacob and I then arrested them without any incident.

An agent and I drove the two buyers to the FBI office while another agent drove the van. Once there, they placed the coke into evidence.

The buyers didn't offer any information and refused to cooperate during the interrogation. Instead, they wanted their attorneys. They were then booked into the federal system.

Although Jacob and I both loved the action of these cases, they kept us on edge. They had proven themselves dangerous over and over again. We always kept in mind that a lot of police officers got shot while working these types of drug deals. Knowing the risks kept us on our toes.

Don't Fly Away, Yellow Bird!

During the summer of 1993, I finally submitted my application to the FDLE for the position of special agent, my dream job. I had just completed all of my required credits for my bachelor's degree at Barry University.

The timing couldn't have been better because a special agent position happened to be open in Miami, so the process went quickly, well, quickly for such a job as this. Over the next couple of months, I underwent physical and psychological testing, a background check, and attended an oral board.

I felt confident that I would be chosen for the position, but one never knows until it actually happens. So I continued to move forward with my career with the Florida Highway Patrol.

While sitting in heavy traffic on U.S. 1 in Cutler Ridge and thinking about the FDLE application process, I observed a dark-skinned slim man wearing a yellow shirt and yellow shorts running across the busy highway. If that sight wasn't odd enough, the fact that he carried a money bag and a gun set off all kinds of alarms.

Another trooper, Ray Valdez, was in his car ahead of me. He jumped out and began to chase the man on foot.

"Yellow bird" had a good head start on Ray, so I wheeled my car out of my lane. I hit my siren and emergency lights to stop oncoming traffic, sped across the southbound lane, and pulled onto the next parallel road. I advised the dispatcher that Ray and I were chasing someone who I suspected to be an armed bank robber.

I spotted Yellow Bird running south. He had discarded the yellow shirt but still wore the yellow shorts. Sometimes perps will try to get law enforcement off track by removing clothing they know is part of the original description. However in his case, getting rid of that shirt didn't distract our attention away from him at all because he still wore those yellow shorts. They became a flashing neon light as far as we were concerned.

I drove ahead of him and parked. I immediately jumped out of my car, drew my gun, aimed it, and yelled at the top of my lungs, "Stop! Police!"

Yellow Bird took one look at me and obeyed. I ran over and handcuffed him.

A few minutes later, Ray recovered the money bag containing five hundred fifty-one dollars, a firearm, and the yellow shirt that Yellow Bird tossed during the foot pursuit.

Just as Ray and I had surmised, he had just robbed the bank across from where we were stopped in traffic. We arrested him for armed robbery, aggravated assault (for pointing a gun at the bank teller), resisting arrest (since we had to order him to stop), and possession of a firearm during the commission of a felony.

Later on, Ray and I reenacted this event for a filming of the television series *Real Stories of the Highway Patrol*. We were awarded the Troop E Heroism Award for apprehending this armed robber.

I would like to think my keen aptitude for identifying criminal behavior led me to recognize this felon. Admittedly, the gun and money bag helped.

Ultimately, though, this incident proved what my keen fashion sense already knew: when robbing a bank, don't wear a bright yellow outfit.

The Unexpected

Fairly new Trooper Manny Perez loved his job.

In the early morning hours on the Dolphin Expressway's eastbound lane, he conducted a traffic stop for a possible DUI. This stop would change Manny's world forever.

While standing near the driver's door of the stopped vehicle, another car heading east swerved off the roadway and struck him. The driver sped away, leaving Manny lying on the pavement fighting for his life. Unfortunately, the impact ripped off Manny's arm.

A passerby who witnessed the accident called 911, and fire rescue responded. Since this took place just a mile from Jackson Memorial Hospital, timing worked in his favor.

After the ambulance transported Manny to the emergency room, the doctors decided to rush him into surgery and reattach his arm. They hoped their efforts would succeed. Manny also suffered other severe injuries that put him in critical condition.

As a felony trooper, Lt. Fagan asked me to assist with following up on leads called into the Crime Stoppers tip line so that we could identify and arrest the hit-and-run driver. At least we had a start from witness accounts. They stated the suspect vehicle was a blue Oldsmobile, which we soon confirmed through the car parts left at the scene of the accident.

One of the leads was an anonymous tip that the blue Oldsmobile had been seen parked at a drinking establishment in North Dade County called The Tree. I searched the phone book but didn't find a bar named The Tree. I also searched the state database for a business and liquor license with that name and got the same results. I then began to go into other bars in the area, asking people if they knew of a place called The Tree.

After a day and half of looking, I learned from an old man in a seedy bar that there was *a tree* in the north end. It was a known meeting place for working folks to congregate on a daily basis with their alcohol.

When I arrived at the tree in question, I saw that it was just a large shade tree that grew in the midst of a grassy parking lot. Hundreds of discarded beer cans and liquor bottles intertwined with long grass blades and weeds. There must have been fifty men hanging around and shooting the breeze with their drink of choice.

I approached a man standing at the front of the group. He looked tired, and his tan shirt and matching pants were splotched with black stains that looked like grease from working on cars. Before I could reach him, he yelled, "Hey lady, what's you doing in our hood? Looking to arrest us?"

"No," I responded. "I'm looking for some information about someone who drives a blue Olds. He almost killed a trooper before leaving the scene."

These guys all seemed genuinely concerned and wished the trooper well. However, they didn't know about the blue Oldsmobile.

After the car's description was broadcasted, a tip came in with a tag number. In fact, the caller gave specific details, such as damage on the car that looked like it contained dried blood. This tipster also told us the possible driver's name, age, and where he might live.

Then another tip came into the Crime Stoppers confirming a lot of the information from the previous tip. This caller said he saw the car in the parking lot of his Miami Beach apartment complex. He then proceeded to give a description of the driver and the apartment where he believed the driver lived. It appeared we were obtaining the pieces of a puzzle, and they seemed to fit together in place nicely.

Lt. Fagan and I felt we had enough compelling information to drive to Miami Beach. We pulled into the parking lot of the tipster's apartment complex, and I spotted a blue Oldsmobile. After a quick inspection, we saw damage that appeared to match the evidence obtained at the scene of the accident. I ran the tag to verify the owner's name, age, and address, all of which matched our tips as well.

We knocked on the door. A dark-complexioned, greasy-looking skinny guy with eyes that appeared too big for his face answered it. He also matched our description.

After we identified ourselves, Lt. Fagan asked, "Are you Johnny Morgan?"

His eyes got even bigger. "Yes, that's me." He spoke with a Spanish accent.

I asked, "Does anyone else live here?

"No."

I said, "We're here to arrest you for leaving the scene of an accident where a trooper was hurt badly."

He looked down. "I know. I left because I was scared."

That's all he said. He didn't tell us why or what caused him to hit Trooper Perez. Frankly, I didn't care. What I cared about at that time was that he hit a cop with a car and left him lying on the side of the street struggling for life without so much as an anonymous call to 911 to get Manny help.

"Turn around," I ordered.

I then handcuffed him. He continued to comply with all of our directives and offered no resistance.

We then read him his Miranda Rights. Afterward, he didn't say anything. We put him in our backseat and drove him to jail where we booked him.

Manny survived but could never use his arm again. Regardless, he persevered and stayed with the Florida Highway Patrol as a duty officer. He proved to be a brave man and continued to serve.

A Kidnapping Interrupted

While Manny remained in Jackson Memorial Hospital recuperating, a life flight from Key Largo arrived with Trooper Cindy Mixon. She had been brutally attacked during a traffic stop.

Earlier that night, a tow-truck driver had been travelling south on U.S. 1 in Key Largo. He saw a car speeding away from the vicinity of where an empty highway patrol car was parked on the roadway's shoulder.

He stopped to find out where the trooper was. While walking around the highway patrol car, he heard moaning. He followed the sound and found a female trooper lying on the ground. Blood covered her head and face.

She had difficulty breathing because of the large amount of blood coming from her mouth and flowing down her neck. Barely conscious, Cindy tried to spit out half of her teeth which had been knocked loose during a vicious attack.

The tow-truck driver ran over to Cindy and laid her on her side so that the blood could drain from her mouth, and she wouldn't choke on it. He then hurried to her car and used her radio to notify dispatch about the situation and the location. His curiosity, quick thinking, and actions probably saved her life.

Cindy had only been riding by herself for about three months. She had graduated from the academy six months prior to this attack. The first three of those six months she was in training and assigned to ride with her field training officer.

The night of her attack was especially dark due to the lack of stars in the sky. Cindy stopped a driver for speeding. Unknown to her, a woman lay helpless in his backseat tied up with rope. The driver had kidnapped her from a bar.

When Cindy approached the driver's door with her flashlight shining, he jumped out and lunged for her gun. Thank goodness she wore an issued holster with the safety mechanism. In order to unlock the gun from the holster, the release must first be pushed and rocked in a precise manner.

When this crazed man couldn't pull her gun out of her holster, he grabbed her flashlight. She placed her hands on top of her gun to further protect it from being released, so he beat her hands with her flashlight.

He became even more agitated. He took the flashlight and beat her in the face. He knocked out her teeth and broke her nose and jaw. He then began to beat her head. Cindy still hung onto her gun, even as she passed out.

The driver left and ended up dumping his kidnapped victim a few blocks away before speeding off in an effort to get away. He knew he couldn't hide in the Keys. However, if he drove north about fifty miles, he could hide in Miami. This was his only means to evade apprehension.

His kidnapped victim flagged down another vehicle. The motorist called the highway patrol and told them about her and gave a description of the suspect's car.

Fortunately for us, the Keys provided only one way in and one way out for vehicles, and we wanted to keep it that way. We knew he wouldn't reach Florida City for another thirty-five to forty-five minutes. With time and heavy traffic working in our favor, the FHP and police departments from Miami-Dade and Florida City immediately shut down traffic and set up a checkpoint in Florida City where U.S. 1, SW 177th Avenue/Krome Avenue, and the Florida Turnpike merged together into a single road. By the time the monster came to that point, the police were waiting for him and arrested him, taking one more violent criminal off the streets.

When Cindy arrived at the hospital, they operated on her immediately. Jackson's trauma unit possessed the reputation of being one of the best on the east coast. Miami-Dade County and the Florida Keys law enforcement officers have said, "If I'm shot or seriously injured, I want to be taken to Jackson

Memorial Hospital." We knew we'd receive state-of-the-art emergency care there, and that's what counted.

The shift sergeant sent me to the hospital about fourteen hours after Cindy's attack. The highway patrol assigned its officers to stay with injured troopers or their families around the clock. During this time, we supplied any of their needs and provided security.

I walked into Cindy's private room located two floors below Manny's room. I saw a slim young woman with long blonde hair lying in the room's only hospital bed. I didn't know Cindy, and I had never seen her. From the bruises and cuts covering her swollen face, I couldn't even imagine what she looked like normally.

I noticed that the staff hadn't cleaned Cindy's face, even during surgery. As a result, dried blood matted her hair, and streaks of dried blood still covered her neck. The overburdened nurses don't have time for the niceties of washing blood out patients' hair and from their skin. These tasks must be performed by the patient's family members, friends, or coworkers if it's to be done at all.

When Cindy saw me, she tried to smile. The doctors had wired her mouth together due to her broken jaw. It prevented her lips from moving much.

I went to my car and retrieved some shampoo, lotion, and a lightly scented body spray. I always kept a packed bag with grooming articles, towels, fresh underwear, and clean uniforms in case I couldn't get home but needed to shower or change.

Once I got back into Cindy's room, I managed to move her enough to shampoo her hair and wash the lower portion of her neck to remove the awful metallic smell of dried blood. I then used the body spray on her hair to make it smell better. At least she would be more presentable for her reunion with her family who were driving from the Midwest to be with her.

Cindy's recovery took over two years during which she endured multiple surgeries. Her doctors did an excellent job reconstructing her face and teeth.

Finally, she was cleared to return back to duty. She worked for a few months before leaving for good.

Perhaps Cindy interrupted an insidious plan to hurt or even kill the woman in this monster's car. She probably saved the kidnapped woman from torture or death. When faced with the adversity of her brutal attacker, Cindy fought the fight as hard as she could.

I didn't get a chance to really know Cindy, but in the little bit of time I cared for her in the hospital, I did get to see glimpses of her character. What I concluded was that Cindy was the total package, complete with brains, beauty, and courage.

Sniffer, Sniffer Making Our Job Easier

Two FBI agents who resided in Homestead and worked in its small field office called Jacob and me. They told us they had received information that a dangerous fugitive named Jo Johnson was hiding in Perrine, which was located between Miami and Homestead. Johnson was wanted by the FBI for unlawful flight to avoid prosecution and by the state of Georgia for arson, narcotics, and an assault on a Jessup, Georgia, police officer.

One of them said, "Floy, we'd like your help in apprehending Johnson, and bring Sniffer with you in case Johnson runs."

So Jacob, Sniffer, and I met the FBI agents in the parking lot of a mall. I was thankful for the cool morning breeze because it energized me for the task at hand—apprehending this bad boy.

We all drove to the address where Johnson was reported to be hiding and parked in front a small and shabby concrete-block house with a beige roof. White paint peeled off its exterior walls in large patches, unintentionally creating a motley-color. The yard contained more weeds than grass, and an old car without tires sat on four sets of blocks on the cracked concrete driveway.

We knocked on the door. A skinny woman wearing a pair of short shorts and a tight shirt with a plunging neckline answered it. She rolled her eyes when she saw us standing on her front porch, not seeming a bit surprised or nervous. I suspected we had triggered some déjà vu moments with her.

When she spoke, she revealed a mouth full of rotted teeth. "Whatta you want?" Her tone sounded bored.

She then inched the door a bit wider, just enough to allow us to peek inside. Sitting on the living room couch sat Johnson watching television. His stocky, muscular build stretched the white wife-beater t-shirt he wore.

He glanced over to the door. He saw us, and then his eyes scanned down and froze when they landed on Sniffer. His brown eyes widened, and he stood with his hands straight up in the air. After that, he didn't move one more inch.

That was a smart move on his part. I could sense Sniffer was looking for a bite.

Working Jointly with the DEA and ICE (Immigration and Customs Enforcement)

The last time I worked on a joint operation that involved both the DEA and ICE (U.S. Immigration and Customs Enforcement) together was late summer 1993.

The federal agents had been conducting surveillance on a Hispanic male working at the Kendall-Tamiami Executive Airport, and the DEA called us for assistance. Their information revealed that a plane coming in from Mexico contained a large amount of marijuana. Once it arrived, the suspect would transfer the marijuana from the plane and put it in a brown Ford van that he would subsequently drive north on Krome Avenue.

When Jacob and I arrived at the airport at the designated time, we parked in an abandoned garage that hid us from both the air and from any countersurveillance conducted by the bad guys. We positioned our cars so that they faced opposite directions with our drivers' side windows side by side. While waiting and watching, we passed the time by chatting.

Then Jacob asked, "Do you think this deal is really a go?

I shrugged. "Hope so."

We continued to make small talk. Finally I saw the plane in question fly in and taxi to a stop. My adrenaline started pumping in anticipation of the action.

Sure enough, a brown Ford van drove to the plane. A dark-haired bearded man wearing an airport uniform jumped out of the driver's seat. He ran around to the cargo section of the plane and began unloading crates and placing them in the van.

Once the van started moving away from the airplane, we stopped it. Both Jacob and I drew our guns before we approached the suspect's vehicle. When the driver exited the van, our guns were trained on him. We noticed his name was embroidered on his mechanic's uniform, and his airport identification was clipped to his belt.

I yelled, "Put your hands in the air and walk backward. Then kneel with your hands on your head."

He completely complied. Strangely, he remained calm and nonchalant about his arrest on major drug charges that would land him in a federal prison.

Jacob ran Sniffer around the vehicle, and he alerted us to the drugs by pawing at the rear bumper. We opened the back of the van and saw floor-to-ceiling bundles of brown burlap bundled together with silver masking tape. The entire inside of the van smelled like marijuana.

I cuffed the suspect. When I pulled him up to a standing position, his posture had changed from indifference to acceptance and regret. He slumped his shoulders forward, hung his head, and didn't say a word.

I turned him over to the DEA, and we then moved the vehicle to their headquarters. We all helped unload and weigh the marijuana.

When all was said and done, we discovered that our airport mechanic's shipment contained eight hundred eighty-five pounds of marijuana valued at $1,361,160.

Threats and a Bomb for a Job Well-Done

Uri Bassano had his life turned upside down. One day he was on top of the world, and the next, well, read on.

Uri's legal problems started when he chose to drive a bit too fast in the Florida Panhandle. This act led to a trooper pulling him over for speeding.

The trooper asked, "Where you coming from?"

Uri said, "Mexico."

"Where did you enter the United States?"

"Texas."

"Where you heading?

"South Florida."

Uri's responses sent up a red flag for the trooper, who happened to belong to the Felony Drug Interdiction Team. He had searched many vehicles en route to South Florida, and Uri's car would be no exception. Hopefully, he could search it with consent.

"Mind if I take a look in your trunk?" the trooper asked.

Uri responded, "I don't care. I've got nothing to hide. Go ahead and look."

The trooper took him up on his offer. He opened his trunk and lo and behold, there sat a duffle bag. The trooper opened it and saw it crammed with cash (which would later be counted to equal one million dollars).

This discovery understandably sent up another red flag. Since the money was being transported from Mexico to South Florida, the trooper thought it could be drug-related, so he requested backup and a K-9 drug dog.

The K-9 sniffed the cash and alerted his handler to the presence of drugs on the money. The trooper arrested Uri and confiscated his vehicle and duffle bag. While processing the arrest, the trooper requested assistance from the DEA. He then learned that the DEA had already suspected Uri of laundering money from drugs, so he had been on their radar anyway. Thus this car stop turned into a joint investigation between the DEA and the Florida Highway Patrol.

The plot thickened when intelligence checks revealed that Uri was a suspected member of the Israeli mafia. As a result, the investigation also pulled in the FDLE, adding a third agency to this joint operation.

Then the investigation led to our neck of the woods all the way down in South Florida because Uri owned a penthouse in a very exclusive building in Miami. As a result, the DEA requested our assistance, and Sarge called us. He assigned us to go to that penthouse and search it, compliments of a federal search warrant. The goal was to obtain more evidence of the criminal organization involving Uri.

Jacob, Sniffer, and I joined the DEA and FDLE agents in the search, but Uri wasn't home at the time. No worries because we continued with the search anyway. Once inside, I was in awe of the luxuriousness of his home. Never had I searched a more spectacular and gorgeous premise.

The interior looked as if a top-notch designer had furnished its contemporary layout. Lots of black leather, glass, and clean lines set a modern and lavish ambiance. Furthermore, the apartment overlooked the vast blue Atlantic Ocean.

I was assigned to search the master bedroom and closet, so I became familiar with his wardrobe. I noticed all of the beautiful expensive clothes and couldn't help but glance at some of the designer labels.

Uri arrived home with his lawyer in tow as we finished the search. He looked just like I had imagined. He wore expensive designer clothes with Italian leather loafers and no socks. His long, dark-brown hair was pulled back into a ponytail, and his dark eyes stood out on his handsome olive-toned face.

Uri's cosmopolitan style and smooth mannerism gave him the ability to remain collected during our search. He showed no emotion while we invaded his privacy.

We didn't discover any contraband or financial records in the penthouse, and Sniffer didn't alert us to any narcotics, so we left empty handed.

Evidently, I must have made a memorable impression upon Uri, though. In the fall of 1993, a few weeks after our search of his home, he called me. At the time, my family lived in a travel trailer on my Homestead property while waiting for my house to be rebuilt. I don't know how he got my cell phone number, but he managed to somehow.

When I unsuspectingly answered my phone, a deep voice asked, "Is this Trooper Turner?"

Thinking the caller was another law enforcement officer, I responded, "Yes, this is Trooper Turner."

He then said, "This is Uri. I want my money returned to me now. Where is it?"

Although his voice sounded composed, it contained a menacing undercurrent. My heart beat faster than normal. Why was he calling me? I felt very concerned that he would verbally threaten me and that if he was able to get my cell phone number, how hard would it be for him to find out where I lived? I forced myself to calm down and speak slowly and clearly.

"Mr. Bassano, your money was seized by the trooper in North Florida. You'll be contacted by the Florida Highway Patrol in North Florida regarding any civil proceedings involving your money."

I heard a click and then a dial tone. I didn't know if I should be relieved or even more concerned for the safety of my family and me. Admittedly, I can't remember a time when I appreciated my small arsenal of weapons more.

For some reason, Uri zeroed in on me because I was the only he called. Maybe I stood out among the agents and Jacob because I was the only female, so maybe he thought he could intimidate me.

My husband was at home at the time of the call and freaked out when I told him what had happened. "That's it!" he yelled. "The Israeli mafia's probably going to blow us all up in this trailer."

I must admit that I understood his anxiety. The mob was known to be ruthless. Furthermore, Uri had acquired another name that went well with his reputation. His inner circles called him Uzi, the name of an Israeli-made submachine gun. I suspected he was quite capable of seeking revenge when he felt wronged. He wanted his money, and in his mind, either I represented the barrier that kept him from it or the key to get it.

Fortunately for us, Uri never called me again. Unfortunately for Uri, the state used the civil forfeiture process to seize his million dollars.

A few more weeks went by. When I checked my mail, I saw a twenty ounce soda-pop bottle lying inside my mailbox. At first, I thought, *Why is a soda-pop bottle lying in my mailbox?*

Then I noticed a piece of tin foil and liquid that didn't look like soda inside the bottle. My pulse raced because I knew I was staring at a bomb that was ready, willing, and able to explode.

I immediately stepped away from my mailbox and called for the MDPD bomb disposal unit. They came and detonated it. They informed me that enough gases were in that device to sever fingers and cause second- and third-degree burns to any exposed skin. This type of bomb is referred to as a "works" bomb and is easily made with normal household ingredients.

I didn't suspect the Israeli mafia. They would have constructed a much more sophisticated gadget. Since I parked my marked highway patrol car in my driveway, anyone with a grudge could have planted that bomb.

Hitting Too Close to Family

I had been investigating a local Latin gang named the 307-Street Gang.

One day my youngest daughter went with me to the grocery store located about a mile from our house. While we were in the produce section, I heard her say, "Hi, Juan."

I looked up from selecting a watermelon to see the person she had greeted. I saw that Juan was the gang leader of the 307-Street Gang.

A chill went up my spine and my body froze. I tried to hide my physical reaction to this potentially dangerous situation. How did my daughter know a gang leader enough to speak to him?

This particular gang leader knew me from the investigation. He probably put two and two together and figured out that she was my daughter.

After Juan walked away, I turned to my daughter. "How do you know that guy?"

She shrugged. "Everyone knows Juan."

This is one of the perils for law enforcement officers who live where they work. My perpetual worry about my girls just intensified with this encounter.

RID—Robbery Interdiction Unit

In the early fall of 1993, Jacob and I had been chosen to work with the Robbery Interdiction Unit (RID). By its very nature, RID was hazardous. The unit concentrated on the areas with the highest homicide rate and targeted the thugs who controlled their communities.

Drugs played a major role in these crimes because drug dealers don't stick to just their niche; they like to rob and murder as well. It becomes part of their job description. The robberies were a means to an end—acquiring money to purchase more drugs, and the murders were a means to remove obstacles, threats, and liabilities. They all went hand in hand.

However, the brutal murders and robberies of tourists in Miami over the past six months had created a tremendous amount of national publicity. In an effort to address and stop this heinous crime spree, a multi-departmental task force involving the FDLE, most of the local police departments in Miami-Dade County, and the FHP was established.

The FDLE and MDPD were the administrators. The FDLE further participated by assigning agents from all over the state to serve as supplemental officers. The local police departments and the FHP provided an overall police presence by saturating these areas with additional marked patrol cars.

Two neighborhoods known for extreme violence were located in close proximity. They received the nicknames "Scott Projects" and "Pork and Beans." The sale of narcotics took place on every street corner.

Dealers employed their defensive strategy. We referred to them as armed "dope boys," which were basically lookouts and protectors with guns.

We utilized our offensive strategy called "jump outs." This tactical movement involved us driving swiftly into the suspected dope "hole." We then "jumped out" of our vehicles with guns drawn to ensure the element of surprise.

One time we had observed four men sitting on crates in front of a corner store. One person after the other walked up to them and gave them money. In return, the buyer was given what appeared to be drugs. We drove up very quickly, jumped out, and took down the four men. We then turned over those crates and discovered stacks of money totaling four thousand dollars, about thirty rocks of crack cocaine, and a long knife.

Conducting these types of exercises in this manner offered us an advantage. The lookout and "dope boys" didn't have an opportunity to react by drawing their guns, hiding, or moving their dope or money. As a result, we took a lot of these commodities off the streets.

I found the scariest part to be chasing teenagers who carried guns. I wondered if they were truly capable of perceiving just how serious the consequences were when shooting someone. These children happened to be products of a society that glorified violence and where shootings, illegal activities, and gang warfare thrived. I always felt bad for those innocent families trying to raise their children in the midst of this lawlessness. Many times, the children grew into this violence by default. By our stopping the cycle it in its tracks, the chances of losing more young lives to this lifestyle were diminished.

The RID Task Force conducted numerous traffic stops in those neighborhoods as well. Because all of the RID members worked in the same area, at least two or three of us (and sometimes our entire squad of eight) responded to each car stop, demonstrating a proactive, unified force. We parked our cars behind the officer or agent who initiated the stop. The large number of officers discouraged any violent response from the suspects.

One evening, I conducted a traffic stop for a minor violation. Jacob, Sniffer, and Mark Harper, who was a FDLE SWAT agent, and about four other FDLE agents provided back up for me.

The driver consented to a search of his vehicle. I told him to stand next to the curb. I then asked Mark to keep an eye on him while I looked through his car.

I donned my black leather gloves and began looking under the car seats. I saw a Glock 9mm semi-automatic pistol.

After pulling the gun out of its hiding place, I held it up, barrel pointed down. Admittedly, I allowed myself a stupid show-off moment that told the FDLE agents, "Look what I found!"

My show-and-tell episode deflected Mark's attention from the suspect for just an instant, but that's all it took. The perp now realized he had a small window to escape and run, and that he did.

The FDLE agents ran after him. We quickly established a perimeter. Sniffer found my runner hiding in an abandoned shed.

Not long afterward, Mark would become my field training agent with the FDLE. We still laugh about the runner who took advantage of one of those stupid moments.

Memories and New Beginnings

The Florida Highway Patrol hired a new director.

He had been recruited from the Ohio State Police where he had earned an excellent reputation for taking a progressive stance. Even so, rumors circulated around that the felony teams were going to be disbanded.

When Colonel Ralph Gibson took the reins of the Patrol, he brought all of the felony troopers to Tallahassee for a meeting. We learned from the director himself that the program wasn't going to be dismantled but would instead be enhanced.

After the meeting, Colonel Gibson said, "I'll meet with the entire group at Hooters at seven this evening for dinner."

A colonel meeting with troopers at a restaurant like Hooters was somewhat out of the norm for Tallahassee. We all thought it was pretty cool.

At the restaurant, the group appeared relaxed. We felt this to be a great day for the program. We all had worked so hard to bring it to the forefront. Funny thing, none of the guys seemed to notice I suffered through a bad hair day or even what I wore for that matter.

Not long after this "change of the guard," I experienced a tremendous change as well. In late September 1993, while getting ready for work one morning, the phone rang. The caller identified herself as Pat from human resources with the Florida Department of Law Enforcement in Tallahassee. She informed me that I had been hired as a special agent.

My body went numb. Somehow, though, I managed to write down her instructions of what needed to be done between now and the day of my appointment in Tallahassee, a mere three weeks away.

After the call ended, I held the phone in my hand. Excitement overwhelmed me and took my breath away when I grasped what had just happened. Then once I began to think of all of the things I needed to get done in preparation, my emotions turned to scared, scared of starting a new life, then excited about starting a new life, then back to scared.

I knew I would need to undergo a lot of new training in Tallahassee for about three months, and I didn't look forward to that aspect. I also knew I would miss Jacob and Sniffer terribly. That was an even worse notion.

Before leaving the house to go to work that morning, I sat down to compose my two-week notice to the FHP. I decided to go ahead and submit my resignation now so that I could have a week off before starting with the FDLE. I wanted this time to prepare both mentally and physically. I also needed that time to shop for pantsuits and more fashionable and functional work shoes.

I found writing my resignation letter to be bittersweet. I had served as a Florida Highway Patrol Trooper for eleven years. I reflected back as the memories deluged my mind. I had not only survived the well-respected Florida Highway Patrol Academy, but I managed to graduate from it. That was only the beginning of an action-packed adventure with this outstanding law enforcement agency.

I had gone from patrolling the highways to undercover roles to Troop Felony Team Coordinator, all of which I enjoyed for a variety of different reasons. As a result of all my hard work and passion, I gained the recognition and respect from law enforcement officers at the local, state, and federal levels, many of whom helped to propel me to the next level in my career.

I'm glad that my last couple of years with the highway patrol ended on a high note. Jacob and I seized twelve million dollars worth of narcotics in a two-year period, and we had taken dozen of guns off the streets. Indeed, I had acquired a lot of memories that no one can ever take away from me.

I finished my letter and drove to the station. My mind filled with all kinds of things along the way, again mostly what all needed to be done over the next few weeks in preparation.

I got to the stationhouse and walked into Sarge's office. "Sarge, Tallahassee called me. I got the job with the FDLE, so here's my resignation letter."

Sarge stared at me a moment before holding out his hand for my envelope. "I hate to lose you, Floy, and I'm real sorry to see you go, but I understand. You've been wanting to do this for awhile. I wish you all the best. Hey, before you go, our squad's going to have to get together."

I nodded. My smile now felt frozen as I thought about leaving my squad.

He pulled my letter out of its envelope and walked out of his office. He read my letter as he walked in the direction of my lieutenant's office, I assume to pass it onto him.

As my resignation letter made its way up the chain of command where it eventually found its final resting place in the FHP headquarters in Tallahassee, I knew there was no turning back. That was the bitter part.

I called Colonel Gibson to personally tell him about resigning. "Sir, my long-term goal of becoming a FDLE agent has finally happened. I'm sorry to leave, especially at the same time you came onboard."

Colonel Gibson said, "Floy, you're making a wise career decision. I'm sorry to have you leave the Patrol, but FDLE is an outstanding and respected agency."

The Colonel's comments meant a lot to me. I loved the Patrol and would miss my colleagues. Also, losing my identity as a trooper would take some adjustment.

When my last day as a trooper arrived, I drove my highway patrol car to the station. Jacob agreed to drive me home after I turned in all of my gear and finalized my paperwork.

By around noon, Jacob, Sarge, and the rest of the squad took me to lunch. The combination of excitement and sadness prevented me from having much of an appetite. Regardless, I managed to nibble some on my food, but my mind was focused on this being our last time together as a team.

After we returned, I began to unload my equipment. My coworkers circled around my things like sharks circling their prey, and like sharks, they commenced in an activity that was no less a feeding frenzy. They picked through my stuff, examining each piece and claiming it as their own.

Truthfully, I had wished they could have waited to go through my gear until after I left, but then again, they were guys, and as guys they brought a different perspective to this situation. They probably weren't as attached emotionally, so I gave them grace. To them, it was probably more of a first-come first-serve situation where they had to get while the getting was good. The fact that I would be gone was secondary. Of course, if I couldn't completely wrap my head around the reality that I wouldn't be coming back, I'm sure they couldn't either.

So I watched these guys, who had been my family for over a decade, rifle through my things. Although the FDLE was what I wanted, I still hated to leave them.

I looked at Jacob and Sniffer, and I felt my throat get tight. We had been together for so long and were so close. How would my professional world be without those two? Memories of Sniffer chasing me with the hidden sleeve, Jacob and me crawling through the saw grass with Sniffer leading the way, our various car stops, trying to reload the trucks we searched, the drugs we confiscated, and many other memories all flooded through my mind. Jacob was my best friend, and although we were going in the same direction, we would be on different paths.

As I continued to observe my friends and colleagues, wondering what laid ahead for them, I again looked back upon my life in law enforcement thus far. A tear spilled from my left eye. I recognized the invaluable patrol training I had gained from serving with the Florida Highway Patrol, another commodity that could never be taken away from me. I would come to find out that everything it had taught me, along with my street experience while under its command, would serve me well as I transitioned from trooper to special agent.

Upon walking out of my stationhouse for the last time, it hit me that I was no longer a trooper. My legs felt a bit heavy as I plodded to Jacob's vehicle. I looked over and saw my patrol car parked and unoccupied. Who would it be assigned to now?

Then a smile involuntarily crossed my face as realization replaced the sadness. I wasn't changing careers; I was furthering it. Today, I took off my Trooper Stetson for the last time. Today, excitement could and would prevail over any apprehension I had been feeling about learning a new position. Tomorrow, I would still fight monsters and get the bad guys off the street because that's who I am.

I sighed as my smile grew and my steps got lighter. Oh, yeah. Tomorrow I would take on the new role and adapt to the new identity of Special Agent Floy Turner. Tomorrow, I would start the journey of fulfilling my dream career with Florida's premium law enforcement agency. Tomorrow, I had my whole life before me with the Florida Department of Law Enforcement.

And that, my friends, was the sweet part.

About the Author
FLOY TURNER

FLOY TURNER began her twenty-five-year career in law enforcement in Miami during the volatile cocaine-wars era as a trooper with the Florida Highway Patrol. After eleven years in this position, she served as a special agent with the elite Florida Department of Law Enforcement (FDLE) for the next fourteen years. She has been assigned to joint task forces at the international, federal, state, and local police levels, such as the 9/11 Counter Terrorism Task Force and the Belle Glade Prison Escape Task Force. These assignments have included complex investigations of serial homicides, kidnappings, missing children, child homicides, human-trafficking cases, and illegal narcotics smuggling cases. In 1993, she received the International Narcotic Enforcement Officer's Award and the Heroism Award, which led to her reenacting the apprehension of an armed bank robber on *Real Stories of the Highway Patrol*.

As a FDLE Special Agent, Floy served as the Regional Crimes Against Children Coordinator in the Miami Region of Southeast Florida and was also a member of an Internet Crimes Against Children Task Force, the Law Enforcement Against Child Harm (LEACH) Task Force, the Miami-Dade County and Broward County Child Death Review Boards, U. S. Immigration and Customs Enforcement Human Trafficking Task Force, and Homeland

Security Task Force. She assisted in the development of the human-trafficking curriculum for Basic Law Enforcement Training and Incentive Classes for Florida Police Officer's Standards and has been a guest speaker at many local, state, and federal training sessions, including the FBI's Women in Law Enforcement Conference in 2004. She was awarded the State Law Enforcement Officer of the Year at the Florida Missing Children's Day in 2004, for her criminal investigations that located and recovered multiple missing children who were reunited with their families.

Prior to her retirement, Floy began working as a consultant for Fox Valley Technical College on the development and implementation of various training initiatives for the National AMBER Alert Training and Technical Assistance Program, U. S. Department of Justice, Office of Justice Programs. She was responsible for coordinating local AMBER Alerts with the FDLE Missing Children Information Clearinghouse and established a Child Abduction Response Team (CART) for the South Florida Region. After her retirement, Floy became the AMBER Alert Liaison for the Southern United States and Caribbean and created and coordinated the Child Abduction Response Team (CART) Certification program. She also continued to provide instruction in many AMBER Alert training courses until 2012.

Floy was a member of the Northeast Florida Human Trafficking Task Force, and in 2010, the Organization of American States selected her to conduct human trafficking training at a conference for government officials in Belize. In 2011, she was recognized as Jacksonville's Justice Coalition's Citizen of the Year. She has also received authors' credits as a law enforcement consultant in two best-selling books.

About the Author
SHERRIE CLARK

SHERRIE CLARK is a former police officer with the NYPD, and she is a writer, book editor, and author of the award-winning book SMALL VOICES SILENCED. She's a coach and consultant for aspiring authors all across the country and speaks at conferences where she teaches audiences how to write their books. She cofounded Storehouse Publishing that takes authors and aspiring authors where they're at and helps them write and publish their books.

Sherrie has written, bylined, and ghostwritten over 200 articles, stories, blog posts, press releases, website content, bios, and such, all of which have been published online or in print. Some of the publications for which she has written include the award-winning newspaper *Victims' Advocate*. She served as the Jacksonville Christianity & Social Issues Examiner for examiner.com, a niche she created but has since been used by other writers, and was a volunteer writer and editor for the international organization Stop Child Trafficking Now.

Sherrie created, produced, and hosted the weekly online radio show *God, Where Were You When?* This show aired throughout Europe and as far as Japan and into Africa. She has a Masters of Arts in Clinical Christian Counseling and is a Licensed Clinical Christian Counselor with the NCCA.